Trauma-tragedy

Manchester University Press

Trauma-tragedy: Symptoms of contemporary performance

Patrick Duggan

Manchester University Press

Published by Manchester University Press
Altrincham Street, Manchester M1 7JA, UK
www.manchesteruniversitypress.co.uk

British Library Cataloguing-in-Publication Data is available

Library of Congress Cataloging-in-Publication Data is available

ISBN 978 0 7190 9988 5 *paperback*

First published by Manchester University Press in hardback 2012

This paperback edition first published 2015

The publisher has no responsibility for the persistence or accuracy of URLs for any external or third-party internet websites referred to in this book, and does not guarantee that any content on such websites is, or will remain, accurate or appropriate.

Printed by Lightning Source

For Naomi and for my parents, with love

Contents

Illustrations

Acknowledgements

This project has been supported by many people over the years of its gestation, in many different ways. But thanks are due in particular to Jane Bacon, Tony Gardner, Vida Midgelow, Gareth Somers, Victor Ukaegbu and Mick Wallis for their generosity and support at various times during the process of researching, developing and writing this book. You have all offered me invaluable critique, guidance and inspiration as readers, critics, cajolers and colleagues, but above as all friends.

Thanks also to Franco B and Kira O'Reilly for kind permission to use images of their work, and to Bex Carrington at the University of Bristol Theatre Collection for help sourcing some of them. I am grateful also to the University of Northampton for granting research leave that facilitated the final writing-up of the volume.

Importantly, I want to thank two people at Manchester University Press: Matthew Frost, for commissioning the volume, and Kim Walker, for her help and patience in seeing it through to completion.

To all those who I have not the space to mention here, thank you. All the input I have received, formal and informal, has been instrumental in finishing this project. Any errors, of course, remain my own.

Introduction

Event(s)

What we do is just a shadow of what we want to do
and the only truths we can point to
are the ever changing truths of our own experience
I do not know if I am hangman or victim
for I imagine the most horrible tortures
and as I describe them I suffer them myself
There is nothing that I could not do and everything
fills me with horror

(from *Marat/Sade*. Weiss 1983: 31–32)

Readers and theatre-goers […] despise the pleasurable
and […] value the disturbing, the jagged, the painful
work. It is now virtually unimaginable that a reviewer of a
new play should praise it by saying that it offers solace or
comfort. Conversely the adjective 'uncomfortable' is auto-
matically read as praise. Ancient Stoics and Epicureans
argued about most things but would be united in their
bewilderment at this. I am a twentieth-century person and
I share the general taste for discomfort.

(Nuttall 1996: 1–2)

There is, it would seem, pleasure in the un-pleasurable.

It is interesting that while Nuttall's investigations in *Why Does
Tragedy Give Pleasure?* focus mainly on ancient and Elizabethan
tragedies, he decides to answer the question of his title in the

mid-1990s, a time when (in certain quarters of British theatre, at least) there was a move towards a theatre which sought to address the more violent, more unpleasant, more un-pleasurable aspects of society and culture at that time.[1] It is a historical juncture which, while I do discuss examples from before this point, can be seen to be the time from which my enquiry stems; the point from which, loosely, we can define the 'contemporary' of this book's title.

Nuttall contends that if we were all wicked or evil there 'would be no problem' in understanding why (and how) tragedy gives pleasure (Nuttall 1996: 1). He goes on to juggle the notion of an underlying evil in humankind, both denying it with ease and then reintroducing it as a possibility when reading Freud. The idea that we might derive pleasure from tragedy because we might be inherently evil is the central philosophical dilemma that Nuttall grapples with throughout and which stimulates the deceptively simple question of the title. His detailed and complex reading of multiple writers and 'types' of tragedy belies the simplicity of this question; however, it is that very simplicity which is so intrinsic to opening up the investigation. In this vein, then, I pose four interrelated, overlapping questions that have stimulated the pursuit of this book:

1   To what extent can theatre and performance represent trauma?
2   How can theatre and performance go about this?
3   How could this help us to understand trauma on personal and social levels?
4   Finally, in a world increasingly preoccupied with and exposed to traumas – social, personal, political, violent, psychological, fictional, local, global – what does performance offer as a means of commentary that other cultural products do not?

While trauma has long been the subject of scholarly attention in many other fields, very little has been written on the subject in the context of theatre and performance.[2] My desire to understand the traumatic in performance stems from an encounter with Pip Simmons' revival of his 1975 production of *An Die*

Musik, in October 2000 at Warwick Arts Centre. At the beginning of the play, houselights still up, an actor, who is dressed as and playing an SS soldier, enters and stands downstage, just off centre. He looks at the audience and announces that tonight we will be treated to a performance by some of the 'inmates' and he hopes that we enjoy 'the show'. It becomes clear that the audience members are both spectators of the performance in 2000 and being doubled as a Nazi-sympathizing, 1940s audience who have come to what I presumed to be Auschwitz to be entertained by a group of six Jewish detainees. Throughout the piece, these six were subjected to routines of strenuous physical exercise, degradation, humiliation, and physical and mental abuses, all the while performing for the audience.

I found the piece deeply unsettling, so much so that I struggled to speak afterwards and was only able to try to articulate the experience some time later. The piece offered no resolution to what it had presented: it simply offered the images, demanded the audience's attention and then asked the audience to make up their own minds. This difficult, formative theatrical experience has, at least subconsciously, guided my academic interest in this type of performance. Thus, in an attempt both to satisfy my own questions and to fill the hole in current scholarship, I came to embark upon this study.

Trauma has problematically become an increasingly overused term in today's society, so much so that it has almost lost all sense of meaning in its everyday uses. The word pervades all levels of our interactions in the world, from the most personal and private traumas experienced throughout life, to its most banal use in television insurance adverts which claim that taking out a policy with such-and-such a broker will prevent 'traumas'. We now live in a society which is bound to its traumatic experiences, a society in which, as Christina Wald posits, trauma has become a 'cultural trope' (2007: 3). She further suggests that the rise of this trauma trope has pushed its meaning to 'the point of meaninglessness', but that the relatively recent rise in trauma theory as a focus of academic interest has galvanized trauma as a frame through which to examine cultural issues 'of experience, memory, the body, and representation' (3). Meanwhile, Western academic, artistic, journalistic, psychiatric, psychoanalytic and cultural discourses, in particular, have become increasingly engaged in analysis of traumata and people's experience of them. Contemporary British society has been described by literary critic Roger Luckhurst as a 'traumaculture'. Responding to Mark Seltzer's notion of 'wound culture', the term is borne out of the 'notable academic turn to questions of memory, trauma and identity during the past ten years' and the 'pervasive sense of the organising power of the notion of trauma in the 1990s' (Luckhurst 2003: 28). Indeed, Seltzer convincingly contends that 'the modern subject has become inseparable from the categories of shock and trauma' (Seltzer 1997: 18).

The rise in academic interest in trauma theory outside the psycho-medical disciplines can most easily be seen in the fields of history, literature, cultural studies and fine art. But the history and genealogy of modern trauma theory is littered with narratives and examples which might legitimately be thought of as performative or theatrical. Furthermore, contemporary trauma theory suggests a performative bent in traumatic suffering. This is not to trivialize traumatic suffering, nor is it my intention to detract from the insistence that trauma narratives must be adequately and truthfully borne witness to so as not to diminish the importance/weight of the original event.[3] Instead, I wish to suggest that the increasing take-up of trauma theory as a means of exploring theatre and performance is long since due.

Dominic LaCapra implicitly draws attention to this performative element in *Writing History, Writing Trauma* (2001) when he suggests that trauma sufferers have a tendency to 'relive the past, to be haunted by ghosts or even to exist in the present as if one was still in the past, with no distance from it' (142–143). We might think of this performative element in two senses. The first is that trauma might be seen to perform itself, as it were, within a collapsing of time; in a sense the inability to 'exist in the present' is a traumatic performative disruption/disturbance of time. Adrian Heathfield has suggested that the linear narrative of life is what enables us to live productively in the world. He argues that we constantly 'evaluate and, listening to what the past tells, draw lessons for life in the present' and through this process of evaluative 'learning', 'you might come to believe that you have survived the thing that has ended, you might create a bar between you and it, and so consign it to the past' (Heathfield 2000: 105). While Heathfield's concern is not the traumatic, we can subsume the argument into the current discourse to suggest that trauma-symptoms, which I shall discuss in more detail in Chapter 1, collapse the linear succession of things through their constant performative irruptions. The second element in this consideration of trauma as a performative *dolor* is that the survivor-sufferer might be seen to perform the symptoms of their suffering. LaCapra suggests that survivor-sufferers 'act out' compulsive repetition of actions, words, and situations from traumatic occurrences. And Luckhurst argues that this 'repetition compulsion' is central to contemporary understandings of trauma in which 'individuals, collectives and nations' can become trapped in 'cycles of uncomprehending repetition' until such time as that repetition becomes a process of 'healthy analytic [...] "working through"' (Luckhurst 2008: 9). We might say, following the performative line, that trauma requires 'acting out' in order to 'work through', an argument that those in the field of drama therapy would certainly support.[4] Trauma, then, can be seen to rehearse, repeat and re-present itself in performed 'ghosts' that haunt the sufferer.

Symptom(s)

As will become clear in Chapter 1, trauma, like performance, is a complex and polysemic phenomenon. As a result, in order to explicate my arguments and to unpack this dense and multifarious field of investigation fully, my methodological approach to researching and writing the book has been deliberately fluid. I have drawn upon a diverse range of performance theorists, theatre academics and philosophers, as well as examples of my own practice and multiple examples of performances from a broad spectrum of practitioners. Throughout, I have tried to cross, negotiate and deconstruct the hierarchized binary between Live Art and theatre. This is driven by my belief that an engagement with these two interrelated live events is a necessary move when attempting to understand the wider field of performance and theatre studies. While there are a plethora of differences between these forms, they can profitably be put into dialogue or juxtaposition to offer different dimensions to the consideration of trauma in performance. Perhaps the clearest example of this negotiation can be found in Chapter 5, which contains analyses of Sarah Kane's *Blasted*, the National Theatre's adaptation of *His Dark Materials* and Kira O'Reilly's *Untitled (Syncope)*.

Throughout the volume I make use of descriptive writing which is intended to offer a sense of the moments of performance I am discussing; this element of the writing might be seen as analogous to Clifford Geertz's 'thick description' (2000: 5–10). The usefulness of thick description lies within the describer's ability both to present and interpret context towards opening the event to those who come to it later through the writing. In attempting this one must continually pick through 'piled-up structures of inference and implication' (Geertz 2000: 7). My thick descriptions are, then, dedicated to what happened on the stage, actors' actions, the scenographic design and audience reactions, for example, rather than a discussion of the diegetic action, narrative or character development.[5] It is intended (to take Geertz only slightly out of context) to help 'render them [performances in my case, other cultures in Geertz's] accessible: setting them in the frame of their own banalities, it dissolves their opacity' (14). Description is thus part of the analytical framework of the writing and is a tool through which the arguments and theoretical modelling can develop.

In order to address the questions properly that I set out above, it has been necessary not only to draw upon the diversity of references that I have, but also to ensure that the process has been flexible enough to respond to the multifaceted nature of my two central concerns: trauma and performance. These fields contain contestations and problems, different avenues of approach to the same problem that lead to different propositions depending upon that approach. This is not to say that the arguments contained here are fluid or tentative; rather they are solidly and fully argued, yet they are grounded in theoretical diversity and formed through a writing process which has reflected upon many external influences in order to be able to refract within itself to arrive at the arguments that it does.[6]

Raymond Williams' work has been important to shaping this volume. I will address his work more thoroughly in Chapter 2, but it is worth stating at this point that Williams' writings, particularly *Modern Tragedy* (1966), and his idea of 'structure of feeling' have proved both profitable and influential in the development of this research. As later chapters will both reference and evoke Williams' thinking, I will not dwell on his arguments at this point except to state that the work of this book might, in certain ways, be seen to be supplementing and extending some of the core ideas in *Modern Tragedy*. My arguments suggest a contemporary structure of feeling which is embodied in a performance mode that is acutely concerned with addressing the traumatic: I have termed this mode *trauma-tragedy*.

As one might expect from my title, the other major theoretical underpinning of the book comes from the developing field of Trauma Studies. Chapter 1 critically traces a particular, 'performative' genealogy of trauma theory through Charcot and Freud to Cathy Caruth and other contemporary theorists. The chapter also addresses current critical engagements with trauma and the performing arts in order to position this project within the wider critical field. I will propose a (localized) triangulation of tensions between the desire to forget trauma, the necessity to deliberately relive it to effect a cure and the uninvited intrusive hallucinations of trauma symptoms. This model of trauma will form the basis of considerations of the trauma theory developed throughout the rest of the book.

Moving on from this formulation, I address the theatrics of Jean-Martin Charcot's practice as a means both of articulating the performative lineage of trauma theory and to suggest that trauma symptoms are themselves performative in nature. Through a brief reading of Anthony Neilson's play *Normal*, and linking this to the story of Lucy Blackman's murder in Tokyo in 2000, the chapter further proposes that Post Traumatic Stress Disorder (PTSD) is a false definition of trauma symptoms because they are anything but 'past'. The perpetual present of traumatic experience, I argue, creates a schism in one's understanding of self; thus, trauma-symptoms are modelled as an ever-present doubling of the traumatic wound. As a gateway to the rest of the volume, Chapter 1 concludes by arguing that theatre/performance, more than any other art form, is perfectly placed to attempt a dialogue with, and even a representation of, trauma.

Alongside the first chapter, Chapter 2, which develops a supplement to Raymond Williams' *Modern Tragedy*, forms the theoretical foundation of the book. The chapter argues that Williams' notion of 'structure of feeling' can be used to identify a contemporary, societal 'psychic' trauma (in the West) which pervades daily existence. This reading of contemporary, Western late-capitalist society is modelled through Williams and through Schechner's 'infinity loop' between social and aesthetic drama. The work of the chapter shows that, for contemporary society, Schechner's loop illustrates a constant dramatization of the world using aesthetic orderings and imagery, creating a flattening or disjunction in community. Building on this reading of Schechner, the chapter proposes that the loop itself needs reworking: I refigure the loop to illustrate the almost instantaneous interchange between the social/ritual and the aesthetic in contemporary society. The chapter draws on the work of Marshall McLuhan, Fredric Jameson, Susan Sontag and Jean Baudrillard to develop an understanding of our current structure of feeling. This is traced through the development of Live Art practices and the privileging of the live since the late 1960s. From this base, the chapter examines the chronology of tragic forms that Williams proposes in order to suggest, in light of the contemporary structure of feeling, a new contemporary tragic form and mode of performance, trauma-tragedy, as a means of engaging with and shedding new light on performance works which address trauma.

While I propose that this historical development of tragedy is directly related to our desire for a more 'real' experience at the theatre, relating to arguments that will be made in later chapters, I am not suggesting trauma-tragedy as a genre *per se*. Rather, the work here is to model a theoretical means of analysis and suggest a performance mode through which we can approach a wide canon of work that taps into an emergent zeitgeist and desire for a sense of 'reality' in the theatre. Concurrently, trauma-tragedy is positioned as a means by which society can engage in attempting to understand, contextualize and bear witness to its own social dramas and traumas. It is pertinent and important to note here that while this volume addresses a large and diverse set of performance examples, these are not simply a mix of disparate live events that have been brought together as illustrative of the concerns of the writing. Nor are they only symptomatic in some ways of the contemporary structure of feeling I am discussing. Rather, the performances analysed throughout the book (and many others besides) can be brought together as a coherent grouping of works that can help both to establish an understanding of our structure of feeling and move forward in a more determined/productive way within it.

The possibility that live performance can put the spectator into an experience of trauma's central paradox is explored in Chapter 3. Taking W. J. T. Mitchell's assertion that contemporary art is 'incorrigibly insisting' on attempting to 'transmit trauma as directly as possible' to the spectator (2005: 295), the chapter proposes a formulation of a productive mimesis, primarily after Benjamin and Taussig, in which the mimetic object acts as a mode of knowledge over that which is represented. From this point the chapter moves into a discussion of two performance examples, *BR.#04* and *Still Life*, in order to argue that performance can hold the spectator in a state of flux between a sense of the 'reality' of a performance and an understanding/ recognition of mimesis. Using these two very different performances, I propose that certain moments of performance act as rhetorical, performative Barthesian *puncta* which impact upon the audience to stimulate a state of what I term 'mimetic shimmering'. This places the audience into an experience of trauma's central paradox, and through this performance can be seen to act as a site of and for the rehearsal of trauma. The performative *punctum* is the catalyst to opening the shimmering between reality and representation that causes the audience to stumble in their reading of the performance, which can in turn be associated with a represented experience of trauma's central paradox.

Unlike the third chapter's focus on two key examples, Chapter 4 widens the field of reference, exploring a number of performance examples to address performance as a possible site of witness. Here I discuss what it means to witness and to be witnessed in the context of trauma in performance. The chapter also argues that performance offers an opportunity for testimony which may function as some form of *catharsis* (from trauma). *Cathartic* here is read in light of Malcolm Heath's argument (1996) that (Aristotelian) *katharsis* is not intended to rid a person of their emotions but rather a means by which one comes to 'feel the right degree of emotion in the right circumstances' (Heath 1996: xxxix). The term is also considered through Judith Herman's assertion (2001) that a cathartic experience (in relation to trauma therapy) is less a purging but rather an 'integration' through a 'process of reconstruction' by which the trauma memory/story 'undergo[s] a transformation [... so as to become] more present and more real' (Herman 2001: 181).

The chapter principally focuses on the performance or script itself, rather than the audience experience, in order to investigate theatre/performance's ability to act as testifier of or witness to trauma. The broad range of cultural objects explored in Chapter 4 are read alongside and through trauma theory and psycho-therapeutic research (especially LaCapra 1996 and 2001; and Laub 1995) to foreground the centrality of witnessing within both trauma (theory/therapy) and the theatre. Highlighting the necessity for testimonial/witnessed outlet of traumatic memory, I propose that the theatre can act as such an outlet. I argue that trauma-tragic theatre is not only concerned with illustrating the destructive nature of a traumatic past that is not properly witnessed, but also that it can address the gap between the impossibility of articulating trauma and the necessity of doing so.

Moving away from this focus on the theatrical object, Chapter 5 turns more to the audience experience. From a definition of witnessing that primarily focused on 'theoretical' and 'therapeutic' conceptions, this chapter uses Karen Malpede (1996) and Simon Shepherd (2006) as starting points in a discussion of the kinaesthetic, visceral, phenomenological impact of witnessing, both 'in general' and specifically at the theatre. Employing the philosophy of (theatre) phenomenology as well as scientific theories of bodily perception/reception and Kristeva's semiosis, this chapter examines three distinct yet interrelating performance examples: Sarah Kane's *Blasted*, Kira O'Reilly's *Untitled (Syncope)* and Nicholas Wright's adaptation of *His Dark Materials* at the National Theatre.

The concern here is with the specifics of the *mise-en-scène* and its impact upon the watching audience. Focusing on the dramaturgical structure of *Blasted*, the first section examines how this play uses form to create a sense of traumatic presence through a disruption of audience expectations. From here I move on to address *His Dark Materials* and the creation of a 'presence-in-trauma effect' that is caused through an 'uncanny echo' between the diegetic action, or levels of textual meaning which are natural to the shape of the play, and a ritualized layer of coincidence which creates an 'unexplainable' presence of trauma.

The third performance under scrutiny is O'Reilly's *Untitled (Syncope)*. The analysis builds upon the notion of physical witnessing to discuss the kinaesthetic experience of *Untitled* and its ability to place the audience into a space of traumatic memory and, potentially, experience. Through a personal narrative of being at the performance and drawing upon O'Reilly's own thoughts (from an interview I held with her in 2008), this section considers how being moved about the space affected and augmented my felt connection to the body of the artist. In turn, I investigate how trauma can be part of a (performative) consideration of, in O'Reilly's words, 'what it is to have a body, what a body is and how that engages [with society]' (2008: personal interview).[7]

While this chapter proposes that there is a way of 'accessing' a performance through its visceral impact on the body, it also recognizes the importance of what Bert O. States referred to as 'binocular vision' in reading performance (1985: 8). The chapter thus works through the relationship between the semiotic and the phenomenological not to suggest an ascendancy of phenomenology over semiotics, but to propose that it is one way in which we understand and experience the traumatic (in the theatre).

Having mainly looked at the stage and live performances in the preceding chapters, the book then turns slightly to pull the modelling established in earlier chapters through a consideration of a different but related area. Chapter 6 functions as a development of and bridge from the point that we arrive at with Chapter 5 to the Conclusion, which considers the ethical in performance and trauma. In Chapter 6, I look directly out to the world of the social through the events of Abu Ghraib and then reflect back to examine some fundamentals of stage performance in a discussion of corpsing and drying. While drawing on the theoretical models established in the previous chapters, there is here a slight shift in focus. First, I argue that theatricality and performativity can be employed as mechanisms by which 'traumas' can be inflicted upon a person or persons, or through which we might recognize the performativity of trauma in everyday life. Second, I investigate the theatrical 'failures' of corpsing and drying as specific instances of theatrical trauma. These failures not only unravel the performance event but also impact repeatedly and violently on the performers themselves in an uncanny echoing of trauma-symptoms.

In drawing the book to a close, I consider questions of ethics in relation to performance which addresses trauma. The Conclusion functions both as a means of positioning the notion of trauma-tragedy within the developing scholarship on theatre (and) ethics, an area of study which is related to and developing at the same time as my own, and serves as a means of pointing forward from the results of the investigations contained within these pages.

1

Trauma's performative genealogy

'Daddy!' she screams. 'Daddy!' –
Her voice is snatched away by the boom of the surf.
Her father turns aside, with a word
She cannot hear. She chokes –
Hands are cramming a gag into her mouth.
They bind it there with cord, like a horse's bit […]

Now rough hands rip off her silks
And the wind waltzes with them
Down across the beach, and over the surf.
Her eyes swivel in their tears.
She recognises her killers.

(Aeschylus 1999: 15)

On 22 February 2007 I read an article detailing the gang rape of a fourteen-year-old Iraqi girl and the murder and cremation of her entire family by American soldiers fighting the 'War on Terror':

She kept trying to keep her legs closed and saying stuff in Arabic,' Cortez said. 'During the time me and Barker were raping Abeer, I heard gunshots that came from the bedroom. After Barker was done, Green came out and said that he had killed them all [...] Green then placed himself between Abeer's legs to rape her.'

Green shot the girl dead too, at which point the soldiers set her on fire. The fire prompted neighbours to contact Abeer's uncle, who discovered the bodies.

(Gumbel 2007: n.p.)

In a world where violence is becoming increasingly normalized and pervasive, something in this writing caught my attention and drew me in. The first person testimony carried some kind of authenticity that positioned me as a witness to this atrocity without my physical presence in the scene. Yet the events remained 'unreal' and impossible to grasp fully. In an attempt to work through and objectify the story a little, I ran a performance experiment that attempted to locate the rape in the landscape of imagination as a means to interrogate how and why the perpetrators were able to report such a heinous crime with clinical detachment, seemingly without realizing the trauma they inflicted:

Three men walk on stage; they are wearing their own everyday clothes. They sit down and watch the end of another piece of action. Eventually they start to chat among themselves about childhood dreams and fears. During this conversation they are periodically given bits of clothing 'found' on stage which they change into, eventually becoming 'soldiers'. They all finish speaking with a line professing their childhood desire to be in the army: 'when I grew up I wanted to be a soldier' etcetera. Then, as a group, they stalk the stage like children playing at being soldiers, throwing imaginary grenades and shooting invisible enemies.

The playing becomes increasingly 'serious': the soldiers suddenly rush towards two women, who are stage right, with purpose and aggression. One wrenches a woman half to her feet by the hair and drags her off stage violently; another hits the second woman, knocking her on to the pile of clothes on the floor, the third proceeds to undo his trousers and 'rape' her. Crying, she tries to fight him off and keep her legs closed. As the first rape finishes the soldier who hit the victim takes over. The first soldier walks back onstage and rapes her for a third time, but she cannot fight any more. She has become very quiet. He finishes and the soldiers exit.

The experiment 'failed' when put in front of an audience; the representations seemed clumsy, blunt and misanthropically polemical. As a result, it did not help to work through the story of Abeer nor did it represent any similar trauma with any complexity or 'insight', rather it felt like it became a hackneyed lecture on the horrors of war. However, in the moment of its first rehearsal the scene was clearly disturbing, powerful and shocking for performers and director-spectator alike. The rehearsal room was a difficult place to be in the moment of and after the repeated representations of rape. A silent tension engulfed the space which was broken only once we left the room. We had (unsubtly perhaps) given form and attempted to bear witness to an essentially unknowable experience. 'Unknowable' in the sense that one can never know rape unless party to it, either as perpetrator or victim, and even then the victim is unlikely to comprehend the event fully: the traumatic impact of an event like this exceeds one's ability to grasp it in the moment of its occurrence, rather it is enfolded into the body only to be made 'real' latterly and at a distance from the event and broken body through the aftershock of traumatic reoccurrence (cf. Solga 2006). Traumata are events which are unknowable in the instant of their occurrence; they must somehow be codified, set in relation to other events and experiences, in order that they might be confronted again so that the survivor-sufferer can begin to process them towards some level of comprehension (Solga 2006: 57).

Although 'no genre or discipline "owns" trauma as a problem or can provide definitive boundaries for it' (LaCapra 2001: 96), historically the term has been associated with physical injury, to be studied and treated by doctors and surgeons. Increasingly the term and theoretical model are employed across disciplines but the word is still extensively used in relation to physical injury, surgery and accidents. Trauma is defined medically as 'a term used in a physical sense as a wound or injury – such as a severe blow leading to a fracture' (Macpherson 2002: 634).[1] Trauma's etymological lineage is from the ancient Greek τραῦμα (*travma*), which comes from the verb τιτρώσκω meaning variously to break, cut, hurt, injure, scathe, sear or (most commonly) to wound. The ending of the word, -μα, means the result of the action, so τραῦμα can be considered to mean the result of the cut or wound etcetera.[2] The modern understanding of the word is thus borne out of its ancient roots concerning physical attack, but equally from the notion of a resultant wound, which is now recognized as being either or both physical and psychic. This etymology is appropriately violent for our modern understandings of trauma. The term's use in relation to psychic wounds came much later, towards the end of the 1880s, and the verb form later still (*circa* mid-1900s). This rough timeline accords with the period when understandings of trauma began to be reconfigured within psychopathological practices and discourses (cf. Hoad 1989; and Onions 1966).

During this period the definition of trauma started to shift from physical blow towards that of a shocking event, the impact of which is felt within the nerves and mind of the survivor. In the late nineteenth and early twentieth centuries, there was an extraordinary period of development in 'creative psychological theorizing' across Europe and the United States (Micale 2001: 115). It was during this period that the foundations of modern psychoanalysis/psychotherapy, psychology and psychiatry were developed. This Euro-American movement, initially coming out of studies on hysteria and neuroses, was predominantly led by European figures such as Pierre Janet, Jean-Martin Charcot and Hermann Oppenheim. Charcot's influence on the history of trauma theory (and psychoanalysis more widely) is of particular importance as his theorizations and examinations of hysteria positioned him as the pedagogical leader of the field for some time. The Salpêtrière Hospital in Paris, Charcot's clinical home and the scene of much controversy, became a centre for the diagnosis and study of *névrose traumatique* in the late 1800s. Key to Charcot's theorization on the cause of 'hystero-traumatism' was his belief that the original trauma-event was not the principal cause of 'hysteria' but operated as a trigger to a hereditary predisposition to nervous and/or neurological malady.[3] Although fundamental to later theorizations of trauma, we might also highlight that while a traumatic incident may, in so far as we agree with Charcot, trigger hereditary predispositions to hysteria, we can go further to suggest that such an incident can lay the foundation for a later predisposition that is not necessarily hereditary.

Trauma's theatrical history

> Yes sirree... as the ringmaster would say.
>
> (Didi-Huberman 2003: 187)

The development of trauma theory is underpinned by a history of theatricality, and performativity is inherent within the structure of trauma. Charcot's practices are central within this discourse, but before turning to consider them in more detail I would like to attend to another, less written about but contemporaneous 'trauma theorist', the surgeon Herbert W. Page. His book, *Injuries of the Spine and Spinal Cord and Nervous Shock*, was published in 1883 at a time when modernism, industrialization and the rise of the city were redrawing the cartography of Britain and Europe. Luckhurst proposes that the conceptualization of trauma could only have emerged within modernity and the increasing mechanization of society. He suggests that the mark of modernity was the rise of the city and its subsuming of 'the majority of the British population' by the end of the nineteenth century. He further contends, through Benjamin, that modern city life is comprised of 'a series of shocks and collisions' which in effect spawned a new conceptualization of self: an 'urban self' which existed within a series of 'traumatic encounters' (Luckhurst 2008: 19–20). In *Illuminations* (1955), Benjamin, according to Luckhurst, relies on Freud's ideas of the shock that 'overwhelms psychic defences' to draw a picture of Paris (a surrogate for all cities) as a city of these traumatic encounters (Luckhurst 2008: 20). City life might thus begin to be formulated as a series of traumatic events, of 'shocks and collisions'. This 'shocking' urban lifestyle might further be thought of as stimulating the beginnings of modern investigations into trauma. These nascent inquiries principally focused on train wreck survivors, whose symptoms became known as 'railway spine'. Indeed, Luckhurst convincingly states, in a widely recognized and supported argument, that the 'origin of the idea of trauma was inextricably linked to the expansion of the railways in the 1860s' (2008: 21). It was from his experience of working with these types of survivors that Page wrote his 1883 tome.

In *Injuries of the Spine*, Page argued that the symptoms of railway spine were the result of the shock sustained in a traumatic incident, specifically in the case of train crashes, and not the result of physical injury. He proposed that these symptoms, which he aligned with those of hysteria, indicated 'some functional disturbance of the whole nervous balance or tone rather than structural damage to any organ of the body' (Page 1883: 143). Furthermore, he suggested that this disturbance was caused by an imminent threat of death and 'the hopelessness of escape from danger' in the moment of collision that gave rise to a powerful emotional experience or dissonance that in itself was sufficient to produce shock (1883: 148). Page's musings on trauma are closely aligned with current conceptions of the condition, especially in his formulation of 'nervous shock' where he suggests that the symptoms have been:

> [w]arded off in the first place by the excitement of the scene, the shock gathering, in the very delay itself, new force from the fact that the sources of alarm are continuous, and for the time all prevalent in the patient's mind.
>
> (1883: 148)

However, at the time of writing his book Page had been working for the London and North Western Railway Company for nine years and thus, as Luckhurst contends, these 'modern' arguments might be seen to come from less than objective, 'pecuniary motives' (Luckhurst 2008: 23). Coinciding with the expansion of the railways was a huge rise in locomotive accidents (evidently leading to the examinations and discourses surrounding the effects of them) and, as a result, a rise in compensation claims made against the rail companies because there appeared to be an organic link between crash and damage or symptom, and increasingly compensation was being awarded in the absence of a visible injury (cf. Luckhurst 2008: 23). So, if Page was able to link nervous shock to theorizations of hysteria, he would be 'equat[ing] it with a shameful, effeminate disorder, often dismissed as a form of disease *imitation* (what was called "neuromimesis") or malingering' (Luckhurst 2008: 23; emphasis is original). The legal and perhaps clinical result of this would be to throw doubt on the validity of the victim's symptoms.

It is within this notion of malingering – especially as it relates to *imitation*, pretence and make-believe – that I want to suggest that Page's arguments align the genealogy of trauma with a sense of performativity or theatricality. Page devotes Chapter 7 of his book to notions and instances of malingering within cases of nervous shock, or hysteria, and proposes at the beginning of his conclusions that the possibility of receiving compensation despite displaying no physical symptoms was prompting and prolonging cases of hysteria:

> the knowledge that compensation is a certainty for the injuries received, tends, almost from the first moment of illness, to colour the course and aspect of the case, with each succeeding day to become part and parcel of the injury in the patient's mind.

(Page 1883: 255)

This amounts to a perpetuation of hysteric symptoms through what might be thought of as a neuromimetic performance, through playing the role of a hysteric for financial gain – or, literally, acting (it) out.

This discourse of theatricality within trauma's history continues with Charcot and the theatrics of his infamous *Lecons du Mardi*. In his authoritative and illuminating book *Invention of Hysteria* (2003), Georges Didi-Huberman points out that Charcot's use of hypnosis was a central tool in his 'therapy'. He would put typically female patients into a hypnotic trance and then induce hysterical episodes through various theatrical and 'far from innocent [... public] fondling of bodies' (Didi-Huberman 2003: 176). His techniques varied from exploding packages of gun-cotton under patients' noses to 'masturbating them [...] until they could take no more' and even to 'prescriptions for coitus' (176). These methods were played out in the overtly theatrical setting of his famous Tuesday Lectures with the expressed purpose of investigating, understanding and curing *les névrose traumatique*, but which, as medical photographer for the Salpêtrière, Albert Londe pointed out, did not produce any clinical value (cf. Didi-Huberman 2003: 210). Charcot presided over these theatrics as writer, director and performer; Didi-Huberman gives evidence that each one was drafted and redrafted 'with lines, soliloquies, stage direction, asides by the hero, and so on' (243). It is evident from the moment one begins reading the numerous accounts of Charcot's hypnotic techniques that because his methods involved 'coaching', or structured 'playing' that was designed to achieve predisposed or pre-planned responses, the clinical validity of the experiments is questionable at best and akin to sanctioned rape at worst. Charcot seems more like torturer than trusted doctor or pioneering psychotherapist; indeed the staged repetitions of the hystero-traumatic 'first time', or 'primal scenes' as Freud would later coin it, were as much new traumas as they were repetitions. The relationship between Charcot and his patients was one of performed 'torment' in which Charcot issued 'experimental "blow[s]" [*coup(s)*]' in order to produce attitudes and *tableaux* for the delight of a largely non-medical audience (Didi-Huberman 2003: 176 and cf. 176–210).

The importance of an audience and the rhetorical use of theatrical techniques illustrate the overtly performative quality of Charcot's work. It returns us and lends further weight and pertinence to the psychoanalytic term 'acting out', but here the term is inverted, as it were, for it is the analyst, not the analysand, who is author of the drama. Charcot's theatricalized practice also highlights the dubious and contested background from which trauma theory has grown. Trauma theory as we know it today can thus be seen to have its roots in a succession of violently theatrical traumatic experiences and pecuniarily motivated presentations of performed hysterical symptoms before audiences that, when not motivated by pure entertainment, were there to 'watch', 'see' or 'observe' another in a theatrically framed experimental space.

Trauma's double wound

> Search not a wound too deep lest thou make a new one.
> (Fuller ctd in Christy 1887: 517)

As trauma theory has developed it has moved past both the notion of 'hystero-traumatism' and Charcot's techniques to acknowledge the original event as the primary, causal site of traumatic neurological repetitions. It was under Charcot and in the environment of the Salpêtrière that the young Freud began to formulate his earliest musings on the human mind. Having observed at the Salpêtrière

(1885–1886), Freud later said (1893) that he had been 'completely under the spell of Charcot's researches' (ctd in Luckhurst 2008: 45). It is little wonder, then, that he was so inclined to sexual readings of his patients' maladies and in his writings at the beginning of his career. However, having later rejected hypnosis and indeed many other aspects of Charcot's work, Freud could be argued to have become the founding father, so to speak, of Trauma Studies as it is known today. His ideas developed and radically changed throughout his career, most notably after World War I as a result of his contact with soldiers suffering from 'shell shock'. *The Wolfman* (1918), *Beyond the Pleasure Principle* (1920) and *Moses and Monotheism* (1939) are his best known and, perhaps, most influential texts on trauma. These texts proffered three ideas that were central to the development of trauma theory, namely: the notion of 'primal scene', the first scene of trauma, usually an infantile experience of witnessing a sexual act, which is repressed until adulthood; 'traumatic neurosis', although it is important to point out that Charcot had penned the phrase *névrose traumatique* as early as 1885; and (perhaps most importantly) 'latency', used to explain the psychological return of the event in the mind of an 'apparently uninjured' victim of trauma after an unspecified period of time from the moment of the incident.[4]

In more recent years, Freud's ideas have been developed by a number of writers including Cathy Caruth, Dori Laub, Dominic LaCapra and Judith Herman. While trauma has been redefined and reconsidered over many decades, there is still no single definition or unified understanding of it. Despite common or colloquial understandings, trauma remains a much contested area of debate and clinical study which continues to generate a great deal of literature, from many different disciplinary perspectives. It is with this in mind that I now turn, briefly, to Anthony Neilson's play *Normal* (1991) as a bridge to the work of formulating an understanding of trauma in the context of this study and from the disciplinary perspective of theatre and performance more broadly.

> WEHNER: [...]
> Every one of those victims was someone's daughter, someone's lover, someone's brother, son. Imagine their thoughts. Imagine the details of their thoughts.

> Imagine thinking about your child's last moments on
> this earth, alone, afraid, the child that you made, the child
> that you saw smile for the first time, that you saw walk,
> that you heard talk. What noises did it make in that last
> moment?
> What look was in its eyes? Did it feel pain when the
> blade went in?
> Did it call your name?
> Because maybe she walked out the door that night and
> out of your life and maybe you didn't even say goodbye.
> And you sit there sorting through her things, the tatty
> toys she used to hug, her tiny shoes, her simple books,
> and you pack them away in boxes with your hopes and
> dreams, the ornaments of a life, and you think maybe if I
> had done this or that then maybe she'd still be alive maybe
> she is still alive maybe there's been some mistake and then
> it hits you again the deafening slam of the irreversible;
> she's gone, she's gone for ever
> She's gone
> for ever.
>
> (Neilson 1998: 40)

If you are attacked on the street while walking home, you are
unlikely thereafter to feel the same about dismissing the shadow
that seems to be following you; as the above section from *Normal*
suggests, if your child dies (whether violently or not) you are
going to question the natural order of life, forever entangled in
the desire for forensic knowledge of the events and perpetually
wondering 'what if…'. Trauma-events progressively destroy positive values of self and one's sense of safety in the world through
imaginative restagings of the original event in the mind of the
sufferer (Herman 2001: 51). These small infractions become
ever more problematic as their accumulative effect begins to
manifest itself not as mere nervousness but as the symptom of
psychological distress or, as it is now known, Post Traumatic
Stress Disorder (PTSD).

PTSD, while having been almost unanimously taken up by the
psycho-medical professions since its first recognition in 1980,
implicitly suggests that the originating event is the only trauma,

condemning the psychological return of the event as somehow something other than traumatic. Despite widespread discussion of trauma hallucinations as a 'perpetually reexperienced [...] painful, dissociated, traumatic present' which, Ruth Leys points out, 'refuses to be represented [in the mind of the sufferer] *as* past', the theory of PTSD still persists in both medical and academic discourses of trauma (Leys 2000: 2–3). To use the word 'post' in this context is to deny the very present-ness of traumatic hallucinations (a central component of 'trauma-symptoms'), and so in turn denies the potency and immediacy of these psychic returns.

Outside of physio-medical understandings, Cathy Caruth's succinct definition of trauma is particularly useful for my concerns in this volume:

> [trauma is] an overwhelming experience of sudden or cata-strophic events in which the response to the event occurs in the often delayed, uncontrolled repetitive appearance of hallucinations and other intrusive phenomena.
>
> (Caruth 1996: 11)

Cognate with this is Felicity de Zulueta's proposition that these intrusive phenomena remain with the sufferer like 'a foreign body permanently at work in the unconscious' (de Zulueta 1993: 100). Trauma is thus a perpetually present absence; while the original event is a historical absence, the survivor-sufferer lives under the force of its continual re-performance. These re-presentations, primal scenes in their own right, exert a perpetual influence on the sufferer's movement through the world, contradicting the suggestion of their being *post*-traumatic. Thus, I propose 'trauma-event' and 'trauma-symptoms' as terms to distinguish between the original traumatic moment and its disruptive return.

Caruth's theory that the original traumatic event is not fully experienced or witnessed at the moment of its happening, and is only accessible through a delayed return of the event in repeti-tive nightmares, is at the core of contemporary trauma theory. Dominic LaCapra, in a widely supported argument, has prof-fered that traumatic events numb the senses to the moment of impact and therefore they cannot be registered at the time of their occurrence (LaCapra 1996: 174). In the moment of the event, the body is only concerned in dealing with the immediacy of the event. The survivor-sufferer thus always experiences traumata as a historical phenomenon; the trauma-symptom is constructed in a post-hoc reliving of the trauma-event. While some trauma theorists regard the repetitive nightmares of trauma-symptoms as non-symbolic and absolutely cognate with or true to the original event, others identify a more complex relationship with the trauma-symptom which suggests that the return of the trauma-event is mimetic but always already distorted (cf. Leys 2000: 239–255). A more detailed engagement with the notion of mimesis and trauma can be found in Chapter 3, but it is worth noting here that Leys proffers the suggestion that trauma theory can be seen as 'simultaneously attracted to and repelled by' the idea of mimesis in trauma. This is because there is a sense that while an acceptance of the mimetic quality of the trauma-symptoms at once helps to 'explain the victim's suggestibility and abjection', in the same instant it is also a threat to 'individual autonomy and responsibility' to the trauma-event and memory of it (Leys 2000: 9).

While Leys uses the term 'mimesis' without glossing or developing it, I suggest that there are two ways in which mimesis might be working here. Firstly, the repetitive nightmares amount to an internal mimetic, representational restaging of the trauma-event. Secondly, mimesis constitutes a second wound, or, to put it another way, co-constitutes the double wound of the trauma-event. It is this double and repeating wound which instigates and perpetuates a collapse of narrative time, and which re-presents the trauma-event in the mind of the survivor-sufferer ensuring they are kept in stasis, unable to live in either the past or the present.

Roberta Culbertson proposes that survivor-sufferers experience a 'temporal blanking' in which the mind continuously records the passage of time during the trauma, but the mind leaves 'a particular stretch simply open, the images and experience [are put] elsewhere, not accessible to the normal process of constructing a narrative of one's life' (Culbertson 1995: 175). The primary event is simply too overwhelming to comprehend at the time of its happening, like the soldier rushing into battle, or indeed an actor's first entrance; adrenalin surges forth numbing the moment of impact.[5] Trauma sits beyond or outside the normal range of human experience: we have no field of reference within which to understand the event as it happens and coupled with the surge of adrenalin we experience in the moment of catastrophe, the human body is only concerned with surviving the event rather than understanding it.

However, this original event is revisited time and again after it has passed, re-experienced in flashbacks, physical/muscle memories, nightmares and behavioural re-enactments which constitute the trauma-symptoms. Because of the impossibility of assimilating/experiencing the event as it happens, this reliving can feel more 'real' than the event itself. Distanced from the trauma-event, the body is able to witness it more clearly, evoking emotions, fears and reactions that were absent from the experience of the original trauma.

This disruptive reoccurrence points towards a definition of trauma which moves away from a focus on the event, and the physical injuries it causes, to a focus on the psychological impact of it. Traumatic impact is centred on the refusal of the event to be simply located and in its persistent reappearance 'outside the boundaries of any single place or time' (Caruth 1995: 9). Luckhurst moves the debate into a more explicitly cultural realm, but nevertheless continues on similar lines, suggesting that trauma challenges the survivor-sufferers' capacity for narrative knowledge; 'in its shocking impact trauma is anti-narrative, but it also generates the manic production of retrospective narratives that seek to explicate the trauma' (Luckhurst 2008: 79). The inability of the trauma sufferer to locate the event in a singular time or place highlights the pervasive nature of trauma itself. Trauma is a constant present. It is the unconscious recurrences – so often described by words such as catastrophic, overwhelming, incomprehensible and disturbing – which perpetually tie the survivor of an event to the trauma of its aftermath. 'For those who undergo trauma, it is not only the moment of the event,' Caruth argues, 'but the passing out of it that is traumatic; that *survival itself*, in other words, *can be a crisis*' (Caruth 1995: 9; emphasis is original). The very nature of these intrusions, their untimely/uninvited character, brings to the fore what Herman describes as the 'central dialectic' of trauma: the desire to forget and banish to history the events responsible for the intrusions in opposition to the overwhelming need to speak about (testify) and in some way 'relive' these events in order to comprehend them, and so attempt to heal the wounds (Herman 2001: 1).

However, given that trauma-symptoms occur in irregular, unintentional and unwanted eruptions, I propose that this figures a second and equally important opposition. Rather than one central dialectic, this second tension creates a triangulation of oppositions between the desire to forget the original event, the repetitive and uninvited intrusions of the fragmented memories of that event, and the necessity to consciously remember/relive/ restage it in order to attempt to move beyond and eventually forget it (see Figure 1). It is within these oppositions that traumatic memory operates, creating a shudder of uncertainty in the sufferer's understanding of the world and their place in it.

In addition, I want to advocate that there are other complicating factors bound up within this formulation. Because it is not possible to comprehend fully what is happening in the immediacy of the moment, it is only after a period of latency that we are able to 'see' the event, to witness it properly through reliving, re-staging and narrativizing. This 'proper witnessing' is further complicated by the fact that while trauma-symptoms evade public representation, they are at the same time themselves representations of the original event. In her musings on loss and (its) 'survival' in the introduction to *Mourning Sex*, performance

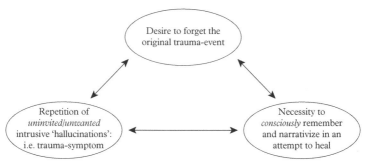

Figure 1: Trauma tensions triangulation.

theorist Peggy Phelan touches on trauma as already existent within humankind from the moment of birth. Her language evokes a sense of evisceration at birth as we are 'severed from the placenta and cast from the womb' only to enter the world as 'amputated' bodies defined by our own mortality (Phelan 1997: 5).[6] During these opening pages she postulates that 'trauma is untouchable [...] it cannot be represented. The symbolic cannot carry it: trauma makes a tear in the symbolic network itself' (5); trauma, in other words, is beyond representation. This, though, is to deny the representational quality of trauma-symptoms and as such I propose that a more accurate reading may be to suggest that trauma is beyond representation outside of the representational trauma-symptoms.

However, the incessant repetition of the trauma-symptoms might be seen precisely to accord with the impossibility of an adequate signifier; the symptoms constantly recur without end because they are never actually represented. By this I mean that despite the representational quality of the trauma-symptoms, the survivor-sufferer has no means of decoding this representation because its irruption in the psyche is both uninvited and is traumatic in its own right. Thus, there is no adequate representation or narrativization of the original event, but enough that that event persists in a cyclical, ritual repetition which perpetuates a disruption of linear time, memory and, consequently, notions of selfhood.

Caruth asks if trauma is 'the encounter with death, or the ongoing experience of having survived it?' (Caruth 1996: 7). Trauma is a disruption of the self, of self-composure; it is a perpetual disruption of personal time which questions understandings of self because it recurs without anticipation continually to call into question our comprehension of the world and our movements through it. For example, surviving the death of one's child is without doubt a traumatic rupturing of the fabric of life. In a striking echo of Wehner's statement from *Normal*, Lucy Blackman's mother, Jane Steare, tried to articulate how she felt after Joji Obara was cleared, in April 2007, of murdering Lucy: 'I only sleep when exhausted. I often awake again in the early hours and begin wondering if this was the time of night she died. I wonder if she suffered. Did she feel any pain? Did she call out my name? I'll never know' (BBC 2007: online).[7] Traumas violate constructions of self and family that have been built up over many years of life experience but no physical harm need necessarily have been inflicted on the trauma sufferer. They call into question all which we might hold sacred, our understandings of safety and privacy. In his illuminating investigation of the impact of separation of mother and baby, paediatrician and child psychologist D. W. Winnicott clearly illustrates the disruptive quality of trauma even in the earliest moments of life:

> [i]n x + y + z minutes [of separation] the baby is *traumatised*. In x + y + z minutes the mother's return does not mend the baby's altered state. Trauma implies that the baby has experienced a break in life's continuity, so that the primitive defences now become organised to defend against a repetition of 'unthinkable anxiety' or a return of the acute confusional state that belongs to disintegration of nascent ego structure.
>
> (Winnicott 2001: 97)

It is clear that the separation of mother and baby is not a physical trauma (in the sense of a wound) but the separation manifests itself physically in agitation, crying and becoming traumatized. The key phrase is 'the baby's altered state', indicating that the separation has caused the baby to begin to question its still nascent construction of self in relation to the mother's presence. The trauma is not the separation itself but the way in which this event alters the 'nascent ego structure'.

There is, here, a slight (Lacanian) complication which needs to be negotiated. While Winnicott might see the separation of mother and baby as anxiety ridden and part of a disintegration of the baby's ego structure, for Lacan the ego is precisely *constituted* by separation from the mother. The separation is a split which is rehearsed time and again in the *fort/da* game which Freud reported in *Beyond the Pleasure Principle*. Lacan repeatedly returns to the *fort/da* game as he grapples with questions of absence, loss and death. Lacan's analyses of the game focused on the infant's desire for a sense of being whole or complete through some form of sublimated return to the mother's womb (cf. Chaitin 1996: 75–76). The *fort/da* repetition according to Lacan, according to Chaitin, is an attempt to 'overcome the deprivation of separation by actively reproducing the trauma' of separation from the mother (76). Thus the child comes to constitute their 'self' as autonomous via a performance, or performative iteration of trauma. Reading separation through both Lacan's take on Freud's *fort/da* and through Winnicott, a paradox emerges: the separation not only causes a tear in the construction of self in relation to the mother (which is traumatic) but also begins to signal the onset of the baby's construction of their independent self. This is, then, trauma as both construction and destruction. Not only are we 'traumatically' born, following Phelan, but also the trauma of separation in early life further comes to 'make' us 'us'.

Returning to the trope of disruption, Phelan elegantly touches upon the schism in self-constitution caused by sexual trauma: 'trauma tears the fabric of knowledge itself: it is a wound in the system of meaning through which the subject knows the world, knows him or herself' (Phelan 1997: 95). So, to answer Caruth's question, trauma is not the encounter with death but is the ongoing *re*-experiencing of having survived it.

Trauma, then, can be seen to rupture the foundations of knowledge by which we recognize ourselves. The psychic wound trauma inflicts can be seen to make the self absent from the body: we cannot be truly present in the moment of original trauma nor in the uninvited repetitions of it in our mind's eye. Put another way: our physical presence in the trauma-event makes us psychologically absent from the experience of that moment until such time as our bodies are no longer present at it. Only then can we become unintentionally psycho-present at the event once more. The repetition of presence and absence, and the desire for constant self-presence, is played out in and is central to traumatic experience. Judith Herman (2001), resonating with Phelan, posits that trauma 'destroys the belief that one can *be oneself* in relation to others' (53; emphasis is original) and that trauma-events worry at and disrupt basic human relationships and attachments, 'shatter[ing] the construction of self that is formed and sustained in relation to others' and ultimately 'cast the victim into a state of existential crisis' through a fundamental violation of the survivor-sufferers' understanding of natural order (Herman 2001: 51). Meanwhile, playwright and theatre scholar Karen Malpede has commented that '[b]ecause theatre takes place in public and involves the movement of bodies across a stage, theatre seems uniquely suited to portray the complex interpersonal [and intrapersonal] realities of trauma' (Malpede 1996: 168). Echoing something similar, Luckhurst comments that 'culture rehearses or restages narratives that attempt to animate and explicate trauma that has been formulated as something that exceeds the possibility of narrative knowledge' (Luckhurst 2008: 79). This paradox surrounding narrative is taken further in Hans-Thies Lehmann's examination of perfor-mance in which he claims that performance can 'question and destabilise the spectator's construction of identity' (Lehmann 2006: 5). This striking echo of Herman's assertion that traumatic events shatter the construction of self is particularly interesting as it once again plots the line between performance and trauma. Not only can trauma-symptoms be considered as performa-tive disturbances of self, time and psyche, but it would further appear, under Lehmann's assertion, that theatre/performance shares this destabilizing power. Thus live performance, more than any other art form, is perfectly placed to attempt a dialogue with trauma, and perhaps, working against Phelan's assertions, even a representation of it.

2
Trauma-tragedy: a structure of feeling

In 1971, Chris Burden stood five metres away from a friend who shot him with a .22 calibre rifle. The bullet was only supposed to graze his arm but Burden flinched slightly as the gun was fired, moving his arm fully into the path of the oncoming bullet. It pierced his skin, tore through his bicep and exited through the flesh on the back of his arm.

Shoot has become one of Burden's best known works and he said of the piece that 'it seems that bad art is theatre […] Getting shot is for real […] there's no element of pretence or make-believe in it' (Burden ctd in Carlson 2004: 113). In 1995 Harold Pinter said that Sarah Kane's work was like 'facing something actual and true and ugly and painful' (Pinter ctd in Saunders 2002: 25). Separated by almost two and a half decades and by a plethora of theatrical or performative differences, the gap between what Burden and Kane both seem to be striving to achieve in their art, and indeed more generally between the Performance Art and plays discussed throughout this book, is not as vast as it might first appear. Pinter's suggestion that Kane's work presents an 'actual and true' experience accords with Burden's seeming desire for a move away from the 'bad art' of theatrical pretence to an authenticity of gunshot wound performances.

The desire for 'authenticity' which Burden identifies ties into Lionel Trilling's proposal that the fact that authenticity has 'become part of the moral slang of our day points to the peculiar nature of our fallen condition, our anxiety over the credibility of our existence and of individual existences' (Trilling 1972: 128). The desire for 'authenticity' is a desire to experience something 'real' in our lives which seem to be, in our 'modern' times, according to Handler, increasingly 'unreal' (Handler 1986: 3). Sociologist Theo Van Leeuwan proposes that authenticity is an evaluative concept and as such has to be understood according to the socio-cultural epoch in which it is being used. Thus, authenticity of performance, irrespective of it being a spontaneous, 'everyday' performance or a performance by an actor, is bound to culturally specific 'social norms' (Van Leeuwan, 2001: 392–394). One conceptualization which seems particularly useful in the context of Burden's desire for 'real' experiences and Pinter's reading of Kane's work as 'actual and true' is that something might be thought of as authentic because 'it is thought to be true to the essence of something, to a revealed truth [or] a deeply felt sentiment' (Van Leeuwan 2001: 393). Authenticity is a 'special kind of modality or special aspect of modality' which is focused on the 'moral or artistic authority of the representation' rather than on any sense of a truthful/accurate copy of an original (Van Leeuwan 2001: 396). Modality, here, refers to:

> the semiotic resources we use for expressing 'as how true' or 'as how real' a given representation is to be taken, and to the ways in which we use these resources. Applied, for instance, to visual representation, the question of modality is not, 'Did what we see in this image really happen?', or 'Does what we see in this image really exist', but 'Is it represented *as though* it has really happened or *as though* it really exists?'
>
> (Van Leeuwan 2001: 396; emphasis is original)

By authentic, then, I am not referring to any sense of a 'faithful', historically accurate re-presentation but to a sense of presenting and accessing cathected experience.[1]

This search for a more truthful or more authentic live experience can not only be loosely seen to stem from the 'happenings' of the late 1960s but is also echoed in the notion of 'traumaculture' and is part of the trauma trope discussed in the last chapter. The move towards the 'actual and true' in performances such as Burden's, or as identified in the work of many of the practitioners

I discuss throughout this volume is, I believe, a central and (re)emergent preoccupation within performance culture today.

Robert Lepage's Dragon's Trilogy *(2005, first premiered 1985) is a little under six hours long and, as such, it is at times both demanding and exhausting. Somewhere towards the end of the second hour a scene begins in which the actors pretend to ice-skate around a rectangular path that marks out the edges of the stage. The sound system streams classical music helping to augment the suggested scene of an idyllic afternoon out. The actors'/characters' shoes, the ghosts of their presence, sit neatly arranged downstage centre on the pebbles that cover the central area of the rectangle. The music builds and builds until the volume and cacophony seem to envelop the whole auditorium and the speakers send reverberations through the seating. The lights slowly fade to red and the actors are no longer 'skating' but have lined up on the pebbles just behind their shoes. The tallest is wearing a naval uniform. They salute the audience. The music heightens the sense that something is going to happen and tension seems to fill the auditorium. The actors, still smiling as if simply out skating, start marching, chomping and crunching their skates across the pebbles as they bisect and cut lines through the stage to the rhythm of the music. Ever faster; ever more violently they move until there is no doubt that the audience is watching 'war'. The music is evocative and emotive; its volume and persistence heighten the sense of violence and fear signalled by the smashing ice-skates. And then it happens: the first of the pairs of shoes is trampled by the blades of an actor's skates, the symbolic ghosts of others decimated as the war machine rumbles, ever smiling, on and on. The stage action has had visible effects as the audience embody their emotions; some cry, others close their eyes and hang their heads in their hands. And then it ends. Blackout and silence. A sense of emptiness and exhaustion descends.*

Restaged in 2005 in the midst of the wars in Iraq and Afghanistan, this scene evokes links to those conflicts and with wars more generally. However, the effect it had on the audience suggests that this theatrical experience presented something that was more tangible, more 'actual and true' and, in a sense, more 'ugly and painful' than the plethora of other representations concerned with war. The scene's theatricality, the very fact that it does not attempt naturalistic representation, gives the audience an impression of the emotional reality of war because it invites a projected, imagined embodiment in the presented action. No matter that the stage action is abstracted and stylized; the scene is visceral, tragic and sad, and the audience's reaction is visibly embodied. The immediacy of the embodied reaction indicates an authenticity of experience which might mirror the experience that Burden was searching for in his work and which might now be seen as part of an emergent contemporary theatrical experience (or as Raymond Williams might have it, as denoting an aspect of modern tragedy which speaks to our contemporary epoch).

Modern tragedy

Towards the close of 'Tragic Ideas', in *Modern Tragedy*, Raymond Williams identifies a number of 'tragedies' that while geographically removed from his seat in Cambridge are nonetheless identified as 'the names of our own crisis', events that, as with all traumas, create schisms which 'put all our lives into question again and again'; his list is, 'Korea, Suez, the Congo, Cuba, [and] Vietnam' (Williams 1966: 80). Twenty-three years after the first publication of *Modern Tragedy*, Williams expanded his list to include Czechoslovakia, Chile, Zimbabwe, Iran and Kampuchea (Williams 1989: 95). Today the list can be extended even further to include Iraq (twice), Afghanistan, Cambodia, Palestine/Israel and the Sudan. This list is far from exhaustive – it could, and probably should, include recent terrorist attacks in America, the United Kingdom, Spain and Bali, for example. Williams' list does, however, indicate the ongoing and (potentially) ever-increasing number of world events that can be, and are, deemed tragedies. We might also include the so-called 'credit crunch', the worldwide (economic) recession, which began, in the United Kingdom, in the latter half of 2007.[2] In *Writing in Society*, Williams makes the point that we are living in a world in which these social dramas (to borrow Turner's phrase) are 'built into the rhythms of everyday life' and that they have become societies' collective, habitual experience because we vicariously experience more drama 'in a week [...] than most human beings would previously have seen in a lifetime' (Williams 1995: 12). The 'tragedies' that Williams identifies are centrally connected to his notion of 'drama in a dramatized society'. They are social dramas played out in a society that has been, and is constantly being, exposed, through the 'mass media', to a vast quantity of social performances/dramas on a daily basis. But while these events are often understood and described as 'tragedies', they give no indication of what the word means for contemporary society.

Tragedy is a term bound to many centuries of theory and discussion but has become increasingly colloquialized and over-used. Williams makes this point at the beginning of *Modern Tragedy* (1966) when he argues that '[w]e come to tragedy by many roads. It is an immediate experience, a body of literature, a conflict of theory, an academic problem' (13). Because of the common use of tragedy, as with trauma, as descriptive of so many events, it is necessary to attempt to define what it might mean in our current time. Through this process of definition, an examination of what might be considered a modern tragic theatrical mode can be made.

Williams goes on to argue that tragedy is an 'action which is not yet ended' (1966: 13). It is a continually morphing theoretical form that must be (re)considered as the societies which employ the term shift their understandings of the world (Williams 1966: 45–46); but, importantly, in searching for understanding Williams specifies that '[w]e are not looking for a new universal meaning of tragedy. We are looking for the structure of tragedy in our culture' (1966: 62). The perpetually changing nature of tragedy which Williams identifies is braided to his central critical framework, that of the 'structure of feeling'. This term is an analytical 'tool' which he developed and regularly modified throughout his career. Despite the criticisms which have been levelled at the notion of structure of feeling (cf. Eldridge and Eldridge 1994), it nevertheless provides a useful means of investigating theatre and performance, especially in light of Williams' own work in *Modern Tragedy*. The meaning of structure of feeling is bound to the importance of a continual re-evaluation of the socio-cultural-historic moment. That is to say, each moment in history has its own social, political, cultural and artistic conventions, all of which braid together in a structure of feeling which is unique, but, importantly, influenced by and emerging out of the structures which have gone before it. In *Drama From Ibsen to Brecht* (originally written in 1952 as *Drama from Ibsen to Eliot*), Williams asserts that structure of feeling is a means of exploring 'the continuity of experience from a particular work, through its particular form, to its recognition as a general form, and then the relation of this general form to a [specific] period [of history]' (Williams 1987: 17). Importantly, he goes on to state that:

> It is as firm and definitive as 'structure' suggests, yet it is based in the deepest and least tangible elements of our experience. It is a way of responding to a particular world in which practice is not felt as one way among others – a conscious 'way' – but is, in experience, the only way possible. Its means, its elements are not propositions or techniques; they are embodied, related feelings.
>
> (1987: 18)

So for Williams the argument or proposition of the art work is not as important as its structure and form, and the feelings evoked by its rhythms. This will be centrally important to developing a concept of a contemporary 'modern tragedy'.

The genre of tragedy has long been the focus of academic ponderings, but, as David Román (2002) points out, there has been a widespread shift towards an attitude that the exploration of what might be understood as 'tragic' has been 'endlessly rehearsed' to the point of becoming 'regressive and irrelevant' (2002: 1). While Román understands and to a degree sympathizes with this view, he remains interested in exploring tragedy in light of new modes of critical thinking and, like Williams, in response to the socio-cultural shifts in the word's meaning. The resultant special issue of *Theatre Journal* begins to track the notion of tragedy at the beginning of the twenty-first century, a time which Román describes as a 'world of terrible suffering and loss, a world that seems at times evacuated of hope, a world in which these feelings have been normalized as well, simply, life' (2002: 2).[3] Although much of the work published in the issue was started before September 11 2001, a great deal of it was informed by and altered after that day (Román 2002: 16). The events of September 11 become a central preoccupation in much of the writing. But, as with all traumas, the terrorist attacks and huge losses witnessed across the world seem too close to the surface of the writing. There is no critical distance from the events, and thus much of the work seems to focus on the specific events rather than on a discussion of what 'tragedy' might mean in the early twenty-first century. Nevertheless, the issue highlights a continuing interest in and contemporary relevance of the term.

The attacks of September 11 were traumas both on an individual level for those directly affected by the events and more widely for American, and arguably global, society. The full impact of the events and the changes in the world that they caused were, like any trauma, inevitably going to take time to process. Writing in the special issue, Harry J. Elam Jr comments that there is 'no doubt, we have been touched and changed' by the attacks (in Román *et al.* 2002: 104). Elam's 'we' is undoubtedly problematic as it presupposes a unified sense of the events' importance. However, it nevertheless usefully suggests that the events of that day were a disruption of previously unquestioned assumptions and therefore a disturbance of the established structure of feeling, in America at least. But, just as with any trauma, a period of latency must be allowed before any impact or change can be felt and before the survivor-sufferer(s) can begin to theorize properly about the impact of the event. It is precisely because of this that Elam, and the other writers of the issue, cannot offer any answers to the questions September 11 asked, nor suggest how (American) society may have been changed.

Cathy Caruth writes that traumas are 'experienced too soon, too unexpectedly, to be fully known and [are] therefore not available to consciousness until [they impose themselves] again, repeatedly, in the nightmares and repetitive actions of the survivors' (Caruth 1996: 4). Of crucial importance, then, is the idea that trauma needs time to settle into tragedy. There has now been time and distance from September 11, and indeed the world has 'suffered' new traumas, all of which have been unconsciously absorbed into our contemporary structure of feeling. In a world so changed in a relatively short period of time, a world where there is more ongoing conflict available for consumption than ever before, and under a cloud of severe economic difficulty, now is the time to reconsider what might be thought of as 'tragic' and if, in light of this, there is a modern/contemporary tragic theatre which might adequately and/or profitably engage with these traumas.

Let us begin by attempting to 'read' or 'define' what might be considered the contemporary structure of feeling for, in so far as we accept Williams' supposition, tragedy and structure of feeling are tightly bound and mutually constructive. Due to the ever-changing nature of social structures and cultural discourses, Williams acknowledges a difficulty in identifying the facets of any structure of feeling while a subject of it (Williams 1966: 90). Nevertheless, he demands that as cultural critics we engage in just such an exercise because in identifying the 'idea of tragedy, in our time' we come not only to understand something of our structure of feeling but also establish a frame through which to interrogate our social, cultural, political and artistic experiences (Williams 1966: 61).[4]

There is a duality in circulation here, between the *post-hoc* nature of fully discovering the structure of feeling and the possibility of determining it through an examination of 'the structure of tragedy in our own culture' (Williams 1966: 62). This paradoxical rotation highlights the slipperiness and problematic nature of structure of feeling, but also defines it as a way of thinking about the world, especially in relation to the traumatic. By this I mean that the constant rotation between the imperative to define or understand the present structure of feeling and the necessity for an objectifying, perspectival distance in order to do so follows a similar pattern to the paradoxical rotations of trauma theory. As I will discuss later, this may help to identify dramatic modes or forms which are engaged in shortening the gap between traumatic event and its re-witnessing and also the gap between tragic expression and the discovery of the structure of feeling, or indeed vice versa. The central point here is that by attempting to understand the structure of feeling while 'in' it, we become better equipped to understand the culture we move in.

In our current structure of feeling, I suggest, this understanding of our culture comes from experiencing the world in more cathected ways than normally made available in everyday life. Thus, while the performances analysed within this volume might at first appear disparate and simply symptomatic of the structure of feeling in some respects, importantly they (and others) can actually be brought together in a coherent figuring to suggest that they can help us both to establish an understanding of our structure of feeling and to move forward in a more determined/productive way within it.

As is well documented, since the late 1960s the live has been increasingly privileged over the scripted; the ascendancy of the live (and of Live Art) has grown from a desire to produce a sense of a more immediate and more authentic experience in the theatre. Williams argues that in order to make an adequate critique of theatre/drama, we must consider the play text and live performance as one entity (1991: 17). Elsewhere he contends that conventions are both enabling (like a linguistic code) and constricting because of a reductive tie to the past (however recent a past that may be). He stresses that the first sense of convention needs to be recovered so that we can understand the links between structure of feeling and dramatic form. Hence, there is a need for tragedy to conform to a sense of tragic convention but that convention must itself be understood to be drawn from history and at the same time always mutable and developing (Williams 1987: 12–16; and cf. Eldridge and Eldridge 1994: 116) Thus tragedy, indeed all art, is 'deeply rooted in a precise structure of feeling' (Williams 1966: 18) and thus the form that tragedy takes is changeable, and while it draws upon tragic conventions, those conventions are similarly rooted in structures of feeling and thus change and develop in line with cultural development.

Our tragedy, then, is not tied to a specific form but to lived experience, to our cognitive and phenomenological understandings of the world around us. Our culture's sense of the tragic can be found in its dramatic forms and in what it articulates as tragic in everyday life; contemporary tragedy might just as easily be a performance by Orlan as a David Edgar or Mark Ravenhill play as a social performance. While a play text may reflect or comment upon a historically specific structure of feeling, that is not necessarily the only structure of feeling it may address or to which it may be relevant. A play text can be used as a mechanism for creating a live performance that is specifically engaged with a structure of feeling that is radically different to the one which existed at the time of the play's writing. Melly Still's 2008 revival of Middleton's *The Revenger's Tragedy* at the National Theatre, London, is a good example of this. Importing into the text numerous contemporary references, such as 'club' music, inter-mediality and numerous scenes of violent realism, the piece had a decidedly contemporary feel. The play was also staged, using the Olivier stage's revolve, in such a way that each scene moved seamlessly and speedily into the next, adding a relentlessness to the experience of being there. There was a sense of violence and ethical implication in watching: the play bombarded the audience with its speed of progression and included them, through direct address and deliberate eye contact, in various moments of violent action (cf. Moreno 2008: esp. 10–11).

The move toward liveness, to a desire for immediacy and authenticity through presenting performance which somehow seems more 'truthful' or more 'real' than other performances, signals a new tragic mode which is culturally specific but never-theless has grown from a historical succession of variant tragic modes. In the second half of *Modern Tragedy*, Williams proposes a number of these tragic modes, all of which overlap and draw influence from one another, and which I will now gloss.

Liberal-tragedy is one in which a person at the pinnacle of their powers and 'the limits of their strength' is in the same moment hopeful of success and yet being defeated, being undone by their own actions and 'energies'. It is a tragedy in which '[t]he self that wills and desires destroys the self that lives, yet the rejection of will and desire is also tragedy: a corroding insignificance, as the self is cut down' (Williams 1966: 87, 105). Williams proposes *private-tragedy*, which ends with the individual 'bare and unac-commodated' and battered by 'the storm he has himself raised'. This is tragedy in which the 'storm of living' is not necessarily the result of personal action but begins at birth and subsumes one in it completely. Thus death becomes 'a kind of achieve-ment' (106) because it results in 'comparative settlement and peace' (120). Williams then goes on to posit the notions of *social-tragedy* and *personal-tragedy*, both seemingly interwoven in the same historical juncture, a point when 'one version of tragedy or the other' must be 'chosen'. Williams suggests that in social-tragedy individuals are 'destroyed by power and famine' and society is 'destroyed or destroying itself'. In personal-tragedy people are suffering and being destroyed by their closest relationships (121).

From this point on Williams' categorizations become a little more fluid, flowing between tragic modes without definition of them. However, I suggest that they might be similarly turned into word couples, and so defined, thus: *impasse-tragedy*, or 'tragic deadlock and stalemate' as Williams puts it. Here Williams suggests that the tragedy is that there is no 'common sense of reality' or, to put it another way, 'common reality is an illusion'. He suggests that the 'individual is isolated, in a permanently meaningless world, so that even the connections within the personality break down' (157). Williams also suggests what we might term *sacrificial-tragedy*, in which the rhythm of tragedy changes from sacrifice as force for renewal to martyrdom for preservation. This is tragedy in which sacrifice is 'not a consummation, [nor] the climax of a general history. It is often a willing event, but to preserve, not to renew. The sense of loss is ordinarily keener than the sense of revival' and so our tragic heroes in this case come to be seen as tragic victims, and our cathected commitment 'is to the man who dies, rather than to the action in which he dies' (157).

These categorizations are by no means discrete; they each take influence from the preceding notions of tragedy and seem to fold into one another at certain moments. Indeed impasse-tragedy might be seen, through writers such as Jameson and McLuhan, and indeed Debord, Baudrillard, Žižek and Stiegler, as particularly definitive of our current individualized society. But what Williams deftly achieves is a workable chronology of tragic forms which traces a distinguishable history and is based in concrete (textual) examples. There is, of course, much that could be added to this list if we were to go further back into the history of tragedy's development and we could interrogate Williams work further in order to expose micro-tragic modes within these wider couplings. We might look further back in history than Williams, to classical Greek and Roman tragedies which could be termed 'anagnorisis-tragedy', in which there is a moment of recognition preceding peripeteia where the fate of the hero becomes apparent to him (and the audience). We might also look at Williams' brief discussion of Hebbel which could be seen to identify a 'grinding of history-tragedy' in which the 'world-historical process', to put it in Hebbel's words (ctd in Williams 1966: 36), grinds the individual down to their ultimate destruction.

We inherit from Williams, then, a series of identifiable, if fluid, tragic modes. We are, of course, in a different socio-historical moment to the one in which Williams' project finished; 'revolution', the 'general' tragic action Williams identifies in *Modern Tragedy* (83), is perhaps not the general tragic action of our structure of feeling, especially given the demise of 'political theatre', a point I will return to again at the end of the book. This leaves us in need of identifying our own contemporary sense of tragedy, which is rooted in our current structure of feeling: as Schechner suggests in a striking echo of Williams, 'all tragedies, probably all dramas, have under their personal and idiosyncratic surfaces deep social sub-structures that guide the sequence of events' (Schechner 2003: 218).

I thus propose that 'the tragic experience of our own time' (Williams 1966: 61) is informed and shaped by our traumatic experiences of life, both as individuals and as a collective society. The desire for immediacy and authenticity of experience has been recognized and taken up by many playwrights who have attempted to put something of the 'real' into their written representations: the call for authenticity has been taken up in writing where there is a drive to embody and bear witness to trauma in the same way that Live Art practices might be seen to make that articulation. In light of this, I am suggesting what we might call *trauma-tragedy* as the tragic mode of contemporary Occident society.

While all tragedy is based in trauma or schism of some kind, contemporary trauma-tragedy is dramaturgically addressing the trauma, not simply by highlighting the existence of world traumas but by trying to embody and bear witness to trauma in an immediate way. Trauma-tragedy can thus be considered an intensification of the trans-historical trope of trauma, a trope which is now particularly identifiable in our current structure of feeling. In trauma-tragedy there is a desire to evoke a sense of being there in an attempt to generate an effect of 'real' presence, or presence in 'reality'. Rather than attempting resolution through form, this contemporary tragic mode is *about* the trauma: it is not about people being ground down by history, nor about coming to some sort of tragic recognition of fault, nor the destruction of society through the fate of a hero. Trauma-tragedy is trying to bear adequate – which is to say more immediate or more embodied – witness to trauma; or, relating back to Williams' definition of structure of feeling, it is a tragic mode which responds to our particular, traumatized world in an experiential and embodied manner, relating experience to physical-emotional feeling.

Trauma-tragedy

> ROBIN *is asleep amongst a pile of books, paper and an eleven*
> *row abacus.*
> [...]
> *There is a box of chocolates next to his head.*
> TINKER *enters and stands staring at him.*
> *He pulls* ROBIN *up by the hair.*
> ROBIN *screams and* TINKER *puts a knife to his throat.*

TINKER   You fuck her?
          Fuck her till her nose bleed?
          I may be a cunt but I'm not a twat.
          (He sees the chocolates)
          Where'd you get them?
          Eh?
          Eh?
ROBIN   They're for Grace.
TINKER   Where did you get them?
ROBIN   Bought them.
TINKER   What did you do, sell your arse?
ROBIN   *(Doesn't answer)*
TINKER *lets go of* ROBIN.
He opens the chocolates.

> *He takes one out and tosses it at* Robin.
>
> Tinker   Eat.
>
> Robin   *(Looks at the chocolate. He starts to cry.)*
>   They're for Gracie.
>
> Tinker   Eat it.

(Kane 2001: 138–139)

Craig Gazey, playing Robin, elongated the '-ie' on the end of 'Gracie' just enough for the audience to register the pain and sorrow in this 'simple' character's voice. Gazey's performance had drawn the audience into a pitying relationship with Robin, but the utterance of these two simple vowels was almost painful to hear. The audience have already experienced fourteen exhausting scenes of Sean Holmes' 2005 revival of *Cleansed*, witnessing expert representations of the injection of heroine into an eyeball, anal rape with a broom handle, incestual intercourse and the severing of limbs to name but a few moments up to this point. But as difficult and as visceral as those scenes were, they had nonetheless been recognizable as representations. The chocolates were different.

Gazey eats, his performed tears in full flow down his cheeks, his sniffling the only sound in the room. Paul Brennan, playing Tinker, throws him another chocolate. Gazey eats. Another chocolate crosses the space and is eaten. Another follows, and another and another and another – each one more difficult to swallow than the last. After twelve or so chocolates Gazey is choking and whimpering, covering his mouth and expelling long, thick, brown strands of saliva through his fingers and into a pool on the floor. He retches and for a moment it looks as if he will vomit: the convulsion is seemingly too authentic to be representation as the actor's body rebels against the scripted action. He regains his composure, wipes his chocolate-covered mouth and eats another chocolate. There is a pause, a beat in which the box of chocolates is turned towards the audience and its emptiness revealed. The audience appear to relax and a collective out-breath seems almost audible.

But 'Tinker takes the empty tray out of the box – there is another layer of chocolates underneath' (Kane 2001: 140). Brennan throws another chocolate; Gazey chews slowly, eventually choking down the brown mush. Another one. Members of the audience put hands to mouths, some retch or choke, others simply look away: the reality of the scene is too difficult for most of the audience to bear, it overpowers the representation and impacts upon them physically.[5] *Gazey is still eating chocolates, his face is flushed and smeared with chocolate, and his crotch is drenched in 'urine'. Brennan throws the empty box at him: 'Filthy little perv, clean it up.' The stage directions read, 'Robin stands in the puddle, distressed'; the live scene could be written, 'Gazey stands in the puddle exhausted, panting, retching.'*

The 'distress' is both physically embodied (at the level of the actor's real discomfort) and acted (at the level of the script): the real and the fiction are interwoven. A metaphysical, paradoxical rotation between presence and absence is portrayed and easily identifiable in this moment. Its evident impact upon the audience and its contemporary pertinence to images of torture such as those which emerged from the Abu Ghraib prison, Iraq, in 2004 (to which I shall return in some detail in Chapter 6) make it a good example of an aesthetic trauma-tragedy. In this scene, trauma and tragedy, real and mimetic, aesthetic realm and social realm are folded in on each other for actor and audience alike. The gap between event and experience, between traumatic action and witnessing, is reduced to an immediacy of experience through the on-stage image.

The scene is precisely *about* the trauma of the event (and not, for example, about its resolution) and imparting something of that experience to the audience in an immediate and (evidently) viscerally embodied manner. This explicitly speaks to the desire for cathexis that is prevalent in our present moment. The desire for immediacy and authenticity of experience is marked, among other things, by the ascendancy of the live and the seeming ubiquity of violent or traumatic images. We are so used to absorbing these images that we have become, to a certain degree at least, anaesthetized by and to them; drawn together and flattened out into a sea of individuals with no sense of communality or connection to society at large. The vast availability of information, and the speed with which it is accessible, enables us to receive images and news from all over the world with such immediacy and in such quantity that we are not given any space to consider these events and their wider socio-political/cultural impact. Through this current desire for images, and the instant information relay that perpetuates that desire, our social dramas have become an ever more apparent part of our everyday lives and as such come to be part of our collective psyche in increasingly virulent ways. If we accept that aesthetic and social dramas are perpetually looped together, to evoke Richard Schechner's 'infinity loop' (Figure 2), and that in this loop there is a 'dynamic positive feedback' between social and aesthetic drama (Schechner 2003: 214), then it stands to reason that our understandings of personal and world traumas are bound to this loop, too.

While Victor Turner is not always uncritical of Schechner's model, he usefully notes that it highlights how:

> social drama feeds into the latent realm of stage drama; its characteristic form in a given culture, at a given time and place, unconsciously, or perhaps preconsciously, influences not only the form but also the content of the stage drama of which it is the active or 'magic' mirror. The stage drama, when it is meant to do more than entertain – though entertainment is always one of its vital aims – is a meta commentary, explicit or implicit, witting or unwitting, on the major social dramas of its social context.
>
> (ctd in Schechner 2003: 216)

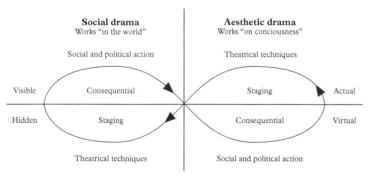

Figure 2: Schechner's 'mutual positive feedback' loop between social and aesthetic performances.
Source: Schechner 2003: 215.

Hans-Thies Lehmann's description of this relationship is perhaps even more explicit, claiming that:

> the real of our experiential worlds is to a large extent created by art in the first place [...] Human sentiment imitates art, as much as, the other way round, art imitates life [...] aesthetically formed drama produces images, structured forms of development and ideological patterns that give order to the social, its organisation and perception.
>
> (Lehmann 2006: 37)

This re-rehearsal of the loop is useful in our present context as it helps to unpack how the rotation is centrally connected to the way we experience the world, to our daily lives and to our interaction with the events which surround us. The loop helps identify a contemporary social-psychic trauma which is part of the way in which we disconnectedly operate in the world.

To advance this idea, I make the following proposition: we exist within two major social dramas which constitute a double trauma. Firstly, the trauma and social drama of world conflicts, which are played out across the world in reality and in ubiquitous and rapidly broadcast news reports and graphic imagery. Secondly, the social drama of psychic disjunction, or psychic trauma, which is a direct result of the world (historical) traumas and, especially in Western late-capitalism, the flattening of experience and individualization of society (I shall return to this in a moment). Both traumas are interconnected on a looped continuum, which might be seen to overlap with Schechner's infinity loop, and are part of our contemporary structure of feeling in which we seek out particularly cathected experiences.

Through the constant dramatization of the world – existing within one's own drama(s) always and being bombarded by drama constantly (drama in a dramatized society), using aesthetic orderings and imagery – we might be seen to live in and through dramas in the social realm which are embodied in the aesthetic shape of stage dramas. The examples of this are numerous but one will stand for many: in late 2007 there was a great deal of media coverage concerning the number of CCTV cameras, unmanned drone helicopters and other authoritarian 'spying' devices which were endlessly referred to, by news media organizations, as 'Orwellian' or as perpetuating a 'Big Brother' culture. Orwell's 1949 novel, *Nineteen Eighty-Four*, is retrospectively evoked as giving shape to and aiding understanding of contemporary social performance. This example supports Baudrillard's posited idea of 'reality' composed of simulacra: the 'map' Orwell drew for us has come to 'engender the territory' of our current social order (Baudrillard 2001: 169). This is not to argue that Orwell foresaw the growth and perpetuation of the close circuit network, but that his ideas have been appropriated into contemporary concerns and the structure of feeling. Consciously or unconsciously we think about the world, order it, and behave in it in a way which reflects our aesthetic dramas and, of course, vice versa – there is constant interchange. Turned upon trauma theory, this loop signals the possibility that the world traumas we create (war, social unrest, terrorism, etcetera) are a direct result of the psychic trauma of society, and vice versa: one informs and creates the other.

   With this in mind, let us now return to the notion of societal psychic trauma which I posited earlier. Social psychic trauma is rooted in our image-driven, mediatized social structure. Marshal McLuhan has extensively argued that exposure to media has both 'psychic and social consequences', and that a media-dominated world (such as the one we, in the West, currently inhabit) is characterized by a sociological 'numbness' and 'mental breakdown' (McLuhan 2001 [1964]: 7–23). He identifies a common psychic flattening, perpetuated by the pervasiveness of the late twentieth-century (and now early twenty-first-century) media, which invades social and psychic space creating, I contend, a common psychic trauma. Perry Anderson's powerful review of Fredric Jameson's work on postmodernity notes that hysteria – which sits prominently on the trajectory of our understandings of trauma and, in Jameson, is gender-neutral – is 'a general condition of the postmodern experience' creating a 'new depthlessness of the subject':

> psychic life becomes unnervingly accidented and spasmodic, marked by sudden dips of level or lurches of

mood, that recall something of the fragmentation of schizophrenia.

(Anderson 1998: 57)

A consequence of technological development in our postmodern era has been the denigration of the subject and a 'metastases of the psyche' resulting in a 'loss of any active sense of history, either as hope or memory' leaving in its place a sense of a 'perpetual present' (Anderson 1998: 56). This in turn is seen to preclude cathected experience or historicity: we are in other words left devoid of a sense of place, time and context the result of which is a desire to experience again.

McLuhan and Jameson employ a rhetoric which closely aligns itself with the language of trauma theory, evoking a sense of dislocation and schism in both society at large and in the individual.[6] There is a sense in which the fragmentation of society, the destruction of community, is (to employ Dominic LaCapra's word) a 'disavowal' of the individual from society (LaCapra 1996: 174). This disavowal can legitimately be seen as part of a psychic trauma which might, in turn, be identified as part of our general condition: it is a trauma that is bound to how we live in the world and how the world's traumas are perpetuated within and through us.

Closely aligned with the psychic flattening and trauma that is created through our technologized society is the way in which technology both shortens the gap between event and its (second order) experience, and proliferates the amount of information available about it, so increasing the number of people who are exposed to that event. In our world of images, satellites and the internet it only takes seconds between an event happening and its representation beaming on to our various flickering screens. In *The Society of the Spectacle* (1967), Debord argued that 'everything that was directly lived has reduced into a representation' (Debord 2004 [1967]: 7). His arguments might productively be thought of as the beginnings of a line of argument that has been taken up and convincingly extended into the twenty-first century by such thinkers as Baudrillard and Žižek. Debord continues by suggesting that society has become 'mediated by images' and that:

> [t]he spectacle presents itself simultaneously as society itself, as a part of society, and as a *means of unification*. As a part of society, it is the focal point of all vision and all consciousness. But due to the very fact that this sector is *separate*, it is in reality the domain of delusion and false consciousness: the unification it achieves is nothing but an official language of universal separation. [... T]he spectacle is both the result and the goal of the dominant mode of production[...] the very heart of this real society's unreality. In all of its particular manifestations – news, propaganda, advertising, entertainment – the spectacle represents the dominant *model* of life.
>
> (Debord 2004: 7–8)

This particular part of Debord's thesis is cognate with the social-aesthetic rotations of the Schechner/Turner model and also with trauma theory's postulation on the separation of self. It further relates to my proposal of a (psychically) traumatized structure of feeling.[7] It seems, then, that in a society of the spectacle there is both an overload of event – in that it is omnipresent in representation – and too rapid a move into representation for the event, whatever it might be, to settle into a sense of 'reality'. But, and as a result of this, the opposite is also true: real events come to be defined by and as representation. The events in America on September 11 2001, and particularly the repeated image of a plane flying into the second of the Twin Towers in New York, is an apposite example: the event was a spectacular, a striking echo of 'the most breathtaking scenes in the big catastrophe productions' as Žižek contends (2002: 15). The representations of catastrophe which are so prevalent in film and news reports but which are always in some way distanced as Other from (Western) late-capitalist societies suddenly entered into 'reality'. Žižek argues similarly that the:

> screen fantasmatic apparition entered our reality. It is not that reality entered our image: the image entered and shattered our reality (i.e. the symbolic coordinates according to which we determine what we experience as reality).
>
> (Žižek 2002: 16)

The distance between event and its representation became almost indistinguishable as the filmed images came to stand in for and define the events. By this I mean that the perpetual repetition of the event's imagery and the immediacy with which it reached worldwide audiences removed the possibility of any objectifying perspectival distance, especially for those societies which similarly treated disaster as an experience (predominantly) of the other. As such it became impossible to separate image from reality, representation from actuality, aesthetic drama from social drama. The perfection of the 'celluloid' moment which was beamed around the world is central to this collapse: Marvin Carlson has suggested that it seemed like 'an all-too-familiar [film]' in which iconic landmarks are destroyed as the terrified public flee and that '[s]uddenly these identical scenes appeared on our television screens, in a horrifying Baudrillardian example of the real projected as a simulacrum of an already familiar imaginary' (in Román *et al.* 2002: 133–134). The image folded into reality; the aesthetic drama became the social drama in an 'instantaneous' articulation of Schechner's loop. By this I mean that unlike Schechner's original loop where the social and aesthetic are separate halves of the same loop with implied distance, difference and passage of time between them, here – and in trauma-tragedy more generally – the loop might be thought to fold in on itself. Modelling this mathematically, we might say that while Schechner's loop tends toward time lapse, in the refiguring of it I am proposing it is precisely instantaneous: we inhabit the zero point, the intersection of the x and y axis while *time = 0*. Thus, an event is always already within all spheres of the loop, instantly aesthetic and social drama.

Of course, the violence of our time may be no more than the violence of any other period in history; but, the advancement of the technologies of communication places us directly and extremely rapidly in the theatre of war and the immediate aftermath of social violence. Thus, the 'realities' of the world's traumas and tragedies are exposed and disseminated as never before. Western society can no longer feign ignorance about the pain and suffering of others – indeed we actively crave the images and reports that bring the conflicts closer to us; we desire 'knowledge' through representation, especially visual. As Susan

Sontag tells us, 'the appetite for pictures showing bodies in pain is as keen, almost, as the desire for ones that show bodies naked' (Sontag 2003: 36). Indeed, Sontag's engagement with the way in which we seek out and crave photographic 'evidence' of atrocity and suffering is particularly relevant to our current concerns. She theorizes that part of our fascination with images of this kind is to do with our desire to be seen to feel the weight of the reality of the situations depicted. She suggests that graphic images have somehow become particularly cathected and are seen to embody a sense of 'reality' or of being in history. Thus, because of our desire for immediacy, for an effect of presence, the content of the image, be it sexual or violent, is irrelevant so long as it provides this effect. In an ever increasingly mediatized world it seems that pictures/images are becoming the currency of memory and 'reality' rather than the spoken word or stories. Sontag contends that photographs 'are a means of making "real" (or "more real") matters that the privileged and the merely safe might prefer to ignore' (Sontag 2003: 6) and that increasingly remembering is the recalling of not narrative but images (80). In other words, witnessing other traumas, like images of war, somehow comes to fill the gap of our own psychic trauma of disconnectedness from the world. The trauma-tragic mode operates in a similar vein, opening up a fissure in our flattened experience of the world and so evoking a sense of presence in trauma. I am not suggesting that trauma-tragedy *is* trauma, but that it is centrally concerned with attempting somehow to bear witness to it (an objective discussed in more detail in Chapter 4).

Žižek has convincingly argued that despite Lacanian notions of the impossibility of experiencing the Real, it is precisely that experience which has become a central desire in contemporary late-capitalist society (cf. Žižek 2002). Elsewhere, he further contends that 'modern art is focused more and more on the Real', and that while an audience is 'supposed to enjoy traditional art, [which] is expected to generate aesthetic pleasure [...] modern art, by definition, *hurts*' and that modern art is thus about the experience of displeasure (Žižek 2006: 147). However, the experience is actually precisely paradoxical: while the artwork might 'hurt' and so be 'dis-pleasurable', it is exactly this experience that the audience seek out for (pleasure) fulfilment through cathected experience. In order to explain my argument more fully I shall turn to another example which Žižek cites in a different context: self-harm. Žižek contends that 'cutters' are 'mostly women who experience an irresistible urge to cut themselves with razors or otherwise hurt themselves' in 'a desperate strategy to return to the real of the body'. For these people, cutting is an attempt to regain a sense of reality or sense of one's 'ego in [one's] bodily reality' in an attempt to ameliorate the anxiety of perceived non-existence. The cutting is thus an attempt to 'feel alive again' and to become grounded in 'reality' (2002: 10).

The example is particularly useful here as it not only highlights the paradoxical rotation between pain and pleasure in that pain, but also echoes the argument I made above concerning an emergent desire to 'experience again' as part of our structure of feeling. The suggestion that we might 'feel alive again' through bodily (as opposed to 'virtual') experiences is cognate with the trauma-tragic mode I am proposing. Socially and aesthetically, the trauma-tragic mode is concerned with embodying an experience that shortens the gap between event and experience and so helps us to rehearse, contemplate or indeed (re)experience our own (psychic) trauma by creating the effect of cathected presence.

The psychic trauma of disconnection from society and the world, created through our technological developments, can be seen to be echoed in the metaphysical rotations of presence and absence, and the 'impossible' search for presence, identified, by writers such as Derrida, as being an inescapable part of the Western condition of being. In the *Paradoxe sur le comédien* (1773), Diderot suggests that there exists a paradox in acting which, retrospectively, may be read as one of the earliest examples of expounding the notion of the rotation of presence and absence. Diderot's paradox suggests that the actor's ability to play different characters was because of their ability to imitate 'the exterior signs of emotion' rather than necessarily embodying, or experiencing, that emotion (Diderot ctd in Roach 1993: 133). Actors, Shepherd and Wallis contend in their reading of Diderot, 'feign, or represent, the feeling by appropriately organising voice, face and body':

> [Actors have the] capacity for reflection, a turning out
> from the self, away from personal feeling, in order objec-
> tively to observe and study, and thus understand, the
> truths of nature... Thus, again and again, the actor may
> weep, touchingly, and always on cue.
>
> (Shepherd and Wallis 2004: 225)

To become believable the actor, under Diderot's formulation,
must absent themselves from the represented emotion. In order
to move the audience, an actor must remain unmoved.[8] This
paradox is cognate with the rotation of presence and absence
which Derrida identified as central to Western metaphysics and
inescapable in the theatre (cf. Derrida 1978 [1967]: 292–316
and passim). It is a debate which Peggy Phelan clearly eluci-
dates, in *Mourning Sex* (1997), in an argument concerning the
trauma of loss and performance's circulation between presence
and absence:

> The enactment of invocation and disappearance under-
> taken by performance and theatre is precisely the drama
> of corporeality itself. At once a consolidated fleshy form
> and an eroding, decomposing formlessness, the body
> beckons us and resists our attempts to remake it.
>
> (Phelan 1997: 4)

The constant struggle to be 'present' is a perpetual repetition
of trauma insomuch as it destabilizes our understanding and
constructions of self. By privileging one aspect of our 'self' as
present, we are by implication diminishing another to being
absent. The theatre is bound to this circulation and is an exemplar
of it: the presence of the actual (physical) action and the absence
of the 'story' represented; the absence of the persons represented
and the presence of the actors; the absence of the person(ality)
of the actor who is in character. Indeed, performance itself is in
constant flux between its 'here and now' presence and its inherent absence through disappearance. Erving Goffman has argued
that this oscillation is part of every day life too. He contends
that in our movement through the world and our interaction
with others we are constantly performing different versions of

ourselves: the presence of the public 'you' creates the absence of the private 'you' (cf. Goffman 1990). To put it another way, we are all always performing a role at the expense of our own presence which brings us back to, and is part of, the social dramas of life. The central edict of traumatic schism of self, highlighted in Chapter 1, seems to me precisely to echo this presence-absence rift and while the performance of self in everyday life might not be traumatic in the same sense as the eruption of trauma-symptoms, it can be seen to articulate similarly the disruption of self within that experience. As such, we might be seen to be rehearsing a traumatic split within the performance of ourselves every day.

This fundamental breach in our constructions of self can be read as part of our psychic trauma, and as such centrally bound to the notion of trauma-tragedy. Artaud, according to Derrida, has stated that theatre must 'restore "existence" and "flesh"' (Derrida 1978 [1967]: 232). This is precisely the goal of performances in trauma-tragedy mode. The trauma-work, paralleling Freud's notion of dream-work (cf. Freud 1999: 211–329, and pp. 60–61 of this volume), in the trauma-tragic mode is not to represent a strict imitation of violent trauma but to attempt a return to experience through theatrical means. Trauma-tragedies attempt to bring the *effect* of trauma into existence – to give it flesh, so to speak. My point here is not that trauma-tragedy can repair the fundamental breach in Western being, a project Derrida suggests is impossible, but that it might produce trauma-effects, such as the absence we experience in trauma-events and symptoms. This type of theatrical experience can explicitly rehearse, or prepare us for, the constant breach in being that is a result of the presence-absence split. Theatrical representations in the trauma-tragedy mode can create a truth effect which, I contend, is absent in other representational forms and which explicitly addresses the contemporary structure of feeling.

Trauma-tragedy is engaging, in social and aesthetic realms, in 'visceral arousal and experience', to borrow from Schechner again (2003: 358); its live performance is a shortening of the distance between tragic expression and traumatic experience which meets the desire for immediacy of experience. The ascendancy of the live and the desire for more viscerally kinaesthetic experiences suggests that the current structure of feeling is one in which we desire a more authentic mode of expression, a more embodied tragic experience in which we seek simply to 'do' the trauma, to make it 'present', rather than solve it through (classical tragic) form. Following Sontag's assertions on the creation of 'reality' through the image, I argue that the contemporary/modern tragic mode, trauma-tragedy, is a form in which we can attempt to bear a more immediate witness to trauma; we can attempt to try to be in it, so to speak. Resolution is no longer as necessary as it once was and so trauma-tragedy instead speaks to world traumas and to the psychic trauma of living. Taking Schechner and Turner at their word, the writing in the *Theatre Journal* special issue can be seen as part of the social drama played out during and just after September 11 2001. It was an attempt to grasp at the history of the moment, an attempt to bear immediate witness to it without letting the event properly settle into consciousness. Román suggests that on September 11 the world, and especially America, experienced 'history happen[ing] in an unexpected, all but unimaginable, way' (Román 2002: 3), but this, as Carlson articulated, is not the case. We had already seen these events in countless representations provided by comic books, photographs and, of course, films. Far from being 'unimaginable' the scenes were thoroughly rehearsed and known, they were part of the ubiquity of the image. This is precisely where the violent shock (to reprise the genealogy of trauma theory) lay though – not because history was happening in an unimaginable way, but because the representations we are so used to seeing and thinking of as 'elsewhere' were folding into reality but yet were being played out in the medium of representation and image. The performance at work in the writing of the numerous performance critics gathered in *Theatre Journal*[5] was a trauma-tragedy insomuch as it was performing an attempt to be present in the historical moment. It sought to bridge the latency/gap between the trauma of the event and its comprehension by tapping out a script on a keyboard. The writing is an attempt to make live the sense of history happening that Román notes. There is a sense in which the trauma of those events was an opportunity to write a social performance in the trauma-tragic mode. There was no necessity to try to solve the event; the desire was to be *part of its history* and to *bear immediate witness* to the trauma of 'the stench, the ominous clouds of smoke, and the clay-colored [sic] human figures', as Bob Vorlicky described it (in Román *et al.* 2002: 125). In *Writing in Society* (1983), Williams stated that:

> the drama of any period, including our own, is an intri-
> cate set of practices of which some are incorporated – the
> known rhythms or movements of a residual but still active
> system – and some are exploratory – the difficult rhythms
> and movements of an emergent representation.
>
> (Williams 1983: 16)

With this chapter, then, I am not intending to suggest any particular genre of performance which might be thought of as a trauma-tragedy, far from it. Rather, I am hoping to set the parameters of an emergent contemporary structure of feeling, and a way of thinking about performances which might be seen to respond and interact with it in various different ways. Trauma-tragedy operates in both aesthetic and social dramas and is a theoretical mechanism by which we might more fully come to understand these dramas, and the traumas which are contained within in them. Rather than looking back at a historical moment of trauma, trauma-tragedy is attempting to bridge or reduce the gap between historical moment, its witness and (that) experience.

3

Mimetic shimmering and the performative *punctum*

The idea that trauma is beyond representation (*vide* Phelan 1997; and Caruth 1995 and 1996) is to consider representation in too narrow a way. The consideration is of representation as accurate copy, but this is to deny the representational nature of the repetitive nightmares and hallucinations of the survivor-sufferer. Admittedly, much trauma theory postulates that these repetitions are in themselves primal scenes of traumatic experience, but this experience is always in relation to a previous one. While the hallucination may not be of the original trauma-event and may be more a remembering of the last time one remembered, it is still acutely related to and imitative of the original. The traumatic event can only ever become trauma-symptom through a reworking in the mimetic realm of memory. The uninvited nightmares of trauma-symptoms and the necessity to speak of the trauma-event in order to work through it are both mimetic iterations of the trauma-event. Trauma demands a referent insomuch as we cannot become traumatized unless we have a means of conceptualizing an event *as* traumatic. The trauma-event must be signified by the repetitive signifier of the trauma-symptom. Thought about in this way, there can be no denying the relationship between trauma and mimesis, for to remember the trauma-event as part of the trauma-symptom is to recreate/restage that event imaginatively.

This is, of course, in direct contradiction to the 'impossibility' of trauma's representation, but it is perhaps time to move away from this slightly narrow understanding of representation and the subsequent reductive assumption about the ability of representational forms. W. J. T. Mitchell shares a similar stance to my own, arguing that while '[t]rauma, like God, is supposed to be the unrepresentable in word and image', society at large:

> incorrigibly insist[s] on talking about it, depicting it, and trying to render it in increasingly vivid and literal ways. Certain works of contemporary art are designed to transmit trauma as directly as possible, to rub the spectator's face in the unspeakable and unimaginable.
>
> (Mitchell 2005: 295)

Mitchell's statement directly foregrounds the centrality of contemporary art in the exploration of trauma, and also indicates a wider sociological desire to investigate and try to understand traumata and (attempted) representations of them. Herein lies a core concern of this project: if we are 'incorrigibly insisting' on trying to render trauma in representational forms then performance, as a mimetic art form *par excellence*, is, I suggest, deeply implicated in this.[1]

Mimesis and the performance of power

Michael Kelly (1998) has usefully argued that 'mimesis aims at influence, change, repetition, or the new interpretation of existing worlds' (237), while Walter Benjamin has suggested that humans have 'the highest capacity for producing similarities' and that this capacity, stemming from our historical compulsion to 'become and behave like something else', plays a decisive role in all our 'higher functions' (Benjamin 2003: 333). In 'On the Mimetic Faculty', Benjamin argues that mimetic powers constitute an ability to understand and identify the interconnectedness of the world and, cognate with Aristotle's arguments on mimesis, enable one to exist productively in it. The mimetic power in Benjamin's presupposed ancient world links to the productive nature of mimesis which is available within Marxist theatre historiography as identified, for example, by George Thomson in the 1940s (cf. Shepherd and Wallis 2004: 215). This Marxist standpoint proposes that mimesis is a process through which, for example, 'the hunter tries to be like an animal s/he hunts in order to know it and so capture it' (Shepherd and Wallis 2004: 215). This is mimesis as mechanism for survival in the world; a productive mimesis that is ultimately concerned with power over an 'other', be that other an object, person, animal or, in the case of traumatic symptom, hallucination and nightmare.

In his influential book *Mimesis and Alterity*, Michael Taussig proposes that '"in some way or another" the making and existence of the artefact that portrays something gives one power over that which is portrayed', later suggesting that this power is created because of and within a 'visceral bond connecting the perceiver to the perceived in the operation of mimesis' (1993: 13; 38). Taussig's arguments on mimesis are particularly important here: in his discussions of shamanism and colonial invaders he postulates that it is not necessarily a visually accurate copy that creates mimetic power but that this rests in the development of representations which share the qualities and essences of that which they represent (Taussig 1993: 47–48). Mimesis, or mimetic power, is not necessarily concerned with accurately representing 'reality', in the sense of precisely copying an object, image or action.[2] Thus the hallucinations, nightmares and abstract associations which manifest themselves within trauma-symptoms can be seen as (personal performative) mimetic acts which, at least for the survivor-sufferer, are representations or iterations of the original trauma-event without being what is conventionally deemed 'accurate', which is to say direct, linear, photo-realistic copies of the trauma-event.

While it is important to note that, like dreams, these hallucinations can only be created from and be referring to past experiences (the trauma-event in this case), I am not proposing that these hallucinations be thought of in the same light as dreams. The distinction can be made apparent by turning briefly to Freud. While both dreams and trauma hallucinations share similar qualities in their emergence from the 'subconscious' and as mimetic of latent memories, it is imperative that the representational quality of the trauma-symptom is not confused with that of dreams. Freud suggests that the work of the dream, 'the dream-work', is to combine, resolve and in some way narrativize disparate, latent psychic material in an attempt to make those materials into the manifest dream-content (Freud 1999:

211–329). The dream-content in turn is a disguised version of hidden wishes or desires expressed in a medium which 'like a safety-valve, allows the psyche to let off steam […] by imagining it in a dream, all sorts of harmful stuff is rendered harmless' (Freud 1999: 388). In contrast, the hallucinations of trauma-symptoms have no such purpose; instead, they are irruptions of the essence of the trauma-event which have a detrimental, invasive impact upon the psyche of the survivor-sufferer. Rather than being readable in the same way that dreams might be, the hallucination of trauma-symptoms is a mimetic re-presenting of the trauma-event which causes the traumatic wound to be reopened and perpetuated through fated repetition.

Taussig continues to develop his conception of mimesis, positing a particularly useful engine for the forthcoming considerations, arguing that:

> [T]o ponder mimesis is to become sooner or later caught, like the police and the modern State with their finger-printing devices, in sticky webs of copy *and* contact, image *and* bodily involvement of the perceiver in the image, a complexity we too easily elide as nonmysterious, with our facile use of terms such as identification, representation, expression, and so forth – terms which simultaneously depend upon and erase all that is powerful and obscure in the network of associations conjoined by the notion of the mimetic.
>
> (Taussig 1993: 21; emphasis is original)

In proposing and collapsing the binaries of copy and contact, image and bodily involvement in that image, Taussig highlights the fact that a representation is always already the copy and the thing itself – image *and* body. Developing his argument further, Taussig proposes that in the operation of mimesis an inescapable and 'terrifically ambiguous power is established' between the capacity to represent the world but in that same instant the capacity to 'falsify, mask, and pose' (Taussig 1993: 42).

The problematic 'always already' of 'reality' and 'representation' is central to much thinking in theatre and performance,[3] but also to understandings of trauma-symptoms (as well as in philosophy and metaphysics more widely). While the appearance of the symptom may be a representation or (re)iteration of the trauma event, for the survivor-sufferer that mimetic action is experienced in the here and now, it is both representation, at the level of the hallucination, and present reality, at the level of emotional and physical involvement in that representation.

In her introduction to *Dissemination*, Barbara Johnson glosses Derrida's arguments concerning such dialectics, highlighting that he suggests Western thought has always been structured in terms of dichotomies or polarities and that:

> these hierarchical oppositions [...] privilege unity, identity, immediacy, and temporal and spatial *presentness* over distance, difference, dissimulation, and deferment. In its search for the answer to the question of Being, Western philosophy has indeed always determined Being as *presence*.
>
> (Johnson in Derrida 2004: viii; emphasis is original)

But as Derrida and many others since have so deftly argued, these binaries are essentially paradoxical dichotomies, in that to discuss the dichotomy is precisely to entangle oneself in, and so prove, the opposition in question. Mitchell succinctly articulates this problem in his discussions of 'the unspeakable' and 'the unimaginable', suggesting that in setting out a law against the representation of something, that law must always in some way 'name, describe or define – that is, represent – the very thing that it prohibits' and thus in effect breaks itself (Mitchell 2005: 297).

In the example of the theatre we may, as Lehmann has, refer to 'real actors' (Lehmann 2006: 36) when we mean humans or to the 'real world' in opposition to the representational world of the stage fiction. However, this is to ignore the fact that the action on stage is, of course, part of that 'real' world. It is in the same instant fiction and happening in the here and now of the 'real'. This is a fairly well-rehearsed and perhaps by now quite a pedestrian point, but it moves us towards deeper complexity in assuming, as it does, that there is the possibility of a 'real' outside of signification. Picking up from de Saussure, and linking to Lacanian theories of the Real, Derrida notes that meaning is constructed through absences and differences, that language relies on phonic or written signifiers and a resultant mental signified.

> [T]he system of signs is constituted solely by the differences in terms, not by their plenitude. The elements of signification function due not to the compact force of their nuclei but rather to the network of oppositions that distinguishes them, and then relates them one to another.
>
> (Derrida 1982: 10)

And so the word 'real' in the context of this project sits in opposition to the word 'representation' insomuch as I am using them as signifiers to differentiate between action which is part of the stage fiction and action which might be thought to be non-fictional, though this is of course a false distinction.[4]

An unsteady mimesis

> [I]n the postdramatic theatre of the real the main point is not the assertion of the real as such (as is the case in the mentioned sensationalist productions of the porn industry ['snuff' films]) but the unsettling that occurs through the *indecidability* whether one is dealing with reality or fiction. The theatrical effect and the effect on the consciousness both emanate from this ambiguity.
>
> (Lehmann 2006: 101)

Lehmann is suggesting that 'postdramatic' structures of performance open up what we might argue – after Derrida and others – constitute fundamental breaches in being: 'indecidability' between real and representation. The statement importantly highlights a rupture in the mimetic order that might be seen as part of the structure of performance which, as we shall see shortly, is crucial to the experience of representations of trauma in performance. He goes on to argue that the 'irruption of the real into the performance' is generally only recognized when mistakes and mishaps occur, or when a performance breaks out of its representational style into a more 'realistic' moment. However, I contend that it also happens when the representation is performed with such clarity and precision as to slip into the realm of indecidability, or more precisely *un*decidability (a distinction I will discuss below), for example, the 'beating' scene in Societas Raffaello Sanzio's *BR.#04* (2003, discussed below),[5] the 'chocolate' scene in Kane's *Cleansed* (1998, discussed in the previous chapter) or indeed various moments in Improbable's *Theatre of Blood* (2005). This in/un-decidability generally occurs in relation to the knowledge that one is watching a theatrical – which is to say fictional/representational – production that is operating within certain practical parameters. Thus the real, in the context of what we might think of as traditionally bourgeois, comfy seated theatre productions, is considered only after recognition and acceptance of the mimetic: it always 'irrupts' into the play, so to speak. Meanwhile, in Franko B's *Still Life* (2003, discussed below), and numerous other Performance/Live Art performances such as O'Reilly's *Succour* (2001) or *Wet Cup* (c. 2000), La Ribot's *Distinguidas Pieces* (2003),[6] Ron Athey and Dominic Johnson's *Incorruptible Flesh* (2007) and indeed in many of Franko B's other works, this delineation is reversed. It is an irruption of the mimetic into the real which unsettles the viewer: the possibility that what we are watching might after all be imitative is unnerving in relation to the presented real action. In both 'types' of performance the operation of mimesis might thus be thought of as 'unsteady'.

This collapse and layering of the mimetic order creates an unease which is cognate with the experience of traumatic reoccurrence. Trauma theory, and our own understandings and experiences of traumatic events/wounds, may thus give us a means by which both to understand and, as performance theorist Adrian Heathfield postulates, to receive the performance as 'an intersubjective phenomenal relation' (Heathfield 2004: 11). The tension or interplay between the mimetic/fictional order and the real/non-fictional order (to utilize that difficult dichotomy again) is central to the embodied experience of performance, and thus its capacity to act as traumatic mirror or indeed to impact as traumatic. This formulation, however, suggests a more complex circulation of tensions than just the dialectic of mimesis and reality. There is a third pole to be considered in relation to these first two: the imputed reality of the referent through the reality of the performance. This idea maps to Kier Elam's formulation of 'iconic identity' in which the 'sign-vehicle' both denotes the thing it is trying to represent and is itself that thing: a dog on stage is a real dog, it is also the representation of a dog which happens to exist in the diegetic world and it further imputes the reality of other dogs in the 'real' world (Elam 2002: 14–15). We might figure this as a tripartite circulation of tensions, unique to live performance: first, that which is on stage, a person, for example, is the thing itself (a person); second, that which is on stage is the mimesis of itself (a character); and third, that which is on stage imputes the presence/reality of that which is represented, itself evoked by the real of the performance (in other words, the 'out there, in the real world' referent is not a mimetic illusion but becomes present through the agency of the reality of the performers/performance).

Bert States has observed that in viewing an image a 'defamiliarized and desymbolized object' is brought to view, becoming 'phenomenally heavy with itself' and in this moment of encounter 'a transitional moment of shock signals the onset of the image: one feels the shudder of its refusal to settle into the illusion' (States 1985: 37). As Nicholas Ridout points out, States' comment highlights that this tension is 'experienced in terms of affect: "shock" and "shudder"' (Ridout 2006: 124). Furthermore, States is here discussing images in general but we can argue that in the theatre, because of the audience–performer and the audience–audience relationships/contracts (discussed further in Chapter 4), there is a particular *intensification* of this shock and shudder. The next part of this chapter turns to explore this inherent tension within the theatrical image. In the two performance examples I discuss below, *BR.#04* and *Still Life*, the tension is palpably present, its articulation made and remade throughout the performances by the spectators.

BR.#04

The opening of Romeo Castellucci/Sòcìetas Raffaello Sanzio's BR.#04 contains much humour and very little action. In a white room, apparently built of marble slabs, brightly washed in the cold white light of industrial fluorescents, a 'cleaner' mops the floor; a white curtain closes and opens again to reveal a baby who has been left centre stage to gurgle and play with its rattle. Once the baby has been removed by an invisible hand from behind the white curtain, an elderly actor with a long white beard enters wearing an orange bikini and flowery sandals. The implied levity and its inherent theatricality is soon worried and complicated by a scene which consciously plays in the borderland between a representational/fictional world of the staged play and a sense of (an irruption of) reality.

As the older actor holds on to two gymnast's rings that have descended from the flies downstage left, balancing precariously as he tries to hoist himself into the air, another actor (let us call him Actor 1) dressed as a policeman enters with a nondescript clear plastic bottle filled with red liquid which he pours on to the white marble-effect floor. He then places four 'evidence' cards around the puddle of 'blood', setting out a recognizable iteration of a crime scene. A second actor (Actor 2) enters, also dressed as a policeman and starts to undress, facing the 'crime scene', ending up in just his white underpants. A third actor (Actor 3), dressed like the others, enters as the still hanging older actor is led off stage by Actor 1. Actor 2 sits over the puddle of stage-blood, semi-naked with his back to us. Actor 3 begins to beat him savagely with a truncheon.

The beating is vicious and lengthy, and as Actor 2 writhes in the 'blood' he becomes increasingly covered in it. With each hit delivered we hear a loud cracking/smashing sound that is timed with the connection between the truncheon and the second actor's body. The beating continues. After a few minutes there are murmurings among some clusters of the audience, and some begin to leave. Actor 3 swaps roles with the watching Actor 1; spectator becomes beater and vice versa. The beating resumes accompanied by the 'crunching' sound effect. More blood is added to the scene, poured on top of the actor who is being beaten. Actor 1 begins to pound the second actor again, but the sound fails to keep up with him (or perhaps it has overtaken him) and the sound and action begin to fracture, *creating an eerie double beating, truncheon hitting actor followed by the crunch of the sound as a second blow is beginning to come down, and so on. The audience became audibly more uncomfortable: as the seeming reality of the violence becomes harder to witness it collapses the spectators' ability to recognize it as imitation. More people leave the auditorium. After a few more minutes of beating, punctuated by Actor 1 repeatedly slipping over in the blood, the third actor rejoins the mêlée. Both actors continue to beat the semi-naked man with renewed vigour – back, face, stomach, hands and feet, all of the body is attacked.*

The scene is overt in its theatricality; it is, as Ridout puts it, 'presenting spades as spades' (Ridout in Castellucci *et al.* 2007: 104). The mechanisms of the imitation are presented to us before the beating begins, and the sound that covers the action seems intended to produce an effective and affecting elongation of the experience of witnessing the action, while not being particularly realistic.[7] The red blur of action is further highlighted and theatricalized by its contrast with the white of the stage and the harshness of the lighting. But the theatricality gives way as the action continues: both the length of the action and its precision create a viscerally embodied sense of the beating as real even as that 'reality' is being undone by the disjunction between readable theatricality and sense of reality, and so a circulation begins. Romeo Castellucci suggests that despite 'the reality of the representation [the exposure of the bottle of stage blood, for example] the scene proceeded […] to become very violent all the same and leap up against the reality of the [stage] blood' (ctd in Castellucci *et al.* 2007: 2), while Chiara Guidi signals the physical impact of the scene, suggesting that she (and by extension the audience in general) 'crashed into the representation' (ctd in Castellucci *et al.* 2007: 3). Bert States has usefully postulated that such moments of blur 'overload the artistic circuit' (States 1985: 37), while Kelleher and Ridout suggest that it is precisely because of the exposure of the theatrical mechanisms in operation that this scene has so much impact (Kelleher and Ridout in Castellucci *et al.* 2007: 2). There is a collapse in the mimetic ordering of the performance; the representation is no longer believable as representation even though we know it to be just that. The action refuses to settle into a comfortable sense of illusion causing a shudder of uncertainty which impacts upon the spectator physically.[8] The duration of the scene (it felt like fifteen minutes) seems to rupture its own mimetic quality as the signified reality comes too close to being real: the represented beating creates a reality effect in which the audience believes the beating is 'for real', the shock of which is palpable in the auditorium and evident in the number of audience leaving.

Although *BR.#04* readily offers the particular reading I am making, it is of course not the only one available. However, it is important to note that while the leaving audience may have been departing because they found it insulting, boring, frightening, unnecessary, excessive or for any number of other reasons, the fundamental fact is that they felt uncomfortable.[9] The performance disturbed the audience; in a tentative parallel with trauma theory we might say that at that specific moment the beating scene created a rupture in their sensibility, driving them from the theatre space.

Adorno has suggested that 'art makes a gesture-like grab for reality, only to draw back violently (*zurückzucken*) as it touches that reality' (ctd in Lehmann 2006: 38). There is no such grab or recoil in the beating scene in *BR.#04*; laying bare the mechanisms of the representation ensures this. However, the audience seems to make just such a grab: we have been set up for this moment by the cleaning of the stage in the first scene and the placing of the baby on stage in the scene preceding the beating.

When the curtain rises, at the beginning of the piece, to reveal the baby sitting centre stage accompanied only by a toy and an abstract silhouette of a head and shoulders cut from sheet metal, the effect upon the audience is palpable but dichotomous, a mixture of affectionate 'ahh-ing' and shocked sucking in of air. The baby seems misplaced, incongruous within the austerity of the space; she is swallowed within it but is never lost to the audience. By this I mean that while the baby is enveloped by the marble room's size, its starkness and, especially in this scene, its foreboding, her relative size and softness fight against this envelopment to raise her perpetually to the forefront of the audience's attention. Kelleher suggests the baby sits in 'unrelation' to the room, and whether she plays and gurgles happily (as on the evening of my viewing) or wails and cries, the 'startling' effect of this unrelation remains the same: we become 'incapable of not watching' (Kelleher in Castellucci *et al.* 2007: 96). Like the pure performance Copeau sees in a cleaner mopping the stage, the baby is unconscious of her role as a performer (Copeau 1990: 75). There is no possible way that the infant on stage has yet developed any deep sense of herself, let alone the complexities which constitute one as an 'actor'. The baby is simply being a baby, and it is captivating. But while the audience read her as 'a baby on stage', she is also a signifier of much more, or at least of many other babies, fictitious or otherwise. Returning to the tripartite circulation I set up above, at once we read her as a baby on a stage, rapidly thereafter as a mimesis of a baby (theatrical sign) and thence her own 'reality' evokes the 'reality' of the referent of which she is a sign. Thus, she unconsciously becomes entangled in a sticky web, to return to Taussig, between being herself, being a theatrical sign and imputing the reality of other babies in the world. The movement between these three modes of viewing this scene is continuous and infinitesimally fast, and so the mimetic instability begins.

Unlike Copeau's cleaner, and the baby of *BR.#04*, the cleaner who opens the piece consciously performs/acts the role of cleaner. She is undoubtedly aware that she is on stage as she performs being a worker. But this performer displays none of the problems that Copeau identifies with actors in his particular historical moment. This cleaner, while performing, does not find herself caught between the poles of 'no longer [being her] self' but 'not yet "other"' (Copeau 1990: 75). So while Derrida might suggest that the inauthentic, or unnatural, is a constant condition of acting and so inescapable, this performance holds to the authenticity one might associate with watching a cleaner clean any space – her mop drips, her bucket overflows and her movements clear away any detritus on the stage floor. Of course we cannot escape from the fact that we know this is not a 'real' cleaner; we know she is part of the theatrical apparatus because the auditorium lights have dimmed and the stage curtain has risen. We might momentarily believe that this person has been caught off guard by an early start, that we have caught the last moments of preparation before the performance proper begins, but it is unlikely. Once more, the theatre becomes entangled in Taussigian rotations of copy and contact, representation and reality – this is an actor performing/representing being a cleaner, representing cleaning but at the same time actually cleaning. We might actually figure the 'sticky web' of this scene with more complexity still because, of course, this could be a 'real' cleaner, persuaded/invited to play the role of a cleaner (herself) onstage so we are left with a cleaner who appears to be an actor playing a cleaner who is representing cleaning but is at the same time cleaning.

The cleaner can, in a sense, be seen to be clearing the space, making it safe, clean and orderly, within both the representational and real economies the scene occupies. The cleaning is creating somewhere where it would be safe, for instance, for a baby, but it is also beautifully paradoxical because the simple act of sweeping away could be read as an act of quiet violence as it neutralizes, effaces and denies difference and *différance* (cf. Derrida 2004: 1–67). It is an imperious, annihilating act of abstraction which, if you like, echoes modernist art according to some feminist anti-patriarchal critiques.[10] However, this violence only rises from the scene once sufficient time has passed so as to stimulate one into questioning the cleaner's function and presence on stage. In the opening few moments of the scene her actions, while interesting, brought with them no great excitement apart from the apparent normality of a cleaner now staged for our viewing pleasure. But in retrospect, the scene is one in which, in Barthes' words, we might 'take a kind of general interest' but which is 'without special acuity' (Barthes 1982: 26). The cleaner scene begins as a performance equivalent of Barthes' notion of *studium* only to cannon towards a *punctum*-like status as the latent tyranny of the abstracting actions become apparent.[11]

This abstracting tyranny is nothing new to the theatre space, a space which has been cleansed of its raucous audiences who were more interested in the theatre of each other than that of the stage. The peripheral spaces of nineteenth-century auditoria were darkened corners in which the 'common people' (as Dickens termed the less wealthy) mingled, freed from the responsibilities and protocols of home and work life (Dickens ctd in Shepherd 2006: 98). The theatre was a place in which to watch and be watched, and not necessarily from auditorium to stage and vice versa.[12] But in the late 1860s, theatres began to make greater use of soft furnishings in an attempt to 'mould the behaviour and composition of the audience' (Shepherd 2006: 100). These furnishings – curtains, carpets and domestically styled chairs – 'implied assumptions about security, class identity and behavioural codes' (Shepherd 2006: 100). New theatre design began to draw focus away from interaction among audience members and towards the stage. Shepherd suggests that theatres, alongside the rise of the restaurant, began to cultivate a 'general way of being in public' that highlighted respectability (Shepherd 2006: 100). There were new seating arrangements that established social stratification; the 'common people' and their bawdy behaviour were slowly being cleared away. A new 'respectable' theatre of comfy seats, dimmed auditoria and silence gradually became the norm. *Différance* was denied as *les bourgeois* were made to feel comfortable at the expense of and safe from the lower classes; or as Shepherd puts it 'the antimacassar as repression' (2006: 100). The 'safety', comfort and (generally) forward focus of audience on the performance of the theatre today can thus be seen to be born from the loins of a very particular bourgeois violence.

Claudia Castellucci evokes another idea of safety or comfort, an appeal, perhaps, to a 'natural' *communitas*, when she suggests that the theatre is 'a natural environment for the human animal' (Castellucci *et al.* 2007: 205). But it is this very 'naturalness' and constructed feeling of safety that *BR.#04* attempts to worry and disrupt. On the occasion I saw the production, the audience was bussed into the suburbs of Avignon and unceremoniously left on a patch of sun-bleached grass outside an austere gymnasium in which the production was showing. Even before the performance began, Socìetas Raffaello Sanzio had already started to unsettle the audience – we had been left in the underbelly of the city, a sub-urban space, not only hoping that we were in the right place but also that the busses would return.[13] So even before this performance of *BR.#04* began there was an air of apprehension, a sense that all may not be quite right. It is an effect that the production itself worked hard to perpetuate.

The costumes and the theatrical trappings in the beating scene which follow the cleaner and baby much more explicitly draw the audience into reading the representation as a sign which is standing in for the event of a real, 'out on the streets' beating. Unlike the baby, in this instance we recognize the mimetic first; the presented scene is received first and foremost as pretend. Despite the supposed 'impossibility' of representing trauma, this scene is undoubtedly a representation of a trauma(tic)-event. But as the action continues the representational quality of the performance is eroded, although the manner in which that representation is presented does not change. There is an irruption of a sense of reality into the representational structure which is deeply unnerving for the audience, unsettling our ability to decode the scene resulting in confusion over what it is we are witnessing. In his discussion of *BR.#04*, Ridout points out that Claudia Castellucci's suggestion of the theatre as a natural space for humankind is anything but the case in this particular piece: 'there is something wrong about being on stage [...] to step onstage is somehow *unheimlich*, a step away from home into a kind of exile [...] the stage is not the place to be' (Ridout in Castellucci *et al.* 2007: 108). Neither, I suggest, is the auditorium.

While the theatre space is familiar, as are the codes and languages of representation, they are made increasingly alien to the point of fracturing. The experience of being at the performance is deeply unnerving. Much in the same sense that Ridout suggests that to be on the stage is *unheimlich*, the same is true of continuing to sit in the auditorium. While we recognize the situation we are in, it is in the same moment strangely different, threatening even. There is a sense that we are watching something we should not, almost as though the Rodney King beating of 1991 is being replayed in front of us. Michael Rothberg has suggested that this type of scene might be described as 'traumatic realism' in which extreme violence is presented as 'a borderland of extremity and everydayness' (Rothberg 2000: 109). It is this very sense of the scene's extremity but familiarity which causes it to feel slightly voyeuristic, a scene stumbled upon which we should look away from but is impossible to disregard. Nicholas Royle suggests that an uncanny experience is one in which there is a sense of a encountering, however briefly, something secret that should have remained hidden (Royle 2003: 2). And

Freud said that 'an uncanny effect is often and easily produced when the distinction between imagination and reality is effaced' (Freud ctd in Royle 2003: 13). To be a spectator at *BR.#04* is to experience this effacement firsthand. It is a violently uncanny experience, in that the onstage act appears to reach out and prick or wound the audience like a constructed performative Barthesian *punctum*. This moment is a rhetorical *punctum*, for while Barthes suggests that the *punctum* is his discovery in a photograph and not a construct of the artist, the *punctum* here (in a much more explicit way than that of the cleaner scene) is a deliberate element of the performance. Nevertheless, Barthes' term is particularly useful in the current context, not least of all because of the language he employs to convey the effect of the *punctum* on the viewer. It is the element of the image which violently captures his attention. He writes that it 'rises from the scene, shoots out of it like an arrow, and pierces me', it is 'that accident which pricks me (but also bruises me, is poignant to me)' and he goes on to discuss the *punctum* as a captivating 'wound' (Barthes 1982: 26–27).

In *BR.#04* the strange familiarity of the violent act which constitutes this performative *punctum* makes for compelling and compulsive viewing but it is painful to the viewer. Freud postulates that to experience the effect of the uncanny is to encounter a feeling of 'helplessness' and, echoing the trauma theorists, to experience a fragmentation of the self as it becomes 'duplicated, divided and interchanged' (Freud 2003b: 142–144).

As the representation wears away, the audience is unsettled as we both recognize the violence and experience it as alien. The reality of the images as representation shimmers, constantly and rapidly in and out of focus with the perception of the representation as violent reality. The spectator is kept in a constant state of flux, never deciding on the images as reality or mimesis. In this process, what we might call *mimetic shimmering*, the images refuse resolution and definition. Unable to decide if the actions of the performance are real or representational, the spectator might be thought of as caught between equal gravitational pulls at each pole of the three-way tension between present reality – mimesis – imputed presence of the referent, without ever settling at one point or finding equilibrium in the middle. It is a state of constant tension, a state of being perpetually unsettled, and it is a state which is deliberately constructed by the performance and the moment of rhetorical *punctum*.

Mimetic shimmering, then, produces an 'undecidability' which is experienced viscerally and painfully but paradoxically also with excitement and curiosity, causing a tension between the desire to look away and a desire to experience it.[14] My use of the term 'undecidable' is taken very much in line with art historian Henry M. Sayre's use of the term, after Derrida, in *The Object of Performance* (1989), in which he suggests that undecidability foregrounds the ethical imperative inherent in watching. Sayre argues that the term positions 'the work's contingency, multiplicity, and polyvocality in the *audience*' and that such works (which Sayre defines as avant-garde) implicate the audience in their content and so demand a personal response (Sayre 1989: xiv; emphasis is original).[15] While there are inevitably elements of overlap between this undecidability and Lehmann's indecidability, the former's focus on the audience is particularly important. Furthermore, I am discussing performance moments which do not explicitly ask the audience to consider whether the moment is real or representational, as the 'smoking break' in Fabre's *The Power of Theatrical Madness* does (cf. Lehmann 2006: 100), but am rather examining performances in which the shimmering between representation and reality erupts precisely because there is no such break in the 'style'; it is the precision of the action which causes it to become undecidable.

Considered through the lens of trauma theory, the paradoxical tension of mimetic shimmering is similar to the paradox between the desire to forget the trauma-event and the desire or necessity to remember/restage it in order to 'know' it and so effect some form of cure. The experience of watching this shimmering in and out of representation is, to some degree at least, to put oneself into and experience the central paradoxical tension of trauma-symptoms. This is not to suggest that one is 'traumatized' by the experience as, unlike the trauma-symptom, there is pleasure and excitement in the encounter with this particular tension. However, being placed within this shimmering borderland might, in light of Taussig's assessment of mimetic power and knowledge gain, be seen as offering up the trauma-event as an object of knowledge. Such an experience may put an audience into a position of bearing witness to trauma in a viscerally embodied manner, and the mimetic shimmer which echoes the tension of trauma-symptoms may act as a mode of gaining knowledge over that which is represented.

Mimesis in reverse

I mentioned earlier that the baby in *BR.#04* elicits a triple reading: the audience read her firstly as a baby on stage and almost instantaneously as a sign within the theatrical mechanisms of that particular performance and as imputing the reality of other babies in the world. It is the ordering that I wish to highlight: first the thing itself is recognized for what it is, a baby in this case; second, that object comes to be recognized within a mimetic economy because of its placement on stage. This second element, the fact that the baby could be seen to represent the baby of the cleaner from the first scene or equally a modern-day baby Moses, for example, disrupts and breaches its ontological status as simply a baby on a stage. Rather than a (mis)recognition of reality which pierces the mimetic, such as in the beating, here the process is inverted or reversed as it is the recognition of mimesis which irrupts into the real.[16] The scene thus holds a similar shimmering in and out of mimesis, but in this instance the mimetic is the catalyst to the shimmering. A similar, if perhaps amplified, shimmer is in operation in performance artist Franko B's piece *Still Life* (2003).

Still Life

The piece's deliberately mimetic title provokes the audience to bring to memory their expectations of still life paintings they may have seen. The title functions as a frame through which the spectators approach the performance: it gestures towards compositional structures, colours, tones and textures. The two words of the title hold a signifying capacity which creates certain expectations and/or assumptions about what the performance might be like even before one has purchased a ticket. After all, as Derrida tells us, 'a title is always a promise' (Derrida 1986: 115).

The small studio was draped in blacks, and an air-lock of sorts, which the audience had to part, separated the theatre's foyer from the small performance space. The space itself was also shrouded in blacks and had had all seating removed. The studio had been sanitized of its usual furnishings and, just as at BR.#04, assumptions of what a traditional bourgeois theatre space should be were disrupted. The studio was hot, claustrophobic and dominated by an illuminated white bed which diagonally bisected the room. The domesticity of the bed's headboard clearly signalled that it was not an abstract sign for a bed nor was it a hospital bed. The bed was someone's bed; a piece of domestic furniture which had been transplanted into a theatrical and unhomely space.

The audience walked tentatively round the bed and eventually settled into their desired (standing/watching) positions.[17] Franko B quietly entered the space, naked and painted completely white. He walked to the bed, lay down, put his head on the pillow and opened the catheters protruding from each of his arms. Blood pumped out of the hollow needles, ran down his arms and began to collect around and under his body, staining the white sheet on which he was lying. The blood puddle slowly grew larger and larger, and its colour was increasingly intensified by the contrast it made with the white bed linen and light box which illuminated the bed. The blood seemed to glow against the whiteness of the performer's body, and the liquid made the soaked sheet stick to him as he turned from lying on his right side to his left. There was another sudden gush of blood as his heart rate jumped slightly with the movement. The performance was not long, as dictated by the rapid loss of blood, and Franko B's exit was as casual and understated as his entrance. He simply sat up, paused for a moment, closed the catheter caps, stood up and walked out.

As the performance went on I was struck by the stillness and tranquillity of the scene: it was beautiful but also lonely and sad. The performer seemed isolated, vulnerable, almost infantile. It was undoubtedly uncomfortable to be part of, and even in the remembering of it, *Still Life* makes me all too aware of the blood pumping round my own body, a precious life force which one can all too easily take for granted. But despite the discomfort of the experience, or perhaps precisely because of it, a strange sort of gift exchange seemed to be taking place: 'to bleed is to give' as the artist has put it (Franko B 2007: n.p.). *Still Life*, and indeed any of Franko B's bleeding work, can be seen as a kind of performance potlatch, so to speak, in which it is not the object of exchange which is important but the fact of it.[18]

A process of reciprocity occurs in which gaze can be seen to be exchanged for blood: the audience becomes witness to Franko B's performance of and insistence on the preservation of gay, sado-masochistic identity established and investigated through his art practice (Mahon 2005: 238–239), and in return he 'pays' the audience with his blood, which holds no real value to us. It is thus the event of the encounter which generates meaning and value to both parties.

In a reductive and problematic argument, art historian and cultural theorist Kerstin Mey groups Franko B and Ron Athey's performances together, claiming that both artists 'inflict extreme physical agony on themselves' and that both put themselves into situations of 'acute suffering' (Mey 2007: 50). While this argument may potentially hold true of some of Athey's performances, although I still find Mey's rhetoric of pain and suffering exaggerated, I think it fundamentally misreads Franko B's work. Although Franko B can potentially be seen to be putting his body at risk through blood letting, the conditions under which he performs are tightly planned and controlled so the risk is negligible. Furthermore, the pain that the artist goes through is minimal: as anyone who has had a blood test will know, the insertion of a needle-catheter generally involves (physically) little more than the sensation of a scratch.[19] Mey further suggests, in a less contentious argument, that Franko B and Athey 'test their own physical and emotional limits' (the loss of blood Franko B experiences is undoubtedly physically demanding) and they further test 'the limits of art and what is bearable for the audience' (Mey 2007: 50). This testing of the limits of what the audience can bear, and indeed the further efficacy of the performance, is less bound to Franko B's 'extreme agony' than it is to the images he creates and significations they conjure. Indeed, the performer's exit and the scene we are left with afterwards were uncannily more unsettling, more 'unbearable' than the performance of Franko B bleeding.

The rhetoric of pain and suffering in Mey's analysis is, as I have said, overstated, but it is perhaps worth asking why she might be making these claims at all and to contemplate why she might be mistaking bleeding for pain and suffering. It seems to me that Mey's reading of these artists' works is bound up in a traumatic projection of some kind: perhaps because of her own traumatic experiences, Mey seems to figure the performers' blood as signifier of (their) 'agony', 'suffering' and 'pain'. I have already argued against Mey's reading but the process by which she gets to it, the idea of a traumatic projection of sorts, chimes quite readily with the next part of my argument and is one which is connected to notions of witnessing which I will discuss in more detail in the next chapter.

The audience is left in the dark studio with nothing but the glowing blood-stained bed and each other to look at. This seemed to generate an awkwardness and unease that had not been present (or at least had not affected the audience as much) while the performer was on stage. Ridout, in his discussion of witnessing the harvesting of a horse's spermatozoa during Societas Raffaello Sanzio's *Il Combattimento*, suggests that in such moments there is an 'anxiety over the propriety of what is taking place' (Ridout 2006: 124). The still life of the bloodied bed acts as a catalyst to realizing the impropriety of the previous action and is also improper in its own right. It seems too 'private' for an audience's consumption. There is simply too much blood; the quantity of it is unnerving in that while small deposits of blood on bed sheets are common in homes around the world, the amount here sits in opposition to the signified domesticity, and so familiarity, of the bed itself and it becomes *unheimlich*.

The biological trace feels excessive as a signifier. Not only does the image suggest a scene of birth or death, but there is something specific about the blood on this bed which seems to unsettle and confuse its reading. The impropriety of viewing this biological deposit is juxtaposed to prior knowledge (and imputed presence) of just such a scene, be it imagined, from film or television, personal history or even another performance. This in turn is juxtaposed to our knowledge that we are allowed to be here, we have paid to be here and no one has asked us to leave. But then maybe we were supposed to go when Franko B did. These juxtapositions create confusion and unease because, left alone, the audience no longer knows how to behave in relation to the bed, the still performing ghost of the absent performer and the imputed presence of other 'real' scenes which the reality of bloodied sheets might be seen to be evoking. A shimmering begins again.

The still life that the title of this performance promises is the bloodied bed, and it is an image which was (and to a certain degree still is) immensely powerful, seeming to signify a great many other images which are part of our cultural and social economies. Barthes has suggested that signified meanings are not at all stable but are open to interpretation in relation to the signifier's context and 'above all due to its function'. He also suggests that signs, in their given context, will precisely concern one group of readers but not another (Barthes 2000: 219–220). The bloodied bed is in a very specific given context; it has been staged in the heart of a liberal, arts-friendly university at the largest arts centre in the UK outside London (Warwick Arts Centre) whose core audience demographic can be assumed to be educated, interested in the arts and aware of the conventions involved in 'reading' visual media.[20] Illuminated and situated in a theatre space, we can safely assume that the audience members are all involved in trying to unravel this piece into some form of understanding. The centrality of the bed image to my memory and understanding of the piece only occurred to me after the event; it is the image which comes quickest to memory and which repeatedly draws me to thinking about *Still Life*. The section of *Still Life* in which the performer is physically present might be thought of, returning to Barthes, as *studium*-like: the tranquillity and arguably beautiful aesthetic quality of the performance is only ruptured once the performer leaves the space. The performative *punctum* of this piece is the (seemingly accidental) discovery of the uncanny image of the bloodied bed.

The emptied space is still filled with the ghost of the performer's presence and his physical presence is still palpable

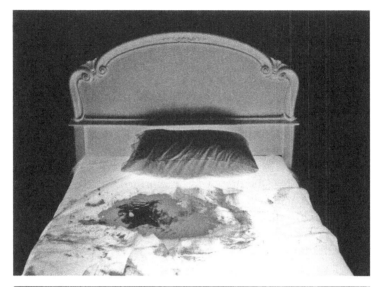

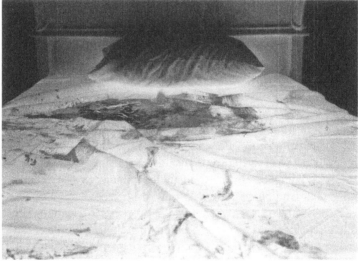

Figures 3 and 4: Performance stills of Franko B's *Still Life* (2003).

in the stains and smells left behind. There is a collapse of the mimetic here too. The (forensic) traces we are left with feel staged, mocked up, perfectly fabricated into a sublimely theatrical image.[21] Not only is it visually and, to borrow from Yeats, 'terribly' beautiful, but it is also framed by the conventions of the space and lighting – there is a sense of the image performing, the image *as* theatre. Even though the central performer has departed, the performance event is deliberately allowed to continue and the audience become performers in relation to the bed and, importantly, to each other, but performing without any sense of how one should perform in this familiar but alien context. The image is also reflexive of other scenes we have seen before, from murder/crime scenes so readily depicted on television shows such as the popular, long-running American crime drama *CSI: Crime Scene Investigation* and the brutality of classical (religious) paintings such as Caravaggio's *Judith Beheading Holofernes*. This is because, as Barthes suggests in his discussion of photography (although the point remains valid across the visual/communicative media), 'it is always *something* that is represented' (Barthes 1982: 28; emphasis is original).

The later example might be closest to the mark, given Franko B's own background in fine art and as the scene's aesthetic is particularly painterly, reminiscent of the vibrancy of Renaissance art. While the associations I have given above are ones I have made, the performance is undoubtedly inviting the audience to engage in just such a relationship of signifier and signified by presenting us with so clearly a constructed image. But in the instant of the recognition of one or more of these imitations the scene dissolves back into reality and we are confronted once more by the bloody bed sheets. There is a constant moving in and out of viewing the performance, particularly the still life of the empty bed, between what is happening in the here and now, mimetic denotation and the imputed presence/reality of (an)other scene(s). The mimetic action, then, is in the hands of the spectator. The shimmering discussed above is in this instance not bound to an explicit attempt to represent a specific scene but to an (unconscious) attempt by the spectator to develop an associative understanding of the piece. The whole performance was a collision of mimetic imitations and imaginings, and a constant reaffirmation of the reality of the situation brought about by the imagination slipping between signified representation and return to the presented image.

Adrian Heathfield has argued of another Franko B performance, *I Miss You!*, that it is 'difficult for us to stand outside of the event' and that we are 'engaged in a vibrant relay between experience and thought, struggling in a charged present to accommodate and resolve the imperative to make meanings from what we see' (Heathfield 2004: 9). Thinking about *Still Life* in relation to Heathfield's assertion, the work is certainly both an immediate and charged 'present' in the way that he writes about it, but more than this it is also experienced as somehow located somewhere else, distanced, 'other'. This is not to suggest that the performance is disengaging, but more that the experience is foreign, unimaginably excessive and almost as if watched from outside oneself. Heathfield suggests that 'excessive performance tends to make evident that the event of its encounter, as the trauma theorists put it, is constituted by the collapse of its understanding' (2004: 9). Heathfield's phrase 'excessive performance' usefully suggests this type of performance is beyond the boundaries of 'usual' representational forms: the spectator meets it as an event which somehow performs outside conventions, necessity, and understanding. The performance of *Still Life* is excessive in that it is beyond (full/complete) comprehension in the first moment of its witnessing. Much like the experience of trauma-events, the audience-witness is consumed by the event of the performance, concerned only with surviving it and much like the return or recurrence of trauma-symptoms, the understanding of the performance is only available to the spectator after the event has passed and in relation to other experiences.[22] In other words, the reality of the event is registered in the bodies of the audience before its mimetic quality is recognized. Just as with the baby in *BR.#04*, the blood is firstly real and secondly mimetic, rather than the other way round as in conventional economies of theatrical mimesis. By this I mean that in most cases we will focus on the representation, of a police beating for example, before that representation slips into undecidability, beginning the process of mimetic shimmering. In the case of *Still Life*, however, we register the imitative, representational, 'fictional' scene only after and in light of the real one. We experience the performance in a process of what we might call *mimesis in reverse*.

The mimetic action is not so affecting as to prevent the sudden moment of realization that at the level of immediate experience there is a man bleeding on a bed in front of you, and for your 'pleasure'. But the beautiful and mesmeric aesthetic quality is composed with a precision which, for me at least, holds the image as art rather than 'reality.' In Freudian terms, the *unheimlich* nature of watching a man bleed returns the viewer to the relative safety of associative pre-experienced images or performances, or, to put it another way, the audience returns to their knowledge of the mimetic quality of art/theatre/life as a means of protection from the uncanny reality of the witnessed event.[23] This return, however, operates in simultaneity with its mirror image. Just as the blood/bleeding is uncanny and therefore returns us to the 'safety' of the mimetic, in the instant we register the imitation or representational quality of *Still Life* we pull back towards the reality of it because the mimicry in this excessive performance is as uncanny and difficult as the reality itself.

It is only after the performer has left that the possibility of mimetic collapse signals the onset of the traumatic image. The light box (making up the bed) which illuminates the scene also generates enough heat to produce a metallic sanguinity which fills the studio. It is a sensory experience, an oral and olfactory 'assault' which I found particularly hard to ignore, and of course I was not supposed to. The clash of the imaginatively made mimetic performance and the reality of the event drive the energy of the experience; the beauty of the image is worried by the reality of the smell of blood and bodies. The key point here is that this very duplicity of the experience of the event holds the audience up to it as both victim-witnesses and as possible complicit perpetrators or conspirators. We are not allowed to ignore the reality of what is happening, nor are we able to deny the pictorial/painterly aesthetic we are presented with. There is in this performance, then, an iteration of the difficulty of mimetic presentation within performance and theatre. Even in a performance that does not claim to be representational in the same way that a play in the tradition of Naturalism might, the mimetic paradox, echoing the traumatic paradox, is once again palpably and carefully made present to and experienced by the audience.

Central to both of the performance examples I have discussed is the idea of mimetic shimmering. The directionality of that shimmering can be both from mimesis into reality, as it were, and, as suggested by my construction of mimesis in reverse, from reality into mimesis. Thus the deconstructive figure of a circulation between real and representation comes to be established. Triggered by one element of the production which seems to rise from the field of signification to peak our interest, this shimmering violently grabs our imaginations and destabilizes our understanding of what we are witnessing. Returning to Barthes, each of these moments, which are common to most of the performance examples I explore, can be viewed as a theatrical or performative *punctum* and it is via these *puncta* that an experience of, or bearing witness to, trauma can take place. These moments of *punctum* may happen more than once in any one performance and, unlike Barthes' premise that the *punctum* is an accidental occurrence, they can exist as constructs of the performance as long as the mechanism of that construction remain 'hidden'. The performative *punctum* is the catalyst to opening the shimmering undecidability between reality and representation that causes the audience to stumble in their reading of the performance, which can in turn be associated with a represented experience of trauma's central paradox.

4

Performance 'texts' as sites of witness

> One of the defining characteristics of a theatrical event is the fact that it takes place in the presence of spectators, in front of a live audience.
>
> (Rokem 2002: 167)

> Western theatre is itself predicated on the belief that there is an audience.
>
> (Phelan 1997: 31)

> [T]o witness an event is to be present at it in some funda-mentally ethical way, to feel the weight of things and one's own place in them even if that place is simply for the moment, as an onlooker[...] The art-work that turns us into witnesses leaves us, above all, unable to stop think-ing, talking and reporting what we've seen. We are left, like the people in Brecht's poem who've witnessed a road accident, stood still on the street corner discussing what happened, borne on by our responsibility to events.
>
> (Etchells 1999: 17–18)

Witnessing brings with it implications of responsibility and imperatives to testify, especially within the specifics of law, medi-cine and history narratives. In trauma discourses there exists an imperative to bear witness and testify to both world-defin-ing traumas, like the Holocaust, and 'smaller', more personal traumas, such as loss, domestic violence or rape. The impera-tive is driven by a desire to comment upon, stimulate some form of action in relation to and potentially come to reconstitute or historicize trauma-events and symptoms. In this chapter I am proposing that performance in general, and trauma-tragedy in particular, might be seen as a mechanism which is more adequately suited to this task than those previously considered within Trauma Studies, such as historical narratives, statute books and legislation, painting, literature or film.

While it is well understood that theatre/performance is about schism of some kind, the particular focus of this chapter is on witnessing and its correspondence with trauma/traumatic schism, and specifically the notion of trauma-tragedy. Examining a series of performances which address trauma and witnessing in different yet complementary ways, this chapter discusses what 'witness' might mean and further what it means 'to be witnessed' – audience to performer, performer to audience and, crucially, audience to audience – in the context of trauma-tragedy. Rather than focusing on individual experiences, though some consideration of this perspective is inevitable, the core focus here is on the idea of a culture thinking itself through: trauma-tragedy as a performative addressing of and bearing witness to traumata.

The theatre or performance event is defined by its existence in a specific time and place, never to be repeated in quite the same way again, for an audience which is unique to that moment. Bodies in space, moving through time and watched by an audience – it is a familiar argument. Keir Elam argues that of 'all successive audience signals, the most significant is its simple presence', and indeed it is 'the spectator who *initiates* the theatrical communication' by buying a ticket (Elam 2002: 86; emphasis is original). Meanwhile, John Freeman contends that the positioning of an audience member as witness to a theatrical or performance event happens because of the frame which is metaphorically placed around these cultural objects:

> It may well be the case that we blink once, if at all, when we witness body modification and adornment in 'life', whereas we blink hard and look away when the same act or image is presented to us within the frame of art. It is precisely this framing aspect of art that makes the things we see so often difficult to bear.
>
> (Freeman 2007: 110)

This arguent seems overly simplistic. I am not sure I could watch a plastic surgeon at work in 'life' yet I have studied pictures and video footage of Orlan's various performances and watched Traci Kelly have her back tattooed live in Hancock and Kelly's *Tattoo* (2007) without once looking away. Nevertheless his point is interesting. The art 'frame' begins a process which places us within what might be loosely thought of as an ethical responsibility to the work which is not present in 'life' – the artwork directly addresses us while in life we have no right to intrude into another person's body practices. It is this ethical responsibility more than the desire to look away which creates any physical or emotional impact an audience might feel.[1] Although not explicit in Freeman's argument, Susan Leigh Foster's notion of frames is similarly useful. Foster argues that a 'frame', by which she refers to any element of the performance from its announcement to the gaze of the performers, guides the viewer 'towards certain expectations about the event by indicating how it differs from daily life' (Foster 1986: 60). Foster notes that the frames 'help define the viewer's role – as spectator, voyeur or witness – in watching the event' (65). As such, within the frame of theatre or performance we are complicit in the acts, firstly, because we can in theory stop them at any point, secondly, because they occur precisely because of our material presence at the event and, thirdly, because we accept the contract that is constituted by the fame.

It has been well argued that the very nature of bodies witnessing bodies creates a visceral human connection enabling the audience to be physically and emotionally moved by what they are presented with.[2] As set out in Chapter 2, since the late 1960s there has been a discernible turn, within some aspects of performance practice, towards a deconstruction of 'the well made play' in search of more immediate, authentic performance experiences. Part of this move was concerned with a reconsideration of the performer–audience relationship: there seemed to be an urgent cancelling of the barrier between the two parties, a collapsing of the delineated theatre space towards a more unified, shared performance space. This collapse and unification is exemplified in performances such as Carolee Shneemann's *Meat Joy* (1964), Richard Schechner/The Performance Group's *Dionysus in '69* (1968), Vito Acconci's

Seedbed (1971) and Marina Abramovic's *Rhythm 0* and *Rhythm 5* (both 1974). The refiguring of performance spaces is, of course, not the only way in which a kinaesthetic connection between performer and spectator, or cathected, authentic experiences can be produced, but as a historical marker it highlights the emphasis increasingly placed on that connection.

Through our muscular and emotional connection to the performance we are able to gain experience or knowledge of that which is presented to us. This idea might be seen to correspond to Paul Crowther's notion (from an art history perspective) of a 'sensuous manifold', an 'integral fusion of the sensuous and the conceptual which enables art to express something of the depth and richness of body-hold in a way which eludes modes of abstract thought' (Crowther 1993: 5). The sensuous manifold is partly constituted by 'empathic experience' and in this way the experience of an artwork might articulate or create awareness of the nature of the human condition (Crowther 1993: 46). Art, in other words, is an embodied revelation and reflection of our enigmatic and enfolded capacity for knowing (in) the world. It is precisely this sense of coming to know the world, or the notion that a society/culture might be able to think itself through, via performance, that is under scrutiny in this chapter.

Witnessing and trauma

As well as formulating a conception of trauma and trauma symptoms, much contemporary trauma theory focuses on the importance of testimony and witnessing. The concepts are engaged with as being means both of moving beyond the trauma event, through a process of witnessed testimony or being borne witness to, such as the therapeutic session, and of testifying to the truth and occurrence of the event itself, a desire to secure a pseudo *memento vivere* to the trauma event (such as the Fortunoff Video Archive for Holocaust Testimonies at Yale University).[3] Psychiatrist Guy Undrill suggests that this desire to engage with processes of witnessing and testimony can be seen as part of the surprising yet 'insistent' parallels and connections between trauma and performance (Undrill 2000: 133).[4]

To be made a witness places someone firmly in the first person; witnessing is the act of being present at the happening of an event. To bear witness, then, is the act of recounting that event to a present audience, to fulfil the role of testifier and articulate the event in some form, to perform it and so give it space to become 'real' for an assembled crowd.[5] This, however, does not dictate the presence of a person as the bearer of witness: while bearing witness through testimony might be carried out by a first-person witness, it might also be achieved through the creation of a painting, play, film, performance or poem, for example, which in some way testifies to the event(s) and so creates the viewer of that 'testimony' as second order of witness to the original event.[6]

There is here an implicit tone of responsibility to and/or for the action and its recounting. To bear witness to the events is to take on the responsibility of imparting the action to others. Undrill picks up on the notion of responsibility within this type of, what we might term, second-order witnessing, arguing that 'the subject that witnesses the other's testimony must bear a solitude of responsibility'. He further contends that the witness must simply be 'with the other in his or her disarray' without imposing attempts to 'cure, explain or meliorate' (Undrill 2000: 135). The latter part of Undrill's argument corresponds with my own in Chapter 2 regarding the construction of trauma-tragedy: the witness must allow the traumatic 'disarray' to simply be and be testified about without intervening towards cure. Likewise trauma-tragedies are simply about trauma; there is no curative bent but rather an attempt to make 'present' the traumatic in order that it might more adequately be rehearsed or thought through. Similarly, trauma theorist and psychoanalyst Dori Laub suggests this responsibility, rather than being towards curative ends, is to the truth of what happens during an event and to being part of its continuing circulation in history (1995: 65).

Echoing the statements by Rokem, Phelan and Etchells, cited at the beginning of this chapter, but extending the notion of spectatorship into witnessing, Simon Shepherd suggests that theatre 'is an art of bodies witnessed by bodies. Witnesses are something more than passive viewers. In the act of witnessing a person attests to the truth of something that is or was present for them' (Shepherd 2006: 73). As witnesses we are undeniably part of the theatrical, performance or trauma event, bound up in its action and responsible (in some form) to and for it. The central difference between being a spectator and being a witness is, then, to do with implication. We cannot escape from the fact of our presence at the event because 'the body', Garner argues, 'is a sign that looks back' (1994: 49). We need also to say that at performance events there are another set of eyes involved: those of our fellow audience members. This second set of eyes is of course present, though configured differently, at other spectatorial art events but unlike those events the audience–audience gaze is mirrored and doubled by the performer–audience one. The key point here is to highlight that this audience–audience gaze is, partly, concerned with (the possibility of) having one's response to the artwork scrutinized. At performance, then, not only are we exchanging glances with or watching each other, but we are also doing so with the performers; we are thus doubly under scrutiny. Through this exchange of glances we might become not only aware of our ontological presence in the room but also of our complicity in the actions presented. The live co-presence of audience and artwork – being able to hear, see, touch and even smell the performers and each other – is a frame which sets up an expectation of both responsibility for and complicity with what is happening on stage, if not in the action of the diegetic world.[7] This double being-seen-watching, common to most theatre and performance to some degree, might be seen to constitute what we can term a basic *implication effect.*

By its very nature live performance ensures that those who go to see it become spectators, watchers, even eavesdroppers, at the event. However, while an audience enters the space with the express intention of viewing the performance, they do not necessarily expect to be made aware of their own presence at that performance. In the moments when we are made aware of ourselves watching, either by performers or fellow audience, we enter into implicated complicity with what we are seeing and are no longer justified in objectifying ourselves as 'outside' the performance event. Rokem has suggested that the difference between spectatorship and witnessing is also partly to do with accidental discovery in so far as 'watching or eavesdropping' are intentional acts but one is created as witness in the accidental encounter with an event (Rokem 2002: 168).[8] The notion of the accidental within the creation of 'a witness' is useful. Even entering a performance event in which we know the performer–audience dynamic will not be delineated by segregating acting space and audience space, or where this dynamic becomes increasingly worried, audiences might, because of the development of theatre spaces since the mid-1800s (detailed in Chapter 3), be assumed to tend to approach a production with a sense of dislocation from the performer(s). Theatre, as Gay McAuley points out, 'consists of human beings *in a defined space* watched by other human beings' and while 'the nature of the defined spaces has varied greatly from age to age and culture to culture', where there is no formal definition the audience will 'make their own' (McAuley 2000: 245; emphasis is original). Historically, this segregation has been worried and broken down through performative means, such as moments in which audience become 'performers' (I will address this specific point in the next chapter) or where the performers break into the audience space, as demonstrated in Anthony Neilson's *Normal* (first performed in 1991).

Normal explores the lead-up to the trial and eventual execution of the Düsseldorf Ripper. The play is heightened and stylized, using direct address, exaggerated props such as 'ludicrously-oversized scissors' and a 'surreal and hideous-looking' hammer, and stylized representations of forests and prison cells (Neilson 1998: 3 and 49). The play is surreal and nightmarish but gives way to a sense of reality and danger during the murder of Frau Kurten when she 'escapes, invading the audience space' (Neilson 1998: 52). The play makes a foray towards the shimmering borderline between 'reality' and representation just this once, but throughout the piece Neilson is constantly battling to try to bear witness to the traumas that 'The Ripper' inflicted upon his victims and those he suffered himself as a child. The stage directions state that the murder scene is 'quite relentless' and Neilson has suggested that the play was intended to show the realities of what serial killers do (cf. Neilson in Sierz 2000: 70); in Alex Sierz's words, *Normal* 'shows how hard it is to kill someone' (2000: 70). The play theatrically articulates trauma visually (the elongated beating) and orally/aurally (continued and prolonged accounts of The Ripper's violence) presenting the audience with both images and dialogue testifying to trauma.

The moment of violence violates the sanctity of the audience's space, puncturing any sense of safety which might be perceived through the boundary between stage and auditorium. In so doing, *Normal* denies the audience the possibility of objectifying the action as somehow 'elsewhere' or disconnected from their presence. The audience at the original staging of the play, as Neilson points out, 'wriggled about [...and] were craning their necks to see what was happening' (ctd in Sierz 2000: 71); they were subjects of the performance. Looked at and potentially touched, the audience is implicated in and made to feel the weight of their presence at the performance. This performance becomes not only an object on to which we project ourselves in the search of pleasure fulfillment, but also an inescapably somatic experience which deliberately implicates the spectator in its action and positions them as witness to it. This type of *dramaturgical* implication effect, complementing the basic implication effect I outlined above, has discernible roots in the development of performance practices since the late 1960s. This moment of *Normal* is a particularly good example of the way in which the trauma-tragic mode of performance can highlight/ foreground the traumatic. The scene is unexpected and fractures from the style of the rest of the play; it may even function as a *punctum* which creates mimetic shimmering. The breaking of spaces here is intended to act in a similar way to the refiguring of space in Performance Art: the move is precisely intended to connect audience to action, both that which is happening in the space and, in a second order, to the testimony contained in the action of the narrative and, thinking back to the last chapter, the realities that imputes. The violence of the scene, both in content and in the way it fractures the structure of the play, is a trauma-tragic experience; it situates the audience in a possible realm of undecidability and deliberately implicates them as first- and second-order witnesses.

In order to break out of the cycle of traumatic re-experiencing, we must give the event proper witness; we must allow it space to become 'real' and palpable, not only to the survivor but to any number of others who become witness to the survivor rather than the event itself. Trauma must have witnesses: the original event must be witnessed to become trauma-symptom; the survivor-sufferer must bear witness to it through testimony/ representation in order to begin to understand the ordeal they have survived; the survivor-sufferer must be borne witness to, their experience must be validated and shared in order for it to be processed and diminished so that they can begin to heal. Psychiatrist Sandra Bloom points out that in order for healing to occur, survivor sufferers need to put the traumatic experience into some form of 'narrative', which can be done through words or by 'acting out' in behaviour (especially in the case of children). By making the experience into a narrative the survivor-sufferer is able to share the experience with themselves and with others in order to prevent the 'traumatic past [being] experienced as being in the ever present "Now"' (Bloom 1999: 6). The acts of being witnessed and of bearing witness through testimony are central to the 'cure' of trauma symptoms.

Trauma-tragedy shares this desire for a witness, to place spectators in a position of ethical responsibility to the work, a position whereby they take up Malpede's challenge of 'receiving of testimony'. Given Malpede's assertion, cited in Chapter 1, that theatre is perfectly placed to attempt to portray the 'realities of trauma' (Malpede 1996: 168), it would seem that live performance has the capacity to function as the space in which trauma can be testified about and borne witness to, through all strata of the apparatus from makers to audience. Boalian techniques of empowerment through theatre and the long history of writing on theories of tragedy and comedy, as well as Turner's social-aesthetic drama model, suggest that performance is a form of artistic practice which has the capacity to function within and beyond the collapsing of community and self caused by trauma events and symptoms. Within the specifics of trauma-tragedies, the performance event is a place where the grand narratives of trauma can be examined and testified to: for example, Pinter's *The Room* (first performed in 1957 and recently staged in 2007) might easily be read as a testimony to the horrors of domestic violence and repressed trauma; his *One For The Road* (first performed in 1984) is a harrowing exploration of state violence and oppression; and Martin Sherman's

Bent (first performed in 1978 and revived in London's West End in 2006) is a depressing testimony not only to the plight of the gay community during the Nazi regime but more widely to the traumas of the many thousands kept or killed in their various camps.[9] Furthermore, although most usually associated with an individual's process of recovery, the possibility of theatre as a site of witnessing is further supported by work in the field of drama therapy which explicitly utilizes theatricalized narrative and exploration through play as a means of helping survivor-sufferers to come to terms with both the trauma-event and the trauma-symptoms.[10]

The importance and centrality of theatre within discourses of trauma therapy and healing, both in the experience of making and viewing (and not only within the context of drama therapy), is summed up by Bloom's assertion that:

> [p]rograms that focus on nonverbal expression – a description that includes art, music, movement, and theatre programs as well as sports – are vital[…] The arts can play a central role in community healing, serving as a 'bridge across the black hole of trauma'.
>
> (Bloom 1999: 7)

Testimony and witnessing can thus both be seen as potentially curative elements in any trauma cycle; it is through testimony and witness that the survivor-sufferer might be able to understand the trauma-event better, placing it in a historical perspective, and so diminish its impact in their present.[11] The diminution of the disruption caused by trauma through witnessing can be seen to function as some form of *catharsis*. By this I do not mean cathartic in the sense of a 'purification' (translated from '*katharsis*') or purging which Aristotle might be seen to propose. Nor am I referring to 'a magic transformation, a purging of evil of the trauma' which Herman discounts (2001: 181). Rather I am considering catharsis in light of Malcolm Heath's argument, as mentioned in the Introduction, that (Aristotelian) *katharsis* is not intended to rid a person of their emotions but is rather a means by which one might 'feel the right degree of emotion in the right circumstances', and that this in turn is considered both productive and pleasurable (Heath 1996: xxxviii–xxxix). In other words catharsis is a means by which an individual, community or culture can come to terms with overwhelming emotions, a means by which the art experience might be able to mediate, think through or balance 'unwanted' emotions, or, in the present case, traumatic memory. The emotions under consideration in Aristotle's work are primarily pity and fear, noting in the *Politics* that 'any feeling [emotion] which comes strongly to some souls exists in all others to a greater or less degree – pity and fear, for example, but also excitement'. He goes on to suggest that this might be thought of as an 'agitation' by which some may become 'possessed' (Aristotle 1981: 473). The 'strong', or 'violent' as Heath translates it, possession by agitation or excitement (also translated as 'enthusiasm') echoes with the definitions of hysteria which so influenced the development of trauma theory. Indeed, Heath picks up on this point, arguing that Aristotle is refer-ring to people who are prone to 'hysterical or ecstatic frenzy' (Heath 1996: xxxvii). While Charcot was able to induce hysteri-cal outbursts through performative mechanisms, Aristotle claims that they might be able to calm it. He suggests that through the experience of music (*Politics*) or tragedy (*Poetics*), people of high emotion, or hysterics, 'inevitably' experience 'a sort of pleasant purgation and relief' (Aristotle 1981: 474).[12]

Although Judith Herman notes that '[b]ecause the truth is so difficult to face, [trauma] survivors often vacillate in recon-structing their stories', echoing the 'impossibility' of representing trauma which Phelan proffers, she also notes the importance of the reconstruction and through it the desire for, or 'implicit fantasy' of, cathartic experience (Herman 2001: 181). Importantly, she goes on to contend that cathartic experience (in relation to trauma therapy) is less a purging or exorcism and rather an 'integration' through a 'process of reconstruction' by which the trauma memory/story 'undergo[s] a transforma-tion... [so as to become] more present and more real' (181). Catharsis is thus both part of the curative process of traumatic testimony and witness, and also centrally bound to theatri-cal experience and, through 'hysteria', to an understanding of traumatic experience. In Chapter 3, I contended that mimesis might be considered as a mechanism of knowledge production, a productive means through which a person might better come to know that which is represented: catharsis operates similarly. While mimesis is concerned with capturing elusive trauma in representation, catharsis is concerned with relief from or balancing of the emotions and memories associated with that trauma. Mimesis and catharsis are both processes of 'coming to know' and both might be seen as constituting theatrical modes of knowledge production and possible means of historicization and reconstitution.

Writing from a perspective analysing the therapeutic possibilities of theatre, Duggan and Granger suggest, through Aristotle, that witnessing performance might be able to connect the audience with 'profound realities' about themselves and the meaning of their lives through a process of 'emotional learning' which is stimulated via catharsis experienced at the theatre (Duggan and Granger 1997: 70). Further, they suggest that because theatre explores the world rather than creating it – 'it is a reflection of the "real" world and is of it as well' – it is able to provide a site of exploration of relationships and emotions. Thus performance 'embodies our human need to give and receive, ceaselessly to rediscover our own true being in an exchange of life' (Duggan and Granger 1997: 73). While I do not necessarily agree that theatre is only of the world but does not help create it (*vide* Chapter 2), this argument is useful in highlighting that performance is able to explore emotional 'reality' in a way which might be closer to, or which allows access to, the truth of those emotions. Catharsis, for Duggan and Granger, is 'an emotional rather than an intellectual phenomenon [...] a discharge of feelings which succeeds in changing the nature of an existing feeling-state, freeing it from elements that disturb and distort it' (1997: 73).

Furthermore, when catharsis occurs, according to sociologist Thomas Scheff, it can be seen to provide a means by which we are reminded of events that we have repressed but which nevertheless need to be remembered and relived (cf. Duggan and Granger 1997: 76–77). In this respect the theatre can provide a space for a safely distanced encounter with and witnessing of traumata in order that it might be more clearly processed and regulated into 'normal' consciousness. Catharsis, then, is a central weapon in theatre's armory when approaching the traumatic, enabling the performance event to act as both witness and testifier.

Theatre and the traumatic gap

I have previously proposed a performativity inherent within traumata and trauma symptoms. Trauma theorist Dori Laub makes a similar connection to the performative when discussing his work with and interviewing of Holocaust survivors and their children. Laub cites a female survivor's testimony from the Fortunoff Video Archive in which she stated that 'we wanted to survive so as to live one day after Hitler, in order to be able to tell our story' (ctd in Laub 1995: 63). The desire to tell the story is part of the survivor's desire to testify to the events, to record them in history. But Laub further suggests that the opposite is equally true – there is a need to testify and be borne witness to in order to survive: the survivor of trauma embodies an 'imperative need to *tell* and thus come to know one's story.' (Laub 1995: 63) Much as LaCapra's formulation of 'acting out', highlighted in Chapter 1, proposed a performativity in trauma, so too does this performance (telling) of trauma in order to work it through. Furthermore, Laub notes that this telling must be performed in the company of a willing audience or witness (even if that witness is potentially inadequate, in that they can never fully comprehend the event) (Laub 1995: 62–65).

But Laub also posits the notion that trauma events cause a 'collapse of witnessing' because trauma:

> [takes] place with no witnesses: it [is] also the very circumstance of *being inside the event* that [makes] unthinkable the very notion that a witness could exist. … The historical imperative to bear witness could essentially *not be met during the actual occurrence.*
>
> (Laub 1995: 65–68; emphasis is original)

Thus a gap between the historical event and its witness is created. While Laub is specifically looking at the Holocaust, his formulation is nonetheless pertinent to trauma events in general. If the trauma event precludes the possibility of a concurrent witness but yet a witness is necessary both for curative and testimonial needs, then this collapse or gap thus generates a need for a latent or belated witness, such as the therapist or, perhaps, the theatre (artist/audience member).

Another Neilson play, *Penetrator*, articulates this type of traumatic gap: there is an explosion of violence towards the end of the play which is the result of the repressed and largely unaddressed trauma around which the play centres. The piece deals with a wide range of issues from misogyny to pornography to internalized homophobia, rape and abuse, but it is ultimately about one character's inability to articulate the difficulties of his childhood, his sexual orientation, and the perceived abandonment and abuse he (may have) suffered. Tadge is incapable of properly expressing himself; he is only able to come close to attesting to his disturbed state in violent (sexual) fantasies, in a language of traumatic experience:

> TADGE: You don't know what it was like. In the dark. All shrivelled up. Just my hatred keeping me alive. Their hands all over me. And you never came for me. Their dirty cocks in my mouth, up my arse. I know how to kill a man. I'm not afraid. I've seen guys get their ears cut off. I've seen lassies with their cunts shot out. I'm not scared of blood on my hands, hot blood pouring on my hands. Let me out there. Let me do what I do.
> *(Sings)* Wounded Arab girl
> Lying in the road
> I'm so horny I could shoot my load
> Fuck her up the arse
> Shoot her in the face
> But save her cunt for the boys at the base.
>
> (Neilson 1998: 109)

Throughout the piece it is increasingly apparent that however disturbing the staged or spoken images are, the real trauma of it is a historic one, something that Tadge cannot, yet, speak about. It is the lack of articulation in the piece that holds the greatest sense of the weight of the play; it is the inability to speak of this historic trauma that drives the action forward and that triggers all of the violence. It is in the representation of this inarticulacy that *Penetrator* bears witness to trauma. By highlighting the destructive nature of a traumatic past that is not properly witnessed, the play addresses and bears witness to the gap between the impossibility of articulating trauma and the necessity to do so.

In an argument which implicitly suggests that modes of artistic expression hold importance within curative considerations of trauma theory, Laub highlights the destructive nature of this gap, which we might also think of as an un-healing, open wound, contending that:

> it is essential for this narrative that *could not be articulated* to be *told*, to be *transmitted*, to be *heard*, and hence the importance of endeavours [... which are] designed to enable the survivors to bear witness, to enable, that is, the act of bearing witness [...] to take place, belatedly, as though retroactively.
>
> (Laub 1995: 69; emphasis is original)

Without this, survivor-sufferers are held in a stasis of silence which, according to Laub, 'serves as a perpetuation of [the trauma-event's] tyranny' over the survivor-sufferer (1995: 64). Silence perpetuates trauma-symptoms but is also unavoidable because, as we saw in Chapter 1, trauma destroys the survivor-sufferer's capacity for narrativization.

It is with this destructive silence in mind that I now turn to an examination of the diegetic world in Pinter's *The Room*, a piece which while very different from *Penetrator* nevertheless echoes its concern with a traumatic gap. Pinter's dramatic works continue to be the focus of much academic attention and his plays' continued relevance to contemporary culture ensure they are regularly restaged around the world.[13] Pinter's relevance to the contemporary theatre scene is further demonstrated in his widely acknowledged influence on other playwrights and of course in his being awarded a Nobel Prize for literature (2005).

The Room's surface of banal domesticity belies a more sinister undercurrent of tension and latent violence contained within the laconic silences which punctuate the play. There is an underlying menace in the play; tension and unease build throughout but nothing is ever made explicit. Silence prevails and its unavoidable abundance holds attention and feeds the spectator or reader's imagination and anticipation. The play's perpetuation of tension through silence suggests that it is within those silences that trauma might be seen to be 'located'.

At the beginning of the play, Rose makes breakfast and incessantly babbles while Bert simply says nothing: his silence holds the spectator or reader's attention in a tangible state of apprehensive desire to know why he will not speak. The sense of an underlying historical trauma, either inflicted or suffered by Bert, is made ever present in its continual absence.[14] Throughout the opening of the play the silence, and Rose's verbal prattling which sits in opposition to it, increasingly suggests a latent trauma in Bert and Rose's past, the impact or re-emergence of which seems to bubble just under the surface of the presented action. The silences seem to contain the puncture wounds of a trauma that runs through the play and the repetition of linguistic metaphors about the weather being 'murder' and a perpetual circulation of the 'darkness' and hostility of spaces outside their little room serve continually to signify this traumatic tension. Throughout the play a series of dialectics are developed which compound a sinister reading of it and replicate the traumatic gap I presented above: silence – speaking; inside – outside; inaction – violence; safety – danger.

The silence in the opening section grows and grows; even with the entrance of Mr Kidd there is no change in Bert's state of engagement. The perpetual refusal to speak suggests that Bert might be caught precisely in the traumatic gap between the impossibility of testimony and the necessity for it. The assimilation of the perceived trauma-event is not complete; it is still in repression and Bert's silences and Rose's incessant nervous babbling are symptomatic of this repression. The silences and distracting domesticity are part of the structure of latency and (violent) re-emergence from repression, which define trauma-symptoms. The silences create tension and are menacing precisely because of their incongruity in the domestic setting; just as with the baby of *BR#04*, the silences sit in unrelation to the rest of the presented action. But these are silences which are anything but silent. Thoughts and memories race through silences; even if there is no meaning intended by a silence, our internal thought processes continue to make meaning from the moments that surround that silence. As Derrida might say, the meaning of silence is defined by its difference from what surrounds it.

In the final moments of the play the action takes an unexpectedly violent turn:

> BERT: [...] I get hold of her. I go where I go. She
>   took me there. She brought me back.
>   *(Pause)*
>   I got back all right.
> *He takes the chair from the table and sits to the left of the*
> *NEGRO'S chair, close to it. He regards the NEGRO for some*
> *moments. Then with his foot he lifts the armchair up. The*
> *NEGRO falls on the floor. He rises slowly.*
> RILEY: Mr Hudd, your wife –
> BERT: Lice!
> *He strikes the NEGRO, knocking him down, and then kicks his*
> *head against the gas-stove several times. The NEGRO lies*
> *still. BERT walks away.*
> *Silence.*
> *ROSE stands clutching her eyes.*
> ROSE: Can't see. I can't see. I can't see.
> *Blackout.*
>
>   (Pinter 1991: 110)

Bert's vocal contribution to the end of the play is an unexpected irruption into the landscape of the piece but even more so is his violence, which seems to rise from nowhere.

In the 2007 production in Leeds, Bert threateningly delivers his line 'she don't mix it with me' (Pinter 1991: 110) from behind and over Rose's shoulder.[15] It was presented in such a way as to suggest that he is reacting to having caught, perhaps not for the first time, his wife's caress of Riley's face (which was staged in such a way as to suggest latent sexual tension). The violence in this production might thus be seen to rise from an emergence of repressed jealousy and anger, but it nevertheless remains a vivid counterpoint to the rest of the fairly placid action. Mark Taylor-Batty contends that:

> the final scene is certainly shocking, I would imagine it's very difficult to perform it in ways that don't make it shocking. It's not only shocking insomuch as somebody gets beaten up on stage and their head gets kicked against a stove and Rose shouts and screams in response to that – yes, those things are 'shocking' – but I think it's shocking for an audience because the level of violence is unexpected, it is sudden, and it is unqualified.
>
> (Taylor-Batty 2008: personal interview)

The unrelation of the violence to the rest of the piece is what makes the act such a shock to an audience. I do not mean shock in a banal sense of the word but use it with specific relation to the shock and shudder outlined both in relation to the development of trauma theories in Chapter 1 and the effect of theatrical images discussed in relation to mimetic shimmering in Chapter 3. Mary Luckhurst, a theatre theorist, argues that the 'brutality' of such images in Pinter's work is disturbing because no insight of the psychological conditions of the perpetrators and victims is offered and because acts of violence and cruelty are generally 'sudden and motiveless' (Luckhurst 2006: 359). *The Room* does not impose explanations or attempt to justify the act of violence; it is simply put in front of the audience. It is precisely the act's sudden and unexplained quality which jolts the spectator and at the same time it bears witness to the latent trauma in the diegetic world of the play. Bert violently 'acts out' in order to alleviate the repressed tension of trauma-symptoms (ironically creating a new trauma-event and thus articulating the need for testimony). Bert's acting out, as with all acting out, is a performative demonstration of repressed trauma and is an action which is echoed and borne witness to in numerous ways in numerous performance works, and not just those in which representations of violence are made. For example, there is Christian's destructive verbal outburst in David Eldridge's *Festen* (2004): the character recounts the sexual abuse he suffered at the hands of his father during the father's birthday celebration, the repressed wound of childhood sexual trauma erupts into testimony precisely because of that repression and silence. Christian's testimony bears witness not only to the character's trauma but also to similar traumas suffered in households throughout the world; it is a double witnessing (cf. Eldridge 2004: 26–29).

At an extra-diegetic level the act of violence in *The Room* also bears witness to imputed violent trauma more generally and, crucially, because of the ambiguity of the ending, its lack of resolution, the play symbolically articulates the cyclical repetitions of trauma-symptoms. 'There is not any kind of frame', Taylor-Batty suggests, 'through which [the audience] can manage that trauma [of witnessing the violent act] – in other words, the audience have to immediately leave the room with that [image] still resonating' (Taylor-Batty 2008: personal interview). The play leaves its audience reeling from the suddenness and severity of the un-clarified violence and they are further unsettled by the lack of explanation for Rose's 'blinding'. Despite the play's age, its lack of resolution has a decidedly contemporary feel. Its cyclical implication (one can imagine the piece simply starting again, the trauma repressed again) ties it to the trauma-tragic mode I suggested in Chapter 2, and thus to more contemporary pieces in which meaning and resolution are opaque and left in the hands of the audience, such as Martin Crimp's *Attempts on Her Life* (1997), Eve Bonneau's performance *'Body' is the first word I say* (2007), and Sarah Kane's *4.48 Psychosis* (1998), to which I turn now.

'Validate me. Witness me'

(Kane 2001: 243)

Sarah Kane's *4.48 Psychosis* is an ambiguous play which, as Alice Tycer has persuasively argued, offers readers and/or spectators the opportunity to 'include their own experiences in the text and/or performance' (Tycer 2008: 26). Indeed the text itself calls for the audience to consider their position in relation to the presented actions and words:

> Sometimes I turn around and catch the smell of you and
> I cannot go on I cannot fucking go on without express-
> ing this terrible so fucking awful physical aching fucking

longing I have for you . And I cannot believe that I can feel
this for you and you feel nothing. Do you feel nothing?

(Kane 2001: 214)

The desire for reciprocal testimony and witness, similar to the
reciprocity discussed in relation to *Still Life* in the previous
chapter, is evident in the insistence of the language. The citation which I used to head this section might be seen as evidence
of the play's explicit call for the audience to 'witness me' (243).
The 'character' – Kane gives no indication of name, gender or
number of characters in the piece – articulates a very clear sense
of the pain of lost love but further requests that the person this
testimony is directed to answer their plea for a demonstration
of reciprocal feeling. The question 'do you feel nothing?' might
be seen implicitly to ask the same of the reader or spectator. In
a production of *4.48 Psychosis* which I directed in 2005, this
line was both delivered to another person on stage and also to
the audience through direct address. Talking to the actress who
delivered the line after the production had closed, she recalled
that 'in asking "Do you feel nothing?" I was aware that some
people would sit there and decide if they felt anything, if they
gave a damn' (Brennan 2005: personal interview). The play is
deliberately ambiguous in this matter and through its ambiguity
asks the performers and audience/readers to actively bear witness
to this question, to at least answer it for themselves.

Much as with *The Room*, Kane's *4.48 Psychosis* suggests
another scene, or indeed a loop back to its beginning, at its
end (the play is littered with repetitions and looping). A 'character' simply articulates a desire for someone to 'please open
the curtains' (245). The utterance is simple, yet it subverts the
conventions of theatrical endings in which a stage direction might
suggest a curtain is closed on the stage or that a blackout might
signal the piece's end. The ending implies that the 'theatrical
experience starts at the play's end and circles back to the beginning'; it does not end at the curtain call, but 'linger[s] with the
audience' (Tycer 2008: 23). The ploy of repetition or cyclicality
is not unique to *4.48 Psychosis* and has been used in numerous dramas and not necessarily to invoke trauma. Importantly,
however, in the particular context of this play – both related to

the author's personal history (the play was problematically called a '75 minute suicide note' (Billington 2000: 5) when it first played in London) and the content of the piece – the shape of it is particularly echoic of the shape of trauma-symptoms.

Caruth suggests that 'the problem of witnessing trauma as a professional is learning the difficult task of speaking of trauma in the terms offered by the survivor' (1996: 17). These 'terms' will, of course, be dependent upon each survivor but if we consider the repetitive and disruptive structure which defines trauma-symptoms, it follows that those terms operate in a similar manner. *4.48 Psychosis* is nonlinear, it utilizes a series of repetitious and thematic reoccurrences which, as Tycer discusses, 'facilitates a trauma-based reading' (2008: 27). The dramaturgical structure of the piece follows a structure which can be seen to mimic that of trauma-symptoms, thus even in its written form and language it can be seen to bear witness to those symptoms. Tycer, who covers this ground well, argues that the play positions the audience as 'active witnesses to an unending trauma that manifests itself through repeated visitations' (2008: 27–30).

In the 2005 production I directed, the repetitive-disruptive quality of the language and themes were explicitly mirrored in the movement and 'style' of the production. Staged in a white-box studio the action took place in one half of the space with the audience flanking it on three sides. There was no stage furniture, just a cast of two women in casual, everyday clothes. Throughout the piece the actors reflected each other and passed the play between them; they repeated and mirrored various movements and gestures, blurring any definition of 'character'. Movements that bisected the space, half collapses, hand gestures and attempted but unsuccessful touches all served to echo the repetitious, collapsing, fragmented structure of the script which, I suggest, parallels the structure of trauma-symptoms. The possibility of repetition at the end of the play was further suggested as the actors swapped positions but repeated the image (and extended silence) of this production's opening, again proposing both a looping back on itself and the possibility of another scene. A repetitive focus on emotional trauma and memories, and performance's ability to subsume the audience into its content, is further explored in Forced Entertainment's *Exquisite Pain*.

'I would have liked to be more unhappy...
I hope one day to really suffer'
(Calle/Forced Entertainment 2007: n.p.)[16]

For a little over two hours Richard Lowdon and Terry O'Connor sit either side of the stage at their innocuous wooden desks, illuminated by open, warm white theatre lighting, and echoing their position are two flat-screen televisions suspended above their heads. Behind the two performers, to the far upstage edge, suspended in the centre of a large black drape, the words 'exquisite pain' are scrawled in blue fluorescent lighting. This is all that occupies the stage for the duration of Forced Entertainment's performance of Sophie Calle's text *Exquisite Pain* (first performed 2005).

'When and where did you suffer most?' (Calle/Forced Entertainment 2007). And so we're off: the next two hours are filled with a litany of testimony about (emotional) traumas, from lost loves to destructive relationships to the death of a father whose funeral the thirteen-year-old son was prevented by his family from attending.

> A man and a woman tell stories of ordinary and not-so-ordinary heart-break, each story accompanied by a single iconic image [...] The woman repeatedly recounts the story of the end of an affair; each time remembering it differently, adding and subtracting details, finding new ways to both remember and forget what happened. The man tells stories from many different people; each a snapshot of sorrow, big or small, that takes place in a growing catalogue of suffering, break-ups, humiliations, deaths, bad dentistry and love letters that never arrive.
>
> (Forced Entertainment, 2008: n.p.)

The performance's main 'theme', then, is bearing witness to these events, all of which have impacted upon their respective authors, Sophie Calle and her correspondents, in variously traumatic ways. Indeed, as Terry O'Connor says, voicing Calle in what has become the performance's tag line, 'I decided to continue... until I had got over my pain by comparing it with other people's, or had worn out my own story through sheer repetition' (Calle/Forced Entertainment 2007). The implication, following Herman, is that the process of comparison and 'sheer repetition', both in Calle's writing and in Forced Entertainment's retelling, represents a reconstitution of self: a form of cathartic closure of the traumatic gap is achieved through the ritual performance of writing and retelling, or testifying. Calle's writing, however, seems to be driven by what might be thought of as a repetition compulsion: she is seemingly compelled to read others' testimonies of trauma, she bears witness to them and in so doing compares the 'depth' of her own traumatic wound. At the same time she is further compelled to repeat and re-experience that wound in her own writing, or testimony. By writing her testimony, which like trauma-symptoms is fractured, faltering and constantly changing, she bears witness to her own traumatic suffering and so begins to diminish its impact. Furthermore, by placing the testimony into the public realm both as a book and especially as a performance, Calle asks her audience to bear witness not only to her trauma/trauma-testimony but also to those of the other contributors. The process of being at *Exquisite Pain* is to bear witness to Calle and her contributors but also to self-reflexively bear witness to our own trauma narratives (by which I mean either trauma we have suffered or that to which we have borne witness).

In the programme notes to *Exquisite Pain*, Tim Etchells writes:

> Two people sit in front of you and make their way through
> a collection of sad stories that belong to other people. A
> kind of bearing witness, a trip through the archive that
> Sophie Calle has collected, and a journey, her journey, of
> remembering and trying to forget.
>
> (Etchells 2008: n.p.)

The bearing witness is in the text; this is not an embodied performance experience in the same way that *Still Life* was, or even in the same way that a production of McDonagh's *The Pillowman*, Neilson's *Normal* or Ravenhill's *Shopping and Fucking* might be. It was a placid performance in the embodied relation between audience and performers; there was even the opportunity to laugh on occasion. Despite the undeniably uncomfortable experience of sitting through the 120 or more minutes of the piece, it would be difficult to describe the experience as being in any way traumatic. Yet there was a sense in which the audience engaged with the testimony in an empathetically embodied way. Although the audience's interest might inevitably fluctuate in a performance of this length with no interval – indeed in both the performances I saw audience members walked out – nevertheless people's engagement with the material was discernible as they leant forward, seeming to listen intently to the testimonies which connected with them in some way.

In his influential *Dynamics of Drama*, Bernard Beckerman suggests that the empathic response of an audience to the stage action is bodily engaged, which can be seen in their posture and rhythms of movement (Beckerman 1970: 149–151). Simon Shepherd takes from this that 'empathy is a response of the whole physical person' (Shepherd 2006: 9). I will return to this embodied quality below. However, first, it will be profitable to identify where/how that embodiment occurs. Under the definitions of witnessing and bearing witness set out above, in *Exquisite Pain* the two performers are testifying about and bearing witness to the (largely emotional) traumata suffered by Sophie Calle and the other anonymous voices. The audience is in turn witness to this and may, at a later point, bear witness to it through latter testimony of their own. Indeed because of the dialogic composition of the piece, in a Bakhtinian sense, it seems that there is an implicit invitation for the audience to put their own trauma memories into conversation with the piece and the testimonies contained therein. The piece invites a personal continuation of Calle/Forced Entertainment's process of comparison and repetition. In this respect, a key piece of the performance's aesthetic and ethical composition is a layering of what we might think of as witnessing levels.

Firstly, Calle and her contributors bear witness to their own trauma events through the process of writing or speaking them in correspondence. Secondly, the Forced Entertainment company bears further witness to these events and their impact on the survivor-sufferer through the process of reading, rehearsal and performance. Indeed, under Etchells' own definition of a witness and their inability 'to stop thinking, talking and reporting' (Etchells 1999: 18), the desire to make Calle's text into a performance could be seen to have been propelled by the text creating them as witnesses to it:

> Sitting on sofas in the lobby of the hotel where we were staying, Cathy Naden and Claire Marshall read the book to me as other guests rushed or drifted past, oblivious. It was clear soon enough that – having spent twenty years devising, improvising and otherwise creating our own performances – we now felt *compelled*, for the first time, to 'do' a text.
>
> (Etchells 2008: n.p.; emphasis is original)

Thirdly, the audience is witness to the testimony of the performers and witnesses to the memory of the trauma event, empathizing, embodying and 'feeling' the stories. Fourthly, the audience may become testifiers to the experience of witnessing the performance (and hence the original testimony again) through stories told in (in)formal settings after the event has passed. Finally, the audience may come to testify about and witness their own similar traumas in comparing them, through a process of repetition, to the performed testimonies: a process of evacuation and assimilation, or relating to Herman's catharsis again, a reconstitution, through comparison via the performance event.

Exquisite Pain operates on the level of embodied empathic witnessing; we are brought into the text by the performers on stage, through both dramaturgical and, especially, basic implication effects, in a way that would not be possible in reading the text. Of course, it is possible to 'feel' an embodied, emotional, empathic response to a read text, but in presenting these stories in a live medium, the audience is able to step imaginatively into the shoes of the testifiers more readily. Shepherd and Wallis employ psychologist Theodor Lipps to expound one theory of empathy which is particularly helpful here: 'empathy (*Einfuhlung*) has two elements to it: perceivers respond to the characteristics or qualities of an object and simultaneously project their own characteristics or qualities into it' (Shepherd and Wallis 2004: 196). The idea of projection into the position of the observed subject is particularly important as the sense of movement it conjures relates it to kinaesthesia. If, as Shepherd and Wallis suggest, 'as a consequence of what the eyes see, the audience's muscular state is stimulated' (2004: 207), then the definition of kinaesthetic response shares much with that of empathy's 'whole physical' response. Both empathetic and kinaesthetic responses are then bodily, and both are central to the creation of a witness in the theatre. I will return to audience response and notions of kinaesthetic empathy in the next chapter, but the case of *Exquisite Pain* highlights how an audience can 'feel' with people whose traumas are being borne witness to through the text and whose voices are being embodied by the performers. By giving voice to these testimonies, the performers invite the audience into an empathetic, kinaesthetic witnessing relationship which is less possible in a reader's relationship to a text. The human voice and the relationship between live, materially present bodies adds emotional weight to the testimony, which in turn creates a deeper sense of having witnessed and borne witness to these memorialized events.

There is a last but important point to make here, in relation to the performance's title. 'Exquisite', of course, is also a mediation between both the depth and acuteness of the pains testified to and the reconstitutive/cathartic 'pleasure' in giving that testimony. The title highlights a series of paradoxical rotations in the experience of performance (both/either from the performers' or audience's perspective): a paradox exists firstly between the enjoyment/entertainment of the theatre experience and the emotional resonance of witnessing the testimonies of pain, and secondly between interest in and responsibility to the testimony and the deliberately 'forced' nature of the experience, such as physical discomfort due to length or potential boredom in the repetition of material.

Towards an (awareness of) embodied witnessing

A trauma narrative, 'the very process of bearing witness to massive trauma', as Laub puts it, begins 'with someone who testifies to an absence, to an event that has not yet come into existence' and furthermore:

> [t]he emergence of the narrative which is being listened to
> – and heard – is, therefore, the process and place wherein
> the cognizance, the 'knowing' of the event is given birth to.
> The listener, therefore, is a party to the creation of knowl-
> edge *de novo*. The testimony to the trauma thus includes
> its hearer, who is, so to speak, the blank screen on which
> the event comes to be inscribed for the first time.
>
> (Laub 1992: 57)

Laub goes on to argue that the listener (and so by extension an audience) comes to be a participant and co-owner of the trau- matic event and in so doing they come to 'partially experience trauma' (1992: 57). In her excellent book *Empathic Vision: Affect, Trauma, and Contemporary Art*, Jill Bennett supports Laub's assertions, arguing that:

> [t]he instantaneous, affective response, triggered by an
> image, viewed under controlled conditions, may mimic
> the sudden impact of trauma, or the quality of a post-
> traumatic memory, characterised by the involuntary
> repetition of an experience that the mind fails to process
> in the normal way.
>
> (Bennett 2005: 11)

In light of this chapter's findings, and recalling the notion of mimetic shimmering, the theatrical experience, echoing Laub and Bennett, within the trauma-tragic mode not only 'validates the victims' reality', to return to Malpede again (1996: 168), but also prepares us for our own traumas by triggering an affective response through what might be experienced as a more authen- tic theatrical experience (*vide* Chapter 2).

Live performance can place its audience in a situation whereby being at the event both activates our traumatic memories and can be seen to rehearse our presence in future traumas, where the performance creates a presence-in-trauma effect through mimicking traumatic impact. Theatre has the potential to destabi- lize and question our individual constructions of self in the same way that the involuntary repetition of trauma can. Furthermore, it is ideally situated as a site of exploration and witness both through its nature as a live, shared somatic event and through its ability to present dramaturgically a mirror of trauma in form and/or content.

Working in both semiotic and phenomenal registers, the embodied sense of presence within trauma, stimulated through the various levels of witnessing and implication I have discussed, might be thought of as a projection of the spectator into the traumatic. Importantly, however, this projection is at a safe distance, so to speak, from the original event: as Laub continues his argument he highlights that the listener 'nevertheless does not become the victim – he [sic] preserves his own separate place, position and perspective' (Laub 1992: 58). The distance is crucial in enabling the embodied projection to impact upon the witness without causing them to slip into traumatic experience themselves. To put it another way, utilizing Bert State's notion of the actor standing in for the spectator's presence in the fiction, we can enter into a situation whereby our absence from the representation of trauma enables us to witness ourselves *in* the trauma – we project ourselves into the presented material (cf. States 1985: 159). Thus the projection sets the foundations for theatre and performance to be a witnessed experience, not only to act as Laub's 'blank screen' itself but also to position its audience in that role.

Although laden with expectation, artistic and conceptual frames, performance works can operate as a 'blank screen', in Laub's sense of the term, on to which an inscription of and testimony about trauma can be made: theatre can bear witness through testimony to (generic and/or fictitious) trauma-events. This might be identified in *One For The Road* (1984), *Mountain Language* (1988), or indeed, more recently DV8's *To Be Straight With You* and Howard Barker's *The Dying of Today* (both 2008). The live event can articulate and mirror the violent repetitions and maddening loops of trauma-symptoms, as exemplified in the structural repetitions of *4.48 Psychosis*, Goat Island's *It's an Earthquake in My Heart* (2001)[17] and Ed Thomas's *Stone City Blue* (2004). The possible penetration of repressed trauma-events and trauma-symptoms into the survivor-sufferer's actions and daily life are attested to in pieces such as *The Room* and *Festen*. A demonstration of the traumatic gap between the impossibility of articulating trauma and the necessity to do so can be found in many pieces including *Penetrator* and *Exquisite Pain*. Furthermore, through theatrical processes we might, in light of the contemporary, 'traumatized' structure of feeling (*vide* Chapter 2), be seen to contemplate and address our past or present traumas and rehearse for potential future ones. Performance further operates as means of creating witnesses; it is itself a witness and can create the audience as further witnesses.

All of the pieces I have discussed in this chapter are first and foremost pieces of performance: although they may, explicitly or implicitly, through content and/or structure, bear witness to or testify about trauma-symptoms and events, they are not necessarily intended as testimonial or remembrance performances like the accounts of those in the Fortunoff Video Archive or Claude Lanzman's film *Shoah* (1985) or even Remembrance Sunday might be seen to be.

Elam has argued that 'it is with the spectator [...] that theatrical communication begins and ends' (Elam 2002: 87) and so it is to the audience that I now turn (and will develop further in the next chapter). The performances I have discussed are in the main performances which an audience enter into as spectators, only to find themselves created as witnesses 'accidentally' (in the sense that Freddie Rokem (2002) suggests we become witnesses, rather than eavesdroppers, through accidental discovery). It is partly because of this dynamic that they are able to make the attempt to articulate traumas: these performances allow the audience to come upon the represented trauma without warning, without dulling the senses to the experience through a pre-empting of the form or content.[18]

By entering into the kinaesthetic space of the performance event, we facilitate a sense of being physically connected to the bodies on stage and to the images they present us with. The performance becomes a charged space in which it has the opportunity (knowingly or otherwise) to attempt to bear witness to our own historical traumas. Through the represented traumas these pieces show or the structures they follow, they have the opportunity to speak to an audience of their own, individual traumas, and those on a more global scale, allowing them the space potentially to come to know them better, to historicize the event through the sensuous manifold of a trauma-tragic theatrical experience. The impossibility of articulating trauma, the impossibility of adequately holding true to it outside of the individual sufferer's experience, seems to signal that all attempts to do so are doomed to failure: as Phelan might suggest, we will never be able to access the reality of trauma because it is beyond representation. Holding true to this idea, we must assume that theatre's attempts to bear witness to trauma will ultimately always fail as they will never be able properly to 'do justice' to the original event nor to the psychological repetitions of that event. But theatre and performance have the apparatus through which they can make an attempt to articulate the impossibility of trauma's articulation in such a way that an audience member could deeply experience that gap and so put them in the region of re-witnessing or rehearsing their own trauma. Theatre and performance, then, can make an attempt to bear witness to trauma that enables an audience to bear witness to their own traumas by accessing them precisely through *inadequate* theatrical representations.

5
Being there: the 'presence' of trauma

All writing about 'the event', trauma or performance, is riddled with failures, lapses and insecurities. Language sits outside the event, incapable of imparting the experience of it adequately; it lacks 'that which would turn inside, make the thing flow and burn, touch and weigh again' (Heathfield 2006: 179). Writing the event is then, potentially, always a failure: a failure to live up to what actually happened; a failure to be accurate; a failure to impart the emotion and experience of the event to the reader of any writing. There is thus a disjuncture between what was experienced and how one conveys that experience. So Heathfield suggests that all one can do is attempt to write about performance in such a way as to elucidate something of the experience of being there, of what it was that happened and that to do so we should 'proceed inside this tear [and] vibrate at the borders of memory [...] cast[ing] word nets towards the event-residues of memory' (2006: 179).

This chapter seeks to explicate something of the effect of 'being there', of being at performance work that in some way addresses trauma within the trauma-tragic mode I am developing. In line with my insistence that trauma-tragedy is not a genre, this chapter considers three performances that are different sorts of aesthetic object. Firstly, *Blasted* is an original, experimental dramatic text that quite closely scripts its staging and which draws upon news events and the traumata of the Balkan conflicts of the early 1990s, tapping into and commenting on a very specific historical moment. Secondly, *His Dark Materials* is what might be considered a modern *Gesamtkunstwerk* and mainstream, popular theatre. It very acutely highlights and embodies the (fantasy) trauma borne witness to in the novels. Finally, there is *Untitled (Syncope)*: a piece of Live/Performance Art developed by the artist in response to 'a whole load of ideas [and] questions about […] what it is to have a body, what a body is and how that engages [with society]' (O'Reilly 2008; personal interview). Despite their generic structural and aesthetic differences, each is an instance in which trauma is theatrically addressed or borne witness to in a viscerally embodied manner. This chapter, then, looks at a range of different sorts of work which trace the cultural contours of the trauma-tragic. The inclusion of this range of performance events is intended to highlight and augment the building argument that the 'experience' of trauma can not only be had in the 'for real' of Performance Art and difficult, violent theatre but also in mainstream, popular theatrical experience. These examples not only illustrate different aspects of the way trauma-tragedy functions but also further highlight the deeply embedded nature of the traumatic in contemporary culture.

The object of scrutiny differs between examples, but in each there is a focus on audience experience. With *Blasted* the focus is mainly on the dramaturgical structure, principally exploring the rupture of the diegesis and through this the rupturing of audience expectation. This is nothing new in itself but is one technique for bearing witness to trauma, and it becomes important because of the particular referential domain around this play. The cultural resistance to *Blasted* at the time of its first staging was supposedly concerned with its lewd and 'filthy' content, but I hope to demonstrate that it is much more likely to be to do with both the impact of the dramaturgical shape and its rhetorical positioning in relation to the historical real. In the case of *His Dark Materials* the focus of analysis is much more on the whole theatrical apparatus, especially in terms of the production's scenography and the interplay between phenomenological and semiotic modes of meaning-making and presence effects. Finally, with *Untitled (Syncope)* I will shift focus to an analysis of bodily proximity, co-witnessing and kinaesthetic experience. Within this chapter, then, I am not only exploring three different modes of theatrical production but also looking at different aspects of each, setting up a series of analyses, a set of foci, that could be levelled upon any performance, especially within the trauma-tragic mode.

Blasted

'I can't piss. It's just blood.'

(Kane 2001: 34)

Roger Luckhurst (2003) suggests that during the 1990s there was a notable rise in interest in what we might call the traumatological (cf. Chapter 1). In the theatre of the 1990s, writers such as Sarah Kane, Martin Crimp, Mark Ravenhill and Anthony Neilson wrote plays which presented and repeated images which ranged across multifarious notions of traumatic suffering. While these so-called 'in-yer-face' writers should not be thought of as definitive of the whole theatrical movement in the United Kingdom at the time, they succinctly highlight the ongoing concern with the violent, visceral and traumatic in performance. Furthermore, although there has historically been a continuing concern in theatre with the traumatic, this might be seen to peak at particular historical junctures and the theatre of the 'in-yer-face' writers is certainly one such juncture.[1] Much like the 'reality' of Performance Art, many of these writers employ compositional and dramaturgical styles which intentionally try to create a constant sense of traumatic presence, a traumatic 'reality' through theatricality.

Sarah Kane's *Blasted* presents a series of violent events and abuses, self-consciously attempting to bear witness to and portray the traumas of war, rape, domestic violence and loss. Using the Balkan conflict of the early 1990s as a central inspiration, Kane wrote a play that so graphically depicts and describes multiple acts of violence that its original staging in 1995 was met with almost unanimous condemnation in the British press. On the media attention Kane commented that 'I suppose the fact that it's a play about a middle-aged male journalist who rapes a young woman and is raped and mutilated himself can't have endeared me to a theatre full of middle-aged male critics' (Kane ctd in Stephenson and Langridge 1997: 130). But the media furore surrounding the original performance and the abundance of critical attention it received runs deeper than hitting back at Kane's portrayal of journalist Ian. *Blasted*, a 'disgusting feast of filth', as *Daily Mail* critic Jack Tinker dubbed it (1995: 5), grabbed the nation's collective attention. In a society where representations of violence were becoming normalized, it presented violence and trauma in too 'real', too embodied a way for the British public to ignore. It is a play which very definitely tapped into the 1990s turn towards the traumatic. What follows here is an examination of three distinct, but interrelated, components of the play which can be seen to represent, or in some way impart, an experience or understanding of traumata to the audience. Firstly, I will discuss diegetic laughter and its inherent violence within the play. I shall then examine more 'explicit' and incessant representations of violence within the piece. Lastly and directly related to the previous arguments, I will discuss how the form of the piece contributed to the way the play was received.

'Cate: (Stares. Then bursts out laughing)' (Kane 2001: 8)

Peggy Phelan argues that 'trauma tears the fabric of knowledge itself: it is a wound in the system of meaning through which the subject knows the world, knows him or herself' (1997: 95). Cathy Caruth describes this tear as the 'crisis of life' (1995: 5), and this is precisely what the dramaturgy of *Blasted* is engaged in articulating.

A young woman sits cross-legged on an opulent bed eating a sandwich. She looks simplistically content, like a small child. At the foot of the bed stands a bald, middle-aged man. A gun rests lazily by his side in his right hand. He watches the woman as she takes a bite of her sandwich. She looks up at him and, still chewing, says, 'Don't like your clothes either.' The man's body slumps slightly as he examines his clothes. He draws himself back up to full height and strips. He stands there naked, his bald head glistening in the light and his pale white buttocks staring back at the audience. He looks at once funny and pathetic, uncomfortable and determined. He walks along the side of the bed toward the woman. He stops in front of her and says without any hint of nervousness or uncertainty, 'Put your mouth on me.' There is a pause. The woman looks him up and down before emitting a laugh that is at once mocking and pitying, childlike and corrosive.

The man on stage fumbles as he desperately tries to get dressed while asking, 'No? Fine. Because I stink?' She laughs even more.

His face seems to redden slightly as his masculinity appears visibly to crumple before us. Ian manages to escape to the offstage bathroom, gaining a little distance from the still ongoing laughing-attack happening on stage. But this must give him little respite as the bathroom, in the flashy hotel of the staged world, is distinctly open plan with no door to block out the giggling.[2]

While laughter can act as a pressure relief in certain circumstances, it is often employed as a weapon, a mechanism of ridicule and embarrassment. T. G. A. Nelson (1990) has argued that laughter is often malicious, that we usually laugh at someone and that 'people enjoy laughing at other people's physical deformities' (1990: 3 and cf. 2–6). (What was Cate laughing at?) This is not a new argument: Richard Schechner, turning our attention to dramatic form, has argued that:

> from stichomythia, the short, give-and-take dialogic assaults of classical Greek theatre, to the punning wit and quick-flying obscenities enjoyed by such Shakespearean characters as Beatrice and Benedick, through to the laconic exchanges of Pinter' laughter has been staged as a divisive and violent act.
>
> (Schechner 2003: 278–279)

But the diegetic laughter in *Blasted* is more than simply a violent act. It is part of an ongoing power struggle between all three characters, a power struggle which develops into a cycle of traumatic experience that is perpetuated throughout the play and, crucially, is left open/unresolved at the end.

The laughter that is levelled at Ian in the scene above is a direct and powerful attack; the script makes this fact obvious in the stage directions, which tell us that Cate 'stares. Then bursts out laughing' and that when asked if it is because Ian 'stinks' she 'laughs even more' (Kane 2001: 8). In Ostermeier's Avignon production (2005) the overt nature of this laughter as an explicit and deliberate attack was palpable as the actress playing Cate stares first at Ian's face, then his genitals, and then starts to laugh. This is most certainly a laughing at rather than with, and for a man as determined as Ian is to assert his masculinity – 'I don't dress like a cocksucker' (18) – it is most certainly a wounding laugh.

Similar to Ibsen's extensive psychological stage directions, Kane, in this scene, writes a detailed economy of embodied emotion into the stage directions. Crucially, the inclusion of the direction that Ian 'fumbles with embarrassment' (18) is centrally important in understanding the impact of Cate's laughing-attack on his construction of self. Embarrassment is a physical and uncontrollable reaction. Nicholas Ridout discusses the etymology of the word in detail, concluding that to embarrass is 'to do something to someone by speech or action, to act or speak in such a way as to introduce obstacles or complications' (2006: 81). The complication in the present case is a complication of the power structure between Ian and Cate. Ian's embarrassment is an obstacle to his ability to figure himself, and act as, a man. In accordance with trauma symptoms, his sense of self is ruptured, disturbed, torn. Cate's laugh and the fracturing it causes in Ian's understanding of himself is a psychologically violent attack which marks the beginning of a traumatic cycle that rumbles throughout the play. Felicity De Zulueta argues that this type of traumatic experience will remain with the sufferer like 'a foreign body permanently at work in the unconscious' (1993: 100).

Before this point in the play, Ian has been the dominant male, an archetypal male bully, an aggressive racist who carries a gun, swigs gin from the bottle and talks down to women. In her work on violence and pain, De Zulueta notes that culturally and historically aggression has equated to masculinity, suggesting that men are socially moulded to aggression as a means of displaying their 'psychological spirit' which is 'the very spirit' that constructs the masculine ego and enables men to 'feel that they [are] men' (1993: 33). Ian is aggressive from the beginning of the play, asserting himself as the dominant male without a trace of femininity. But having his manliness, his 'man-hood', laughed at begins to feminize him, collapsing his power hold, and while he immediately tries to recapture his dominance over Cate through both verbal and physical abuses, his construction as the dominant masculine power is constantly in flux from this point onwards. The macho-misogynist character Ian portrays, both the staged character and, referentially, the equivalent role in the social real, is ruptured as his mother-figure (for, as I will discuss in a moment, this is what Cate becomes) attacks everything that makes him a man. Ian is stripped of his defences; he is no longer the powerful and dominant chauvinist he purports to be but is a helpless, naked and pitiful middle-aged man. Indeed, his construction as a man is not only attacked here but is physically assaulted again when Cate bites his penis and when the Soldier rapes him; he is thus twice penetrated (teeth into penis and penis into anus) and twice feminized.

'He eats the baby' (Kane 2001: 60)

The Soldier's raping of Ian is a turning point in the traumatic cycle of *Blasted*. No matter what has happened up to this point, Ian manages to re-establish himself as somehow powerful; even in the first moments of confrontation with the Soldier he is defiant to some degree – throwing a defensive 'Oi' at the Soldier as he rifles through Ian's jacket (38) and even asking, 'You taking the piss?' (39). But Ian's aggressive stature, already damaged by his attack at the hands of Cate, is completely destroyed as the Soldier rapes him. The humiliation is doubled as, once finished, the Soldier rapes Ian for a second time with a revolver (so, then, a third penetration). Mezey and King point out, in their investigations into male victims of sexual assaults, that we live in a society in which men are expected to defend themselves and that failure to do so, especially in the case of a sexual assault, becomes a 'mark of masculine inadequacy'; 'passivity', they contend, 'is equated with femininity' (1992: 80). They go on to argue that the sexual assault is intended to produce submission and to humiliate, that it is a fundamental attack on a victim's sexual integrity (Menzy and King 1992: 80). Ian submits. The attack eviscerates him of any power as he simply 'registers pain but he is silent' (49). The rape, much like the laughter, ruptures his sense of self: it is traumatic physically and psychologically.

Towards the end of *Blasted*, in a reiteration of the power struggle at the opening of the play, Cate unloads Ian's gun, his only means of escaping the perpetual trauma of his life. It is she who continues the cycle of trauma. Indeed, she seems to suffer the effects of trauma similarly as she 'bursts out laughing, unnaturally, hysterically, uncontrollably. She laughs and laughs and laughs and laughs and laughs' (57) in an episode that closely resembles the fits she has earlier in the play, fits that are stimulated by traumatic experience.

The very end of the play sees Cate feeding Ian, and Ian thanking her, which has, for some, been seen as a sign of minimal hope, reminiscent of Len's mending the chair at the end of Bond's *Saved* and the platitudes at the end of *King Lear*. Nevertheless, the traumas of the play are still active in the on-stage world. The power structure of the play's opening has been completely reversed and Ian is left dependent on Cate. Devoid of the aggression that so defined him at the opening of the play, he is returned to a childlike state: he is in need of nourishment and protection at the hands of another. He has to be mothered by Cate. Left in this abased and infantilized position, he will forever live and relive the traumas that have brought him to this point. However, despite Cate's newfound 'power' over Ian, she is nonetheless still bound to their cyclical-traumatic relationship (she came back) and has endured further trauma in order to be able to feed herself and Ian:

> Cate enters carrying some bread, a large sausage and a bottle of gin.
> There is blood seeping from between her legs.
> (Kane 2001: 60)

My account, here, has been mainly concerned with the place of trauma within the diegesis. However, Cate's bloody return is part of a dramaturgical ploy which I suggest is part of a cycle of traumatic encounter for the audience. I will discuss the structure of the play in more detail below. Here, however, it is worth noting that while instances of sublimation/resolution are built into the diegetic narrative, once achieved they are then taken away: the trauma is perpetual both within the world of the play but also in terms of an encounter with the piece from an audience perspective. For an audience the process of this cyclical encounter (trauma – minimal resolution/sublimation – trauma) unsettles the possibility of 'understanding' the traumatic aspect of this play. It is the coupling of (inadequate) representations of trauma alongside a dramaturgical structure which echoes traumatic reoccurrence that is so important in understanding how this piece disturbs and disrupts the audience.

Blasted showers its audience with image after image of horror and trauma; it quite literally blasts them into confronting numerous traumatic events it is attempting to portray and bear witness to. Historically, cyclical trauma can of course be seen in tragedies such as Aeschylus's *Oresteia* trilogy and numerous Renaissance revenge tragedies. However, as discussed in Chapter 2, the cultural function of those pieces differs significantly from the function of trauma-tragic performances in the current, emergent structure of feeling. The repetitive and cyclical nature of trauma is central to the rhythm of *Blasted*. Highlighted in both content and, importantly, dramaturgical structure, the incessant nature of trauma-symptoms comes to define the experience of the play. Perpetrators have the traumas they have committed turned upon themselves: Cate rebuffs and laughs at Ian, but as T. G. A. Nelson warns, laughter can be treacherous because 'people laugh when they feel superior, but the tables may turn so that the laugher becomes the butt' (1990: 6) and so Ian rapes Cate, returning the traumatic experience to her. Ian and Cate's relationship is a perpetual cycle of wounding and re-wounding which neither can escape. This trauma cycle is further continued as the Soldier rapes Ian and later sucks out his eyes; and the pain of survival is revisited upon Ian *ad infinitum* at the end of the play as '[h]e can't even die' (Singer 2004: 140).

> I_AN_ *tears the cross out of the ground, rips up the boards and*
>   *lifts the baby's body out.*
> *He eats the baby.*
> *He puts the sheet the baby was wrapped in back in the hole.*
> *A beat, then he climbs in after it and lies down, head poking*
>   *out of the floor.*
> *He dies with relief.*
> *It starts to rain on him, coming through the roof.*
> *Eventually.*
> I_AN_: Shit.

>   (Kane 2001: 59–60)

While many of the scenes in *Blasted* are powerfully 'realistic' representations, they never actually re-present traumas: Ian does not actually rape Cate, the Soldier does not really suck out Ian's eyes and, as Kane herself points out Ian is 'clearly not eating the baby. It's absolutely fucking obvious. This is a theatrical image' (ctd in Saunders 2002: 66). But this is precisely the point for, as Kane again states, 'in a way [this type of representation is] more demanding [for an audience] because it throws you back on your own imagination' (ctd in Saunders 2002: 66). Kane is suggesting that because the image is obviously staged, the audience is made to retreat to their own imaginations in order to justify the scene, to make it less problematic. Kane's is not a particularly new argument – all theatrical representation has the ability to throw the audience back on to their imaginations, to suspend their (dis)belief. But what is particularly interesting in the case of Kane's work, and indeed trauma-tragedies more generally, is that the representations apply so much pressure to that suspension as to place it/the audience into the shimmering undecidability I proposed in Chapter 3. In the case of *Blasted*, this is achieved precisely because of the excessive nature of the representations and the incessant way in which they bombard the audience.

In her discussion of the excessive nature of Karen Finley's performances, Rebecca Schneider (1997: 101) points to this type of audience engagement, arguing that some performance works refuse to allow the spectator to 'sit back and suspend disbelief' or to simply distance themselves in order to '"appreciate" art'. Schneider suggests that performances such as Finley's are so 'squarely in your face' that they challenge the audience to disbelieve: 'disbelief is the constant question that bangs at the door of the viewer – I dare you to disbelieve' (1997: 101). The perpetual violence (physical and psychological) represented in *Blasted* is on the one hand deeply theatrical – the make-believe of it clear to the audience – and on the other hand it resists the suggestion that it is anything other than viscerally 'real'. It is, then, not so much the actual representations being made that have an impact on the audience but their ability to stimulate what might be thought of as an experience of the visceral-imaginary which short-circuits the audience's ability to recognize the theatrical.

The Soldier sucking out Ian's eyes is a good example of this. While we know that the act is not actually carried out, our 'suspension of disbelief' creates the effect of embodied violence and so we cannot disbelieve it. The play in performance (and to a certain degree in reading it) puts its audience into a position of discomfort in watching: rather than representing pain there is 'pain in the representation' (Lehmann 2006: 166). As with many plays of the time, and many performances which deal with trauma, *Blasted* triggers, or at least attempts to trigger, what Stanton B. Garner (1994) terms a 'neuromimetic transferral'. Garner contends that in neuromimetic transferral, representations of pain cross the threshold between performance space and audience space, invoking an 'impulse to close one's eyes during simulated blindings on stage', not merely in an aversion to the representation of pain or violence but, more crucially, as 'a deeper defence against its sympathetic arising in the field of one's own body' (Garner 1994: 181). While Kane believed that the theatricality of *Blasted* was obvious, she echoes Garner in contending that theatre has the capacity be 'visceral' and put the audience 'in direct physical contact with thought and feeling' (ctd in Saunders 2002: 15). By employing a series of disturbing theatrical images which represent events and situations outside the realm of most people's experiences, and which had a visceral impact, she created felt reactions in the audience. In each of the productions I have seen of *Blasted*, there have always been visible signs of the piece's visceral nature among the audience, from grimaces and recoiling to fully turning away.[3] To coin Garner's oft-quoted pun, the embodied *I* is moved, emotionally and physically, by the embodied *eye*'s engagement with the stage images (cf. Garner 1994: 4).

'There is a blinding light, then a huge explosion' (Kane 2001: 39)

In looking at trauma in the diegetic world of the piece and the stage images it presents, I have motioned towards the importance of the structure of the play and the relationship this has to audience reception. Kane pointed out in an interview with Stephenson and Langridge that 'all good art is subversive, either in form or content. And the best art is subversive in form *and* content. And often, the element that most outrages those who seek to impose censorship is form'. She went on to suggest that she is using, like other 'controversial' playwrights before her, 'non-naturalistic forms that elude simplistic interpretation' (ctd in Stephenson and Langridge 1997: 130; emphasis is original).

The first half of the piece is fairly 'naturalistic', staged within the walls of a hotel bedroom that looks 'so expensive it could be anywhere in the world' (Kane 2001: 3). The style is thus cognate with the 'kitchen-sink' realism of much post-World War II theatre. It is a comfortable style, one which most theatre-goers would be familiar with, even if the opening line of the play suggests that its content may not be quite so safe. But Kane exploits this sense of familiarity to destabilize the audience's expectations and involvement with the play when the situation is fractured and, literally, blown apart. Halfway through the play a soldier barges into the room and shortly after this a bomb blows the world of the play apart, transporting its action and audience into the ravages of a civil war. This diegetic rupture was intended to bring the audience face-to-face with 'the paper-thin wall between the safety and civilization of peacetime Britain and the chaotic violence of civil war' (Kane ctd in Stephenson and Langridge 1997: 131).

It was a dramaturgy that made its audience feel unsafe and exposed because their expectations of the dramatic universe are destabilized by the form (cf. Aston and Savona 1991: 32–33). Augmenting this position, drama therapists Mary Duggan and Roger Granger (1997: 42) contend that a play's structure is how an audience recognizes 'the theatre as a theatre, a place specifically designed for theatrical presentation' and because of this familiarity, 'we know what it is *for*; and we are not alarmed.' By extension, then, the fracturing of form might be seen to instigate a questioning of 'what it is for', a destabilizing of the audience's comfort, and so instill a sense of alarm.[4]

Kane makes the point that it is a play about articulating the way in which traumas tear the fabric of people's lives without reason or warning:

> At some point during the first couple of weeks of writing
> [in March 1993] I switched on the television. Srebrenica

was under siege. An old woman was looking into the camera, crying. She said, 'Please, please, somebody help us. Somebody do something.' I knew nobody was going to do a thing. Suddenly, I was completely uninterested in the play I was writing. What I wanted to write about was what I'd just seen on television. So my dilemma was: do I abandon my play (even though I'd written one scene I thought was really good) in order to move on to a subject I thought was more pressing? Slowly it occurred to me that the play I was writing was about this. It was about violence, about rape, and it was about these things happening between people who know each other and ostensibly love each other... And then I thought: 'What this needs is what happens in war – suddenly, violently, without any warning, people's lives are completely ripped to pieces.'

(ctd in Sierz 2001: 100–102)

And this is precisely what Kane does when she plants the bomb which blows the stage world from the safety of a Leeds hotel to the war-torn former Yugoslavia. Kane believed that 'the form is the meaning', and that the reaction against *Blasted* was not so much to do with content (though this is clearly part of it) but because of the way the play required its audience to confront the familiar images of war, torture and domestic violence in ways which could not be passed off and ignored:

The press were screaming about cannibalism live on stage, but, of course, audiences weren't looking at actual atrocities, but an imaginative response to them in an odd theatrical form, apparently broken-backed and schizo-phrenic, which presented material without comment and asked the audience to craft their own response. The representation of violence caused more anger than actual violence. While the corpse of Yugoslavia was rotting on our doorstep, the press chose to get angry, not about the corpse, but about the cultural event that drew attention to it.

(Kane ctd in Stephenson and Langridge 1997: 130–131)

Kane's point is important. The form of the piece creates a presence effect for the spectator by staging representations which collapse or reverse our usual understanding of the mimetic quality of performance (*vide* Chapter 3). These representations, to evoke Schneider again, dare the audience to disbelieve them, the result of which is a neuromimetic reaction against and as protection from what is shown. The representations, however, are made doubly powerful through that staging strategy because it collapses the audiences' – or at least the audiences' of the early-mid 1990s – expectations of what a trip to the theatre should be. Kane suggests that if *Blasted* had been a socio-realist play, it would not have been met with the same commotion and crucially she goes on to say that the 'appalling' tensions of the first half of the play are a 'premonition of the disaster to come. And when it does come, the structure fractures to alloy its entry' (ctd in Stephenson and Langridge 1997: 130). The form is the meaning.

Blasted employs a dramaturgical strategy of holding the traumatic wound open, bearing witness to the repetitive and intrusive structure of traumatic experience. It embodies and creates (or created in its historical context) a *presence-of-trauma-effect* through a collision, or interaction, of its different meaning-making elements. The diegetic laughter in the play is both a repetitive mechanism through which the characters inflict violence upon one another and an endemic illustration of the trauma contained within the piece. The more explicit and incessant representations of violence within the piece push the audience to a point where they have no choice but to confront the represented violence on stage, placing them phenomenologically 'in' it. Lastly, the form of the piece is central to the way the play is received. It is employed as a dramaturgical strategy through which to illustrate to and implicate the audience in the trauma(s) of the piece. The relationship between these elements can be seen to create a fundamental disturbance of its audience, a visceral experience which might, if successful, position them within a phenomenological experience of trauma and so, perhaps, as Kane implies she wanted, they might come to be moved to take ethical action in the 'real' world.

His Dark Materials: staging the impossible

Although the National Theatre's production of *His Dark Materials* (2004) is very different to *Blasted*, it contains similar turns towards the traumatological, if not in such explicit content as its 'in-yer-face' predecessors, then most certainly in its attempt to deliberately and viscerally stage 'unstageable' acts of trauma. *His Dark Materials* is a significantly different cultural object from those previously analysed in this volume: it is not what we might think of as contemporary 'avant-garde' writing which could be seen to define the work of Kane and Neilson, nor is it an example of Performance Art or devised performance work. It is a mainstream, big-budget production which attempted to appeal to as wide an audience as possible. Given that it is an adaptation aimed, primarily, at children, it is perhaps not a play that we immediately associate with representations of traumata. However, it is this piece's difference from others within the book that makes its inclusion so important, precisely because it highlights the pervasiveness of the traumatic structure of feeling I am identifying, and which is reflected in and formed by all strata of cultural engagement.

In his lucid and valuable critical review of the production, Mark Berninger concludes that it was hugely popular, a *Gesamtkunstwerk* that 'tuned in with the zeitgeist at the beginning of the 21st century' (2008: 164). What is at stake in this section of the chapter is not the success or failure of the production, but a more specific focus on what it is that was translated from the books into the stage version, namely the traumatic. Throughout the books different traumas abound, the prose bearing witness to it in a succession of detailed narrative passages across all three novels. Historically, children's literature and theatre have always set certain focus on trauma and cruelty, but it is the particular way in which the traumatic is addressed now, and the way in which that is reflective of the contemporary structure of feeling, that is under scrutiny here. While there is of course much more contained within the novels of *His Dark Materials* than its traumatic elements, what is interesting is that in appropriating the novels for the stage, the National's adaptation very specifically foregrounds the traumatic, re-embodying the various modes of its articulation and bearing witness to multiple traumata.

The constancy of a 'subterranean' seam of traumata within the world(s) of the stage play is signalled in the opening few moments of *Part I* of *His Dark Materials*. Timothy Dalton, playing Lord Asriel, Lyra's supposed uncle (the fact that he is her father is not yet known by Lyra or the audience), discovers Anna Maxwell Martin, playing Lyra, eavesdropping on his private meeting in the 'Retiring Room'.[5] Dalton violently grabs Martin's arm, twisting it into what appears to be an agonizingly unnatural, painful position, and although the lines aren't uttered on stage, the presence of Lord Asriel's words from the novels are powerfully evoked: 'what the hell are you doing [in here]? ... I'll break your arm' (Pullman 2007a: 14). This violent action explicitly maps the underlying violence and aggression which is to become a leitmotif of the production through the repetition of similar 'traumas'. The fact that the violence is meted out by uncle/father on niece/daughter is also important, setting up the fragility and abusive nature of many of the relationships within the play.

Dæmon bonds

In *His Dark Materials*, one of the closest and most important attachment bonds is that between a person and their 'dæmon' (which takes on an animal form that can change shape until such time as its human reaches the age of puberty). Very near the beginning of the National's adaptation, an Oxford scholar called Hopcraft asks, 'Why, if a man ran away from his dæmon, would he experience, first discomfort... then pain... then a grinding sense of loss, and finally death?' (Wright 2004: 10).[6] The question makes it textually clear to the audience from the outset of the piece that this relationship is at the very core of human existence in this fictional world. But the importance of the dæmon bond is signified and highlighted through a number of different theatrical/dramaturgical layers; sound, lighting, set and, of course, an embodied/acted layer, all interact to both semiotically and phenomenologically iterate and reiterate this central element of the story to the audience.

Through Bert O. States' notion of 'binocular vision' (1985: 8), Stanton B. Garner has convincingly argued that semiotics and phenomenology are 'complementary ways of seeing that disclose the object two ways at once' (Garner 1994: 15). Meanwhile, Mick Wallis has usefully postulated that by acknowledging the semiotic and the phenomenological, we are able to read and map the 'play of signifiers below the level of signification' in order that we might more fully become aware of 'a multifarious flow of possibilities' and so navigate the 'multivocality' and 'slippery signification' of the stage image (Wallis 2005: 70). Here, we might also turn to Julia Kristeva's notions of the semiotic and the symbolic, and *genotext* and *phenotext*. Philosopher Noëlle McAfee, glossing Kristeva, proposes that 'a text operates at two levels: at the semiotic-genotext level it is a process by which the author organizes or manifests semiotic drives and energies; at the symbolic-phenotext level it is a structural and mappable piece of communication' (McAfee 2004: 25). While these terms are primarily concerned with the analysis of literary texts, we might productively appropriate them into the current context: if we take the whole of the theatrical production as our 'text', the terms become constructive and easily applicable analytical tools.

Although Wallis is not employing Kristeva's framework he makes a similar move in his analysis of *The Fate of Sparta* (c. 1788), arguing that it might be possible to identify different levels of textual meaning within a theatrical performance. The first level is that which is natural to the shape of the play, much like the mappable phenotext. The second is a ritualized layer of coincidence, what I refer to as an 'uncanny echo', which creates an unexplainable presence, paralleling the energizing genotext. Wallis usefully turns to Catherine Bell's idea of 'ritualization' in elucidating his argument: 'the repetition of a basic binary opposition or series of oppositions at various levels of a text or textual system so that a key opposition is both naturalized and appears to subtend from some transcendent principle' (Wallis 2005: 77). Ritualization is, as historian/archaeologist Richard Bradley (2005) highlights, echoing Wallis, 'both a way of acting which reveals some of the dominant concerns of society, and a process by which certain parts of life are selected and provided with an added emphasis' (Bradley 2005: 34). Bell discusses it as a process which is culturally specific or responsive and consists of a 'set of activities that construct particular types of meaning and values in specific ways' (Bell 1997: 82). The model is useful both because of its cultural specificity (relating it cognately to structure of feeling) and because of its explicit focus on the productivity or meaning-making capacity of binary oppositions, such as might be seen in a semiotic-phenomenological reading of performance or the embodied-scenographic relationship I am exploring here. Wallis' central argument, then, is that this layering and ritualization operates as a system of production of phenomena and that such constructedly coincidental repetitions operate as 'a mode of productivity not only of meanings but also of phenomena'. The idea is that there is 'interplay between signification and constructed [phenomenological] presence' (Wallis 2005: 70–74). The dæmon bond is one such presence, a presence which is established not only through the progression of the narrative fiction, but coincidentally through the staging structures of the piece. It is a constructed phenomenon, an unexplainable, uncanny presence which the audience experience fully but which is inherently 'absent'; it cannot be pointed at, seen or heard but is constantly 'there' nonetheless.

Throughout *His Dark Materials* it is indicated that a human necessarily comprises of 'something' plus a 'dæmon' complement or part, without which they become very damaged, something sub-human. Thus, there is no separation or distinction between the dæmon self and the human self. Read like this, the dæmon–human relationship points to various models of this type – for example, the ancient model of the soul (a model Pullman resists)[7] and more modern psychoanalytical, psychological models like Freud's superego and id; and while the soul, superego and id all perform in different ways, importantly, in each case the models refer to something which is inseparable. The relationship is a deeply embedded one, the 'existence' of each part dependent upon the other. The action within the plays performs the relationship in such a way as to indicate that dæmon and human constitute one inseparable self and cannot be disconnected without terrible and lasting consequences.

Throughout the books and the seven or so hours of performance, a theme of separation and split is repeated time and again, and whether it is imposed upon one character by another or self-inflicted, the action is always 'violent', a tear, a disruption, a trauma. So deeply painful are these separations for the characters within the diegetic world(s) of *His Dark Materials* that they can be seen mimetically to echo the central edict of trauma theory, namely that trauma is an event outside the realm of human experience, the impact of which manifests itself in a disruption of the survivor-sufferer's understanding of self.

'The parting is agonising' (Wright 2004: 63)

A large building, displaying the letters G. O. B. on its roof, dominates the stage. It is an austere-looking structure, cold and institutional, penal even. A sliding door which covers almost half the length of the building is open, revealing cage after cage of quivering and agitated animal-like figures. A girl, holding a similar creature in her arms, stands by the opening; she is completely dwarfed by the structure's size and dominance of the space. The girl's shrinking stature is further compounded by two extra-diegetic elements – the enveloping size of the Olivier auditorium and an underscore which plays 'danger' music.

This genotextual 'mood' music is particularly interesting for while it is most certainly outside the world of the play (the characters are unaware of it), it creates – or at least augments – a meaning which is part of and central to the scene on stage. The music throughout the play, particularly apparent in this scene, is part of the *Gesamtkunstwerk* feel of the production that Berninger (2008) and MacDonald (2007) have both highlighted. It is very much a meaning-making tool, a mode of expression, insomuch as it is expressing what is internal; the thoughts, feelings and emotions of the characters on stage are established not only by their actions but also through the music which, because we are so attuned to its seamless presence, creates a phenomenal experience of 'what it's like there', in the diegetic world.

Two men appear and roughly grab the girl; they close the door to the cage room in a flurry of panicked action as the scene fluidly moves to the interior of the 'Bolvangar' camp. Again the scenography is the overwhelmingly dominant part of the stage image and its juxtaposition with the comparable smallness and seeming fragility of Maxwell

Martin serves, as I will develop, to heighten the traumatic expression of the scene. A huge 'scientific' laboratory slices into the space on the drum revolve, the central component of which is a Kafkaesque machine comprising a chair reminiscent of the electric chairs of countless films, connected by a long, covered, rectangular trough to a raised cage. The connection is bisected by a third item, a large guillotine-blade, and just as the prisoner in Kafka's In the Penal Settlement *is confused and frightened by the torturous 'Harrow', so too does the girl embody a sense of fear and confusion as she sees the blade and the rest of the macabre device. She is manhandled into the chair and bound down as the creature she holds to her chest is torn away from her by one of the men. The instant the creature is touched the music screeches and the lighting changes; we know something terrible has happened. Girl and creature scream in agony, and as the distance between them increases the discomfort for both seems to increase: the creature writhes and wriggles, desperate to return to the comfort of the girl's bosom and she in turn struggles against her bonds. The traumatic focus of the scene is brought to the fore as their screams fill the auditorium despite their small size and the dominance of the scenography adds to the audience's sense of fear for the two characters now bound by cage or chair. The girl screams out repeatedly, 'You can't touch him! You can't touch him!', as a lighting effect makes 'visible' the bond between her and the creature, her dæmon Pantalaimon, a bond which we are sure is about to be violently severed.*[8]

The reaction to the Bolvangar scene is primarily a phenomenological one; each audience member will embody what is happening and so experience it in a slightly different way. Yet what is particularly interesting is the way in which there is a dual-layer meaning-making process in operation between the scenography and the actor which gives the effect of making the traumatic phenomenally present. Firstly, the scenographic elements of the production might be seen to 'naturalistically' augment the embodied and textual actions. This is to say that the design elements of the production are passively adding to what is already on stage: they are mappable symbolic-phenotextual components of the stage image. However, there is a ritualized second layer in which the meaning is uncannily echoed through the scenographic elements: rather than a coincidental meaning-making process there exists an energizing semiotic-genotext which motivates and adds greater meaning to the patent stage imagery. The juxtaposition between the enormity of the 'machine', the stage and auditorium spaces, and the cacophony of the sound effects against the actor's screaming and struggling sets the audience on the track of traumatic witnessing. The scream is at once dwarfed by the staging and openness of the Olivier space and in the same instant is piercingly 'real', creating an experience which is viscerally embodied.

Despite its obvious theatricality, the scene I have just described is hard to witness; the screams of Lyra and Pantalaimon resonate in the audience's ears and rattle through their bodies, reaching, as Garner has suggested representations of pain can, 'across the boundary [...] between stage and spectator' to touch and impact upon the bodies of the spectators in a neuromimetic transferral (Garner 1994: 180). Or, to recall my argument from Chapter 3, this might be understood as a moment of performative *punctum* which rises from the general 'scene' of the production to reach out across the space to prick the audience, to bruise them.

One of the clearest moments in which the various elements of this production collide and stimulate each other to generate a sense of traumatic presence is in the Boatman scene in which Lyra and Will cross over into the 'Land of the Dead'. In order to make this journey Lyra must part ways with Pantalaimon, an act which the audience know to be both painful and dangerous, against the 'natural' order of Lyra's world.

The massive Olivier stage is, for the only time in the play, completely bare save the three actors, one of whom is wearing a black body suit as he embodies the dæmon Pantalaimon. High above them a rowing boat appears, as if it is floating in the darkness. The boat descends toward Lyra, Pantalaimon and Will, all of whom stare on in what might be fear or, just as likely, awe and anticipation. A haunting brass/wind instrument which, similar to the music in the Bolvangar scene, might be seen to express the characters' internal, emotional states accompanies the Boatman's journey to the children.

The Boatman very clearly states that Pantalaimon cannot accompany Lyra in the boat. As she begins to move away from Pantalaimon, the small puppet is animated to appear agitated and Samuel Barnett, voicing Pantalaimon, repeatedly pleads with her, 'No! No!' Maxwell Martin (Lyra) climbs into the boat: her character's determination to rescue her friend Roger dictates that she must tear herself away from her dæmon. As the boat begins to move away it is enveloped by the darkness of the empty space, highlighting both the physical distance between Pantalaimon and Lyra, and the growing tear in their unseen but palpably felt bond.

This element of the scenographic design is part of a structure of repetition across the various 'texts' of the performance which helps to create its meaning; it is another uncanny echo of the textual story. Without the empty space the phenomenological sense of emptiness, isolation and violent rupture which is made present in this scene would have been lost. This scene is one in which the ritualized interplay between signification and constructed presence is at its most effective, heightening the emotional resonance of what Butler describes as 'one of the most heart-rending events in the story' (Butler 2003: 108).

As the boat moves further into the darkness, Barnett's voice quivers through the space in a remarkable moment of emotionally charged vocal work as he simply cries out 'Lyra' in a prolonged and agonizing vocalization of the pain of this separation. The sound is tortured and imbibed with a palpable sense of emotion.[9] The emanation created an awareness of both the character of Pantalaimon and his puppeteer, the presence of whom is made manifest in a way which does not happen at any other point in the play: it is this tripartite presence, Lyra–Pantalaimon–Puppeteer, which helps to explain the deeply embodied and emotionally resonant experience of the scene.

During this scene there are a number of things happening which centre around the body of the puppeteer who, as just stated, is made palpably present in a way that has not happened before. The body and actions of the puppeteer are central in this presence conundrum, a conundrum which we can begin to unpick through Eugenio Barba and Nicola Savarese's (1991) arguments on 'pre-expressivity'. Barba and Savarese define the pre-expressive as the way in which a character's energy is brought alive scenically rather than psychologically. It is the quality of the scenic elements of the production, such as the set, lighting, costume and (especially) the actor's actions which creates presence and meaning (1991: 187). They argue that 'the totality of a performer's performance... [is] made up of distinct levels of organisation' and that there is a basic level of organization which is common to all performers: the pre-expressive (Barba and Savarese 1991: 187). Pre-expressivity does not take into account the usual elements of a performer's presence on stage; no heed is paid to intentions, emotions or identification etcetera: '[i]t is the *doing* and *how the doing is done* which determine what one expresses' (187; emphasis is original). In short, the 'psycho-techniques', as Barba and Savarese term them, are ignored in favour of a focus on the performer's physical presence and actions.

In the scene directly preceding that with the Boatman, Barnett plays the character of Lyra's Death; although still clothed in the black body suit he has worn throughout, he is unmasked and for the first and only time we see the actor's face as he 'becomes' another character. Once the scene concludes, Barnett pulls the mask back over his face to continue his role as puppeteer. This switch from puppeteer to discernible character and back again is unsettling, it produces a different relationship to his role and it destabilizes the energy which has captivated the audience's attention by a change in this body's mode of pre-expressivity, a mode which is discernibly different from the others on stage at the time. Depending upon which theatrical conventions a play is operating within, there are seamless ways in which the same actor can take on various roles, but here, despite the evident skill involved in the switch, it becomes strange and uncanny. The movement between character and puppeteer complicates the spectator's relationship with this on-stage body; it becomes indeterminable, pushing the audience into what might be thought of as a shimmering uncertainty, where we question what the body is doing on stage.

This switching back and forth within the pre-expressive level of the performance establishes the puppeteer's body as what Watanabe would term a 'fictive body': a body that sits between the levels of character (fictional) and actor (everyday). It is a body which is at once present and absent.[10]

The puppeteer in the Boatman scene is performing his own absence: he is wearing a black costume in order to minimize the impact of his physical presence, yet he must be there in order to animate the puppet of Pantalaimon. Furthermore, because the audience saw his face in the preceding scene, they are all too aware of his physical presence on stage. His vocalic emanations further add to this metaphysical circulation: his voice is his own but is supposed to be for Pantalaimon while his body is semiotically 'not there'. This difficult circulation clearly articulates States' suggested 'problem' of a character only being available through 'an actor who is not the character but who forms the entire perceptual ground from which any such essence as character can appear' (States 1992: 373). It is this present absence, or the performance of absence, which is so important in triggering the phenomenological reaction to the Boatman scene. Far from being a conventional character who witnesses the action, the puppeteer is a witness from outside the diegetic world while the character he animates is palpably present within it. However, that character is an inanimate object (a puppet) and so cannot witness; the puppeteer can act as witness to the action, but is supposedly absent. In this scene, however, he is made palpably present through his animation/vocalization of the puppet, thus making himself present as witness to the trauma. This circulation operates in a manner similar to the way in which the 'mood' music I mentioned earlier does: while the puppeteer is extra-diegetic, 'absent' from the story; his palpable presence is part of the meaning-making process for the audience. His presence both expresses the emotions of Pantalaimon/Lyra and echoes the audience's presence as witnesses to the onstage traumata. The structure of repetition, the uncanny echo which motivates or energizes the phenotextual reading, is again made evident: now through the presence of the puppeteer's genotextual body.

The voice work, the shimmering uncertainty surrounding the fictive body of the puppeteer and the embodied manipulation of the puppet collide and circulate with the echoic darkness of the stage space (and auditorium) to create and underpin a phenomenological experience of this traumatic split. The Boatman scene is not experienced within a cognitive field in the first instance.[11] Rather it seems to rupture the symbolic divide between audience and performance spaces to create an embodied impact. The confusion between the conceptual and the intuitive creates a sense in which the scene seems to reach across and touch us both emotionally and physically. George Lakoff and Mark Johnson (1999) have persuasively argued that:

> [o]ur sense of what is real begins with and depends crucially upon our bodies, especially our sensorimotor apparatus, which enables us to perceive, move, and manipulate, and the detailed structures of our brains, which have been shaped by both evolution and experience.
>
> (Lakoff and Johnson 1999: 17)

This is not to suggest that the experience of the Boatman scene (and others) is outside a sign system, but rather that the first-order experience of it, stimulated by the collision of or relationships between signs, is a bodily one. It is only after this experience that the cognitive meanings of the signs begin to slip into focus: the corporeal underpinning of all semiotic reception, while unconscious and automatic in most of our daily existence, is here forcefully foregrounded and manipulated in the creation of a presence-in-trauma effect.

The Boatman scene is, again, a moment of performative *punctum* which captivates the audience; it is pertinent to them but is also viscerally/emotionally painful to them. It is emotional, 'slightly overwhelming' and 'felt, very strongly, in the pit of [the] stomach and tightening of [the] throat', as a colleague put it to me.[12] Butler reiterates this point beautifully, noting that '[o]n stage an actor was saying goodbye to a puppet and in the auditorium there were members of the audience in tears' (Butler 2003: 108). There is a sense when watching this scene that it is a deeply private and overwhelmingly 'real' pain that is being put before the audience. So uncomfortable is it that through a series of embodied and phenomenologically experienced spatial and body-to-body relations this moment in *His Dark Materials* creates what Jonas Barish might call a moment of 'ontological queasiness' (1981: 3) in which the spectator is set into a position, as Nicholas Ridout suggests, of not knowing if they 'want to "be" there or not' (2003: 3). To be at the event of the Boatman scene is to experience the effect of presence at traumatic severance, so to speak.

It is through the scenographic system[13] and its ritualized, uncanny echoing of the embodied and textual elements of the theatre event that *His Dark Materials* is able to make present both the dæmon bond and the subsequent phenomenological experience of its split. It is the layering of stage imagery with Pullman's original story which is so evocative for an audience: the staging echoes or repeats the other performance texts to produce a sense of traumatic presence.

To write of the experience in this way is potentially, however, to attempt to write about the ungraspable (cf. Wallis 2005: 71). But that is of course the point, for to write or think about traumata and performance events is precisely to engage in attempting to write, grasp, (re)present the un-writable, un-graspable, un-(re)presentable. It is entirely appropriate, then, to talk of a phenomenological presence-in-trauma effect that is caused by the staging of separation in *His Dark Materials*. While Phelan claims that to represent trauma is impossible, this production makes, if not a representation of trauma, then at least an embodied articulation of it. To read and write about the experience of traumatic separation in relation to *His Dark Materials* is to become entangled in a web of presence effects; the invocation of the presence of the dæmon bond through stage effects and strategies, and through this the effect of being in (or at) traumatic separation.

The importance of the space-body relationship cannot be underestimated in creating the presence-in-trauma effects. The mechanical sublimity of the Olivier's drum revolve and its ability to slice so seamlessly through the scenes of the play and the worlds of the fiction, like the National's very own Subtle Knife, are central to the embodied experience of the audience. Gay McAuley has convincingly argued that in theatre-going, while we are trained to watch the stage the experience is principally one of 'being there', a phenomenological experience 'of the space in relation to oneself, of one's self *in* the place, of the "height in the air," of the "feeling" (what ever that is) of being in a theatre' (McAuley 2000: 256). One might add to this description the relation of one's body to the bodies of the actors, to their voices and movement. The experience of the theatre is a phenomenally active one, experienced in and through the body. By opening up the stage space in the moment of Lyra's separation from Pantalaimon, and through the continued dramaturgical and scenographic strategies, both natural to the story and constructedly coincidental, the audience is opened to a phenomenological experience of traumatic separation which is created by both the experiential and referential elements of the production.

Untitled (Syncope)

> 'a mixture of materials... skin and stone.'
> (O'Reilly 2008; personal interview)

Having discussed at length the representations of pain and separation in *His Dark Materials*, and the possibility that this might offer an effect of accession to a corporeal sense of subject, I am now going to turn to a very different performance and a different illustration, or understanding, of trauma in performance. Moving from the analyses of the dramaturgical structure of *Blasted* and the scenographic system of *His Dark Materials*, the final element of this chapter explores the phenomenology of bodies in the creation of presence-in-trauma effects.

Kira O'Reilly contends that 'all wounds speak. All wounds are a sign that something's happened; something that's happened in time, some sort of break for better or for worse'. Through this she proposes that performance can occupy 'gaps in language', those elements of human experience which are beyond 'grammar and syntax', such as the traumatic, and so a 'visual, non-verbal element [of communication becomes] really vital' (O'Reilly 2008; personal interview). O'Reilly's art practice seeks, then, productively to speak to or about trauma in order that she, and we, her audience, might learn about her body and our/the body. She offers an understanding of trauma that is concerned with an exploration of the physical borders of the body; the actual boundaries between inside and out are ruptured in the act of slicing through the skin, a 'traumatic' act which helps to produce knowledge of self, world, politics and performance.[14]

The following part of this chapter comprises two distinct but complementary sections, each addressing O'Reilly's performance *Untitled (Syncope)* (April 2007). The first section offers a personal descriptive account of the performance which might be thought of as an introduction to the second section, a more critical/analytical reflection on the experience of being at the performance of *Untitled (Syncope)*. My intention is to offer these sections in order that they inform and reflect upon one another by engaging with the performance in different ways.

The Touch and the Cut

Standing in the labyrinthine darkness of the SHUNT Vaults below London Bridge Station, I am struck by how memories return to us when we least expect them, triggered by anything from ambiguous sounds to specific images or spaces to floating scents that tug at our senses as they waft by. Engulfed by the dank and musty crumbling walls of the vaults, listening to the soft murmur emanating from the unseen bar, my haptic senses begin to tingle into action. The softness of the sandstone walls on my back and the uneven concrete floor press against the surfaces of my body and I am returned to memories of childhood nightmares in which I am surrounded by intimidating buildings, lost and vulnerable. Able to run only as if through water, I cannot escape whomever or whatever my imagination has conjured to chase me. But I always wake up in the end, returning to my bed and my world.

The performance proper has not yet begun, but our sombre procession from one end of the maze of arches and chambers to the other feels like it might be part of it. We reach one end of the main concourse and huddle together, staring into the blackness at the other end. As I peer through the sequential railway arches into the darkness, I am struck by the stillness and silence of the audience; there is an aura of reverence and anticipation that I assume is due in part to the knowledge, among some, of O'Reilly's previous work and in part to the surroundings. We wait.

I suddenly see something move. There is a figure coming slowly towards us; she is naked, walking backwards. I think I see a baby looking over her shoulder towards us. As she gets closer, I see she is wearing a burlesque showgirl headdress and bright red high heels, which we can now hear clipping the floor. I realize the face looking at us is not that of a baby but the artist's face reflected in a small circular mirror: she is watching us watch her. When she is only about five metres away, a slow knocking sound begins; it is somewhere between a clock ticking and a hammer hitting a block of wood. I cannot locate its source. As the woman draws ever closer, the audience position themselves in a horseshoe shape around her. She is so close it is possible to see every contour and muscle of her body.

I am drawn in, captured by her image. I want to absorb every detail. Her skin is littered with the traces of past wounds: small, neat scars all over her body from ankle to neck. She stands among us, catching our gaze in the mirror. She holds my eye for what seems like an age, I notice her crimson lipstick mirroring the colour of her shoes, and then her eyes move past mine around the semi-circle, and back again. Her gaze returns to mine, she reaches out and takes my hand leading me away from the rest of the audience. My heart quickens as the security blanket of being part of the group evaporates and I am suddenly aware of their gaze on my back. And although I am comforted by the familiarity in the performer's touch, I feel very alone. Exposed. I notice the scalpel she clamps to the face of the mirror like a sinister clock hand. I am led through two arches into one of the other chambers, the audience following. And then I am released.

The woman places the mirror on the floor, the scalpel now in full view. She stands straight, raises her right arm above her head, points two fingers to the sky and breathes in. She breathes in and in and in and in. There is no exhalation. The sound changes to a faster clicking, like a metronome counting out the beats of her inhalations and movements. Her elongated body starts to tremble under the strain of her breathing, her face reddens, her abdominal muscles contract and the scars on her body seem to flash angrily.

Whether through lack of blood or its increased flow, some of O'Reilly's scars change colour in the moments of greatest strain, paradoxically adding to the theatricality of these moments, increasing the desire to watch, and making the scene all the more difficult: the performer was not only naked and vulnerable, but the very fabric of her physical being, the inner functioning of her body, was now on display.

Her body suddenly relaxes, her arm drops and her muscles go limp as she finally breathes out. She repeats this process, once more with her right arm raised but this time only exhaling: out and out and out and out. And then twice more (one in, one out) with her left arm raised. With each repetition, her muscles tense more, the veins in her neck bulge and her body shakes under the strain. She goes limp as she finally exhales after the fourth action.

After a moment's rest she steps forward, picks up the scalpel, stretches down to her right calf and cuts. She turns to her left calf next, where I have a clearer line of sight, and as she stretches the skin on her calf I see the purple trace of a previous cut. Unconsciously I tense my calf muscles, half expecting to feel the impending incision myself. She draws the blade along the purple scar line, slicing into her flesh and reopening the three-inch wound. Blood oozes out slowly and as it collects along the cut it tumbles down towards her ankle, puddling between the skin of her foot and the edge of her red shoe. These opening moments give way to a series of repetitive, strenuous and visceral movements, her body (and ours) in perpetual motion through the space. The metronome's pace quickens and grows louder as she tries to keep up her taut automaton-style movements with the pace set by the mechanical ticking, all the while teetering in her high heels. She never speaks.

Captivating wounds

In their discussion of the impact of architectural space on the senses, Bloomer and Moore (1977) have argued (cognate with McAuley's foregrounding of the phenomenological experience of space, highlighted above) that it is our haptic senses which 'contribute more than the others to our understanding of three-dimensionality, the *sine qua non* of architectural experience' (33). Defined as 'the sense of touch reconsidered to include the entire body rather than merely the instruments of touch, such as the hands' (Bloomer and Moore 1977: 34), the above statement might similarly be applied to performance, and especially O'Reilly's *Untitled (Syncope)* at the SHUNT Vaults, London. The ability to understand the three-dimensionality of the performance (space) is, of course, central to all performance experiences, but it was explicitly played with throughout this kinetic and kinaesthetically charged performance. The architecture of the space is leant on, brushed past, climbed upon and hidden behind while the performer repeatedly moves through the audience, touching, bumping into and moving them. Throughout the piece the sensation of touch is palpable, whether it is between performer and scalpel, bleeding calf and dirty wall, or one audience member and another.

O'Reilly's work directly engages with notions of complicity and witness, probing at the limits of the audience–performer contract, constantly asking questions of our position within that relationship. Throughout her own commentaries about her work, and indeed during our dialogue, O'Reilly has always highlighted her desire to engage directly with the audience, to deliberately deconstruct, in the Derridian sense, the hierarchized binary distinction between spectator and performer. As she noted in our conversation, the desire is that her performances have 'a sense of assembly; here *we* are rather than just me and then you lot. It's a bunch of *us* that might then be organized into you and me but there are moments where it is "us"' (O'Reilly 2008; personal interview). Her central tool in this investigation is the body: the site of art actions and discursive engagements with the world; O'Reilly is manipulating her own body and ours. Even in the simple act of making eye contact (used both as dramaturgical and basic implication effect, *vide* Chapter 4), be it through the mediation of the mirror or more directly as later in the performance, O'Reilly makes the audience aware of both the act of watching and their centrality within the performance. The eye contact acknowledges the reciprocity at work in the creation of the piece: the contract between performer and audience is two-way; without either party it would simply not exist – we are created as a group, an 'us'. Furthermore, linking to the tripartite relationship of gazes established in Chapter 4, the creation of a unified sense of 'us' is compounded as the audience-to-audience relationship in this production is explicitly foregrounded: we jostle for viewing positions, occasionally make eye contact and move through the space, illuminated, together.

This 'us', however, is created as a deliberately paradoxical relationship. While we may all be 'here', in the performance together, there is still a sense in which the audience is intruding or stumbling upon something they should not. In responding to O'Reilly's work David Houston Jones has suggested that 'it asks searching questions of our capacity for voyeurism: works like *Inthewrongplaceness* [2005], *Succour* (2001) and *Marsyas* [2004] make us complicit in the spectacle of violence, be it medicalised or inflicted by the performer on her own body' (Jones 2007: online). The centrality of the body sits precisely within O'Reilly's desire to create a more united sense of performance event, and it is through this that the audience is placed in the voyeuristic position that Jones identifies. Through kinesthetic and haptic systems, we are made increasingly aware of our own material presences during the performances. We read O'Reilly's performance through our bodies and as such her work presents us with a series of problems or dilemmas in which we are not only made aware of our material presence, but also, through our continued attendance and acknowledged looking (O'Reilly has met our gazes, we have met each others'), of our complicity in these acts of performative wounding. The 'us', then, is double-edged: the audience is at once made to feel part of the performance and, because of this, responsible for it, which in turn creates an uneasy tension between a desire to watch and a compulsion to look away.

In *Untitled (Syncope)* the physical contact was unexpected, startling even – I had not expected the tall, scarred and naked woman, whose formality/rigidity placed her at a distance from my own presence in the room, to reach out, gentle and tender, to seek my hand. The moment was both familiar and unsettling, and it became central to my experience of the piece. Throughout the forty-minute performance I could not help but think back to the glances and touch I shared with the artist. The experience of being physically led away from the audience group circled in my mind constantly, the sense of her hand on mine palpable throughout. The performance was both beautiful and incredibly difficult to be part of; I found myself desperate to watch and desperate to hide at the same time. The experience was a deeply visceral and connected one: I very clearly felt the musculature of my own body and its relation to the performer's physicality. The performance space was shared, unbounded, desegregated and, critically, through this there was the possibility of generating a sense of being more fully present at the performance. The connection I felt to Kira O'Reilly's body kept drawing me to make associations in my memory; it put me in a space where I began to reconnect with moments from my past – the first time I bled, my first memory of pain, the image of watching a friend's forehead split open on a curb, and the memory of guilt and help-lessness when a loved one tried to commit suicide. I did not want to remember.

The performance dynamic at *Untitled (Syncope)* was such that the audience was unlikely to be engaged in a process of self-elimination as the performance could not be viewed from a distance, physical or emotional; our physical presence in the room was central to the aesthetics, meanings and intentions of the work. By constantly drawing the audience through the space, our bodies were made apparent to us. O'Reilly created a kinaesthetic bond between performer and audience, and between spectator and spectator, a bond which was both physi-cally and emotionally experienced. The experience of watching someone willingly slice into their flesh connected on a bodily level in the anticipation of pain I expected to feel – I felt strangely culpable, as though I should have stopped her, but in the same instant was prevented from doing so because of an overwhelming compulsion to continue the experience (a shim-mering begins again).

The touch and the cut, both acts which press on the bodies of the audience in different ways, give the performance a strange sense of familiarity and extremity, and it is this dichotomous mix which (*vide* Jones) causes it to feel slightly voyeuristic. The familiarity is generated through an awareness of the violent act: society is used to representations of violence; as discussed in Chapter 2, we are bombarded by them. However, in this instance the violent act, while not 'extreme' in a spectacular sense, is too close, too personal and too 'real', and so becomes extreme in its significations. Being at *Untitled (Syncope)* is to experience the effacement of reality which Freud suggests happens in an uncanny encounter firsthand. As with Franko B's *Still Life*, this is a violently uncanny experience which reaches out and (posi-tively, productively) wounds the audience.

(Re)iterating the performance; or, presence effects

If we accept that the actor or performer might represent a person who represents us in the given situation – who stands in for us, as States would have it (1985: 159) – we are able to create the effect of being present in the represented experience. By choosing to position these three different performances side by side, my intention is to suggest that this presence effect can be created in any theatrical setting, rather than to propose a certain genre of production which might achieve it.

As I discussed in Chapter 1, trauma causes a shudder in the make-up of a victim's understanding of their self and the world in which they move; it makes them question their understanding of the ordering of life. Theatre's capacity to invoke this questioning of self is bound to the live nature of the event and the kinaesthetic connection between bodies in a shared space, making it the ideal site for traumatic exploration. Simon Shepherd (2006) asserts that, 'effects are produced in the spectator simply as a result of materially sharing the space with the performance. Many of these effects, bypassing the intellect, are felt in the body and work powerfully to shape a spectator's sense of the performance' (36–37). Therefore, '[t]here is a kinaesthetic empathy between the spectators' musculature and the performers' (Shepherd 2006: 46). Shepherd's argument helps to establish the unique quality of theatre/performance as a felt experience, an experience in which the audience is viscerally connected to the work being presented.

Garner's reflection that the staged body looks back at us highlights the importance of the body-to-body relationship which is unique to the theatrical experience. It is this relationship which might enable us to bear witness, or at least attempt to bear witness, to trauma in a way that is closer than any other to the authenticity of the original event – through our bodies. Karen Malpede (1996) argues that witnesses, whether in the theatre or elsewhere, offer up their bodies to the testifier in order to help bear the burden of the trauma. This formulation is useful in the context of being a witness at the theatre; as she goes on to suggest, witnessing is a corporeal/visceral experience that 'resonates inside the bodies of both the teller and the receivers of testimony', and through this embodied exchange both parties are changed in some way (Malpede 1996: 168). As set out in Chapter 4 (especially in relation to *Exquisite Pain*), within a performance event there exists a cascade of witnessing levels: performer stands as witness to the trauma-event whether fictional or not, then the audience stands as witness to both that witnessing and to the performance event itself. As a result of this cascade of witnessing orders, a performance event can become a serious play space through which traumata can be explored because the cultural place of aesthetic performance, and the performance contract established therein, can act as a buffer or mediation between original trauma and its (re-)experience.

Through the process of viscerally bearing witness to trauma it is conceivable that we are not only 'validat[ing] the victims' reality' (Malpede 1996: 168), but also preparing for our own traumas. We can be placed in a situation whereby being at the theatre rehearses our presence in (future and previous) traumas, where the performance creates something which might be akin to an experience of trauma. There is transhistorical precedent in this claim: arguably since Aristotle, theatre has been attempting such rehearsals, as evidenced in development of arguments around theatre as cathartic experience. My point here is, then, both to highlight the transhistorical nature of this phenomenon but also, more specifically, to look at it in relation to the current traumatized structure of feeling and its operation within the trauma-tragic mode.

'The problem of witnessing trauma as a professional is learning the difficult task of speaking of trauma in the terms offered by the survivor' (Caruth 1996: 117). Live performance would seem to offer a solution as it is a medium that we cannot help but connect to on a human, bodily level. If we return, for a moment, to Shepherd's notion of 'kinaesthetic empathy', we can begin to stitch together the ways in which the theatre may be able to explore, attempt to bear witness to and present a certain type of experience of trauma. Each of the performances explored in this chapter uses differing performance mechanisms which stimulate a visceral, corporeal experience of the live event; each performance is able to stimulate an embodied reaction within the audience. This reaction is caused by the performances' ability to excite the visceral-imaginary: the stage-work, echoing the dream-work, produces a sense of reality through its capacity to short-circuit the audience's ability to see the event as theatre, even if only for a moment. Furthermore, if this experience is set up within a framework which places the audience in a situation of responsibility and complicity with the action, the bodily experience of that audience will be doubly powerful.

As I cited in Chapter 2, Artaud, according to Derrida, has stated that theatre must 'restore "existence" and "flesh"' (Derrida 1978: 232). Although Derrida argues this is impossible, the productions discussed here are making attempts to bring trauma into existence, to give it flesh through the phenomenological experience of it. I have addressed three different sorts of performance and analysed various aspects of them to propose that through dramaturgical structures, scenographic systems and uncanny echoes, and the phenomenology of bodies, performance (especially in the trauma-tragic mode) can create for its audience presence-in-trauma effects. Our kinaesthetic connection to the performers/performance generates the sensation of being present in the trauma through its representation, through performance. In this respect the performances analysed here are very clearly operating within the trauma-tragic mode I am proposing: they are about the trauma(tic).

6
Another view

I have so far focused upon explorations and analyses of formal, 'staged' performance events; through two case studies, this last chapter pulls the arguments out into what we might think of as social performance and then back to the stage, though to address the process of being on stage rather than analysing the performance event. The first argument proposes that there exist moments of socially engaged – which is to say widely circulated – instances of trauma which are created and sustained through theatrical means. This case study moves away from theatre events to analyse theatricality/performativity in relation to photos from Abu Ghraib prison, published in 2004. The second section focuses back on the theatre event but through the specific lens of the 'traumatic' phenomena of corpsing and drying. This part proposes that these phenomena might not only unravel the performance event for both audience and performers but also impact, repeatedly and violently, on the performers themselves in an uncanny echoing of trauma-symptoms. Both parts of this chapter address what we might think of as an economy of trauma which can be identified in the structures and mechanisms of theatre and performance.

Theatre as trauma

To suspend one's disbelief entirely at the theatre is, perhaps, impossible, although this is potentially a question of time. An audience member might, for example, be drawn in and captured by the stage image 'entirely' for a nanosecond. The notion of suspension of disbelief came from Samuel Taylor Coleridge's autobiography *Biographia Literaria* in which he calls for a 'willing suspension of disbelief' which constitutes 'poetic faith' (Coleridge 1817: online). The 'willing' is important and problematic. As a phrase it could mean that it requires will on the part of the spectator if they are to move past disbelief. It also suggests, importantly, that an audience might always already be predisposed to seduction by and into the fiction (perhaps searching for an experience of purgation or catharsis). An audience may empathize and/or sympathize with a character's plight; they may even be so moved by the action as to show physical signs of an emotional attachment, such as crying when Lear 'howl, howl, howl[s]' in *King Lear* or when Lyra is torn from Pantalaimon in *His Dark Materials*. An audience may embody the physical impact of the truncheon crashing into flesh in *BR.#04* because the phenomeno-kinaesthetic impact of the scene is experienced physically and immediately through the body. However – and this is the problematic element – to ignore completely the fiction of what one is witnessing, to be wholly captured by a performance for the entirety of the performance (let us assume it is longer than a nanosecond), is, no matter how willing the spectator, potentially impossible. Western audiences, on the whole, will enter the theatre space aware, to varying degrees, of the conventions and limitations of the theatre or performance event. The audience knows that Lear's eyes will not really be ripped out and understand that no matter how visceral the experience of witnessing the beating in *BR#04*, the actor being beaten will not die from the enacted wounding.

There are, of course, notable exceptions to this in Performance/ Live Art history. Marina Abramovic's *Rhythm 5* (1974) in which she would have died of asphyxia were it not for the fast thinking and action of a doctor in the audience, and *Rhythm 0* (1974) in which she might have been shot are obvious examples, but they are the exception rather than the rule. Indeed, even the 'excessive performances' (Heathfield 2004: 9) of Franko B's blood-works operate within very specific and defined codes and precautions surrounding his health and safety. These codes are identifiable even if one is not familiar with the work. Medical catheters and tape signify a sterile and controlled condition under which the performances are seemingly regulated: the sense of control is identifiable if perhaps not obvious.

At best, and it is a positive experience, the closest most (Western) audiences will come to entirely suspending their disbelief is during scenes like the beating in *BR#04*, scenes which can induce a mimetic shimmer which, as I suggested in Chapter 3, causes the audience to stumble into undecidability. This shimmer is not, however, the same as a willing suspension of disbelief, rather it is a reaction to the precise operation of the theatrical mechanisms employed at such a moment: the shimmering is a result of being overloaded by the clashing of the signifiers which are put into play. Furthermore, the movement of the mimesis into and out of focus is a temporary experience caused by a performative *punctum*. As I suggested in the previous chapter, in such moments there is an eruption of Barish's 'ontological queasiness' (1981: 3) where the spectator/witness/ audience member is set into a position of uncertainty regarding their position in the event and their desire to be part of it.[1] In the discussion of Abu Ghraib images that follows, I suggest that this ontological queasiness is a specific performative disruption which can be used to describe a moment in which 'not wanting to be there' is superseded by the threat of death in being there. That is to say, not wanting to be there is an understatement in the 'theatrical' context I am about to discuss.

A man, judging by his height and stature, is standing on a small, apparently unstable box which is barely wide enough to accommodate both his feet. His body is clothed in a dirty brown garment which resembles a sheet with a hole cut at its centre, from which the head protrudes. His head and face are covered by a black hood which rises to a point, and seems to be deliberately signifying many other 'hoods', both garments and people, which circulate in our contemporary fields of reference – from the Ku Klux Klan to 'hoodies'[2] to execution hoods depicted in so many films. The man is standing cruciform: arms outstretched, palms facing out, his thumbs pointing skyward. Wires snake from each of his fingers, twisting out to the wall behind him.

At least two photographs are taken of this man, from different angles and, judging from the difference in the elevation of his arms, at different times. There were numerous other images put into circulation at the same time as this one, but it was the photograph of this hooded figure which was to become 'the lead icon', as Adrian Kear puts it, of the released images (2005: 114). Žižek comments on the theatrical nature of the images, stating that when he first saw the 'ridiculously theatrical pose' of the hooded, electrode-laden prisoner, he thought it was 'a shot from the latest performance-art show', and goes on to say that the poses and costumes of the prisoners (in all the photos) 'suggest a theatrical staging, a kind of *tableaux vivant*' which is reminiscent of much Performance Art (2008: 146). All of the photographs released are, to varying degrees, theatrical in nature and as such, while I will make reference to the specifics of some images, my arguments refer to a generalized sense of the collected content of the photographs.

The emerging argument here is that it is precisely the theatricality of the scenes which produces their trauma. It is important and productive here to highlight that 'theatricality' is not intended to map precisely on to the idea of fiction. For example, we might say, in the context of what happened in Abu Ghraib, that to be personally theatricalized by an enemy is to be reduced to a resource, a sort of fiction if you like, rather than the truth of one's own being. But the experience of that reduction is of course painfully, viscerally real. Hussein Mutar, one of the people imprisoned in Abu Ghraib, highlighted this paradox when he testified that the American soldiers 'were torturing us as though it were theatre for them' (BBC 2005: online).[3] Mutar's use of 'theatre' seems to indicate a meaning of entertainment rather than fiction, yet this objectification of the prisoner as a figure of entertainment is precisely to fracture the reality of their being which is a traumatic reality. The soldiers demonstrated their seemingly absolute power by using captives as playthings, as props in a gratuitous theatre of trauma.

The photographs indicate that theatrical disruption of time was used in constructing the staged images. This in turn suggests that while the soldiers could have potentially been aware of the 'fiction' of the theatrical scene, the prisoners are constantly under the illusion of a reality of torture, informed by a cultural knowledge of torture and a phenomenological or embodied knowledge of pain. The trauma contained within these constructed performances comes in the expectation of physical torture which creates, for the prisoners, a psychological schism. This traumatic disturbance is further compounded by the fact that in making the prisoners aware of the posed nature of the images (the prisoners are, I contend, in the main, aware of the cameras) a traumatic, performative *mise en abyme* comes to be constructed: the events of the posed images are rehearsals for, or representations of, 'real' torture and are, at the same time, torture themselves.

An audience member who purchases a ticket and goes to the theatre of their own volition might legitimately be assumed to understand, to a certain degree at least, the conventions of theatrical representation. However, in the context, or 'frame' to use Erving Goffman's term (cf. Goffman 1986), of Abu Ghraib it is unlikely that the rules of this particular theatrical game are known to the prisoners. Given the power relations in operation, the particulars of the physical space and the timeframe in which the events happened, we can assume with some degree of certainty that, for the prisoners, there was no clear understanding of the events as play: while Mutar may have recognized that the guards were entertained by the events, as if at the theatre, the prisoners' position within that entertainment holds no sense of playfulness for those prisoners. Entry into the performances depicted in the Abu Ghraib photos might be thought of as akin to stumbling into a production in which the spectators' position as audience is confused with a position as participant. The stumbling entrance is not into a performance that is instantly recognizable as representation, but rather into a production of such commitment, verve, design and accomplishment that the theatrical artifice is virtually indistinguishable from 'real' life. Thus another undecidable circulation between knowing and not knowing the events as theatrical comes to be constituted.

The evident orchestration of the bodies depicted in the images suggests a certain level of planning and an articulation of ideas before the flash has popped; it would seem that a verbal rehearsal of the image has taken place, however fleetingly, in advance of the creation of the image. There is an overt, if perhaps not intended, theatricality about the Abu Ghraib images; all contain elements of representation and artifice – artifice which is admittedly only known for certain to some of those involved, but artifice nonetheless. It is precisely this aspect that makes the staging of these scenes so deeply unsettling to the third-hand viewer and so troublingly traumatic for the pictured victims. Although the prisoners may know they are being posed for photographs, a point I will develop below, that can be seen to be part of the theatrical mechanism producing the trauma. While it might only be posing for a photograph in the first instance, that might very well be a rehearsal for 'the real thing' in the second; and so the *mise en abyme* figure I suggested above, and shall develop below, comes into circulation.

There is a sense in which the soldiers' 'repertoire of improvisations', Bourdieu's *habitus*, is natural to the 'field of practice' that Abu Ghraib constitutes and more widely to the one the soldiers operate within on a daily basis.[4] The soldiers have acquired a 'language' through a certain type of acculturation via their training (formal and, perhaps more importantly, informal), and the culture of expectation to participate which might be seen to exist both within American culture in general (I am thinking here of sporting activities and fraternity houses)[5] and within the military in particular, which enables them to function 'productively' within this economy. Within Western culture there is a particular type of *habitus* available to all through the general development of society and the politico-legal frames within which we operate. However, military training radically alters this frame of reference, not only by providing military personnel with a very particular *habitus*, but also by creating a mobile field of practice. The highly formal, organized structures of teamwork and hierarchy within which the military operates become constant fields of practice which interact naturally with the *habitus* acculturated through training. So while Abu Ghraib presents a very specific setting, one with a particular history of torture, which is layered upon the existing field of practice and *habitus* of the soldiers, it is not simply the specifics of that setting which coincide with their *habitus* to cause the events. What is so disturbing about this is that it suggests that far from being 'a few bad apples' that carried out these events, as former President George W. Bush put it in

2004, this type of activity is a mode of operation to which soldiers (particularly American soldiers) might be seen to be predisposed through training and acculturation within the specifics of the current traumatized structure of feeling. This performance-led, Bourdieudian model signals implications that are wider than just what happened at Abu Ghraib: the analysis suggests that the soldiers' *habitus*, and the field of practice within which it operates and which they take with them, will enable the soldier to make what we might call a natural turn to this type of performance of trauma. By this I mean that the soldiers can be seen to be equipped to perform such cruelties with minimal prompting because of the cultural context within which their *habitus* is developed and the field of practice in which it operates. The prisoners, on the other hand, have to adapt what we might call their base-*habitus* to the new specifics of the Abu Ghraib field.

The prisoners encounter this setting without the natural or trained *habitus* necessary to cope with the situation. The prisoners' ability to present themselves 'appropriately', their capacity to adopt the correct 'face', to turn to Goffman's term (cf. Goffman 1967: 5–15), is gained through the acculturation which might be seen to happen from the moment of first incarceration. Bourdieu insists that *habitus* is generally established in early life: as Swartz glosses, *habitus* is the result of 'early socialization experiences in which external structures are internalized' (1997: 103). Importantly, however, Bourdieu caveats that *habitus* develops and adapts with each new encounter and new situation. So, taking *habitus* within Bourdieu's own terms, while early socialization experiences are evidently part of what we might term the Abu Ghraib *habitus*, it is the specifics of the context which create new acculturation experiences and so the *habitus* necessarily has to 'improvise' within that given context. Or, to put it another way, the existing structures of the *habitus* form part of the improvisatory ability of those in the Abu Ghraib performances but also enable the actors to reform the *habitus* in order that they perform 'properly' within the new field. Randal Johnson, glossing Bourdieu, suggests that in order:

> to enter a field (the philosophical field, the scientific field, etc.), to play the game, one must possess the *habitus*

which predisposes one to enter that field, that game, and not another. One must also possess at least the minimum amount of knowledge, or skill, or 'talent' to be accepted as a legitimate player.

(Johnson in Bourdieu 1993: 8)

The resonance of performance structures is clearly identifiable: the soldiers are seriously and skilfully performing their roles as prison guards and tormentors, and the prisoners, because of the seriousness with which the guards approach that performance, or 'impression', are similarly performing their subservient roles with due diligence.[6] So not only are the prisoner-observers 'tak[ing] seriously the impression[s] that [are] fostered before them' (Goffman 1990: 28), but the consequences of these performances are also to be taken seriously given the particular context.

This play of seriousness was extended to third-level observers (soldiers and prisoners being first and second) in the press publication of the images in April 2004. The images might be thought to circulate and operate within an economy of theatricalities in which they function differently, and are open to view as theatrical at different levels, depending upon which audience one is reading them 'through'. In their global publication the images became openly consumable, no longer confined to the corridors of the prison and the private imaging devices of the soldiers but available to scrutiny and dissemination. Through this, the humiliation is extended indefinitely.

The majority of the photos depict soldiers who acknowledge the taking of the image, wide smiles and thumbs-up or pointing in an echo of the disturbing social performance of what has become known as 'happy slapping' which was prevalent in the media at the same time.[7] It is this acknowledgement of the camera/photographer, and hence an acknowledgement of the object of the image at a later point, which begins to signal the 'staginess' of the scene. Connected to this notion, Kear has argued that despite the trophy nature of the images, 'souvenirs of the "tour of duty" in Iraq', the quantity and pervasiveness of the photographs suggests 'a more orchestrated use of the camera as an integral element in the scenes they depicted' (2005: 115). The integral nature of the camera is, I believe, two-fold: it functions both as an audience and as an extra tool for humiliating the prisoners. I will explore both aspects in turn.

The camera acts as an audience which is explicitly acknowledged and openly referenced. Kear suggests that as more and more images flooded the media it became increasingly apparent that the scenes they depicted were 'self-evidently staged' (2005: 115) rather than snapshots of actual/real – which is to say physical or violent – torture. Take for example the image of the prisoner forced to stand on a box, arms outstretched with electrodes attached to his fingers but not to a power source. The 'torture' is staged in that no electrocution has taken place, nor will it if the wires stay disconnected. The trauma of this torture lies in the expectation of pain and violence, an expectation which is established through theatrical techniques. The stage is set, so to speak, but the expected action has not been seen through. The action is in fact intended to be left as a physical 'what if': the staging of the images signifies an intention towards violent torture but does not actually carry that intention through to action. But, of course, it could still happen, thus leaving the prisoner to wonder *what if* they do it 'for real' next time.

This *what if*, or 'shimmer', thinking back to Chapter 3, is vitally important in understanding the traumatic impact of this theatricalized event. By placing the prisoners into this shimmering uncertainty, the soldiers are able deliberately to ratchet up the seriousness of the play: the cruelty of the event is compounded by the fact that the act of posing is *torture as play*. The excessive nature of the event, recalling discussions of excessive performance in Chapters 3 and 5, is made present to the third-hand viewer precisely because with close reading they can identify the movement between real and representational torture, and recognize the gratuitous nature of that torture. The theatricalized, *mise en abyme* torture has no function – it is simply for play and the degradation of the prisoner.[8]

The presence of the camera, returning to the two-fold integral nature of it, adds another layer of humiliation and theatricality to the proceedings: it is an extension of the soldier-audience as it captures the event to film or microchip and through this enables a continuation of spectatorship outside the context of the original event. The camera is a prop in front of which people perform and pose in the knowledge that they are under a distributable form of observation: the soldiers are engaged in precisely this type of posing – thumbs-up and grinning smiles are the staple attitudes of the majority of those pictured. Those prisoners who are not blindfolded or hooded are obviously aware of the camera's presence and it is likely that those whose sight has been removed are equally attuned to the clicking cameras, at least haptically.[9] However, the knowledge of the camera's presence can only serve to heighten the sense of exposure and add to the undecidable quality of the event. While the soldiers stare directly into the camera, playing to it, the prisoners, by contrast, never seem to turn their eyes toward the lens. Furthermore, the removal of sight by blindfolding or hooding effectively blinds them to the 'playfulness' with which the soldiers continue to approach the event.

Bruce Wilshire argues that 'we grasp what actually is only after we have imagined what it might be' (Wilshire 1982: 5). The prisoners are perpetually stuck in the 'might be' even if they come to realize that the event constructed for the photograph is 'make-believe'. Amelia Jones usefully proposes 'not-real' and 'not-fake' as alternatives to the use of 'real' and 'fake' (and, potentially, then, mimesis and representation), and the problematic slippages associated in those terms (cf. Jones 2006: 71–78). We might profitably think of the prisoners in these events being stuck in Wilshire's 'might be' through a focus on the 'not-fake' nature of the staged event. The fact that the prisoners are 'blinded' removes the possibility of their receiving the torture as 'play', even if they had recognized it as 'not-real' up to that point. Once the blindfold or hood is placed on the prisoner, the situation is rendered 'not-fake' for them; or, at least, an undecidable circulation between knowing and not knowing if the torture will become 'real' sets in. This creates a presence-in-torture effect which is itself a trauma for, as Edwin Henri astutely noted, it is not necessarily the infliction of physical pain which is the worst aspect of torture:

> waiting for a flogging sentence is exquisite psychological torture [...] knowledge of a violent death, the anticipation of it, the waiting for it [...] is torture in a very real sense.
> (Henri 1966: 146)

Henri is here discussing the anticipation and fear one feels in waiting for a torture the victim knows to be coming. In the case of the Abu Ghraib prisoners, the fear is intensified by not knowing for sure, by the undecidability of the theatrical moment. The images depict the performance of torture, the artifice of it, rather than the 'real thing'; although, of course, the performance of this not-real torture is in fact torture itself. It is this shimmering uncertainty which is central to the trauma of these events and that is stimulated through theatricalized action. The theatrical nature of the event is constituted differently within the economy of theatricality proposed above: for the soldiers, the theatricality is part of the excessive, 'fictional' play they are participating in; for the prisoners, the theatricality and shimmering uncertainty of the continuation of the event as theatre is precisely what makes the event traumatic.

For the prisoners involved in these scenes the not-fakeness takes over, overloading and then short-circuiting the capacity for the unknowing (and unsuspecting) prisoner-as-audience-member to rationalize the event as theatricalized, albeit diabolical, fiction. These theatre events employ theatricality to undo or unmake themselves as theatre. Using costume, set, rehearsal, scripts, lighting, actors, directors, stagehands, extras and (crucially) timing to devastating effect, this theatre is a theatre of trauma. The soldiers are playing, acting out their roles, while the captives, despite their convincing performances, are devoid of the knowledge of the theatricality of the situation and so are made present in a trauma-event.

These social performances have been constructed in much the same way as a stage image is built by the actors and director of an aesthetic performance. The smirking grins, overenthusiastic pointing, and the 'thumbs-up' are clear poses and, as Kear points out, the photographs' 'intended focus was the pleasure the young soldiers took in "posing" for them; the presence of the prisoners in contrast seemed to serve as a mere backdrop for their composition' (2005: 115). These composed images are reminiscent of the staged photographs of theatre productions found in foyers and programmes throughout the world: they collapse the digetic event, the moment of staging and the representation of that moment of staging into one image. This posed nature of the images heightens the sense of diabolical play. The soldiers are playing at torture, staging it. They are 'acting up' to the camera by 'acting out' their trauma theatrics. Thus the image functions not only to flatten the tiers of representation in operation here but further connects the event to mechanisms of theatre and representation. The not-fake nature of the trauma of these staged events sits in constant tension with the not-real nature of what is depicted. The play of not-real not-fake is, depending upon one's position in the economy of theatricality, what defines the impact of the event upon the body: the not-fake and the what-if are central to the prisoners' experience of the event, whereas the not-real, 'fraternity prank' (Limbaugh ctd in Warner 2004: 74) nature is central to the soldiers' understandings. The real disturbance held within these images for the prisoners and third-hand photograph viewers is contained within the intensifying *mise en abyme* figure I proffered above. For the prisoners it is precisely not knowing for sure that they are the subject of 'fictional' play that creates these events as traumatic performances. For the viewer of the photograph, the *punctum* of the images is contained in the recognition of the not-realness of the image and hence understanding of the event as functionless. At once the depicted event enters into a mimetic shimmer in which the viewer sees the event as diabolical fraternity prank theatre and as the torture it depicts. This economy of theatricality, then, has at its centre the interplay between the two realms of not-fake and not-real. It is this interplay that creates the trauma-event, and it is an interplay which has theatrics at its heart.

Theatre traumas

While the last section focused on traumas in the social realm that were theatrically done, so to speak, the next section turns to address trauma that similarly operates within the economy of theatricality suggested above but which is specific to the conditions of theatre: corpsing/drying, moments in which an actor can be seen to experience a 'failure' of self which mirrors the catastrophic collapse of self experienced in trauma events.

In October 2002 I directed a production of Christina Reid's *Did You Hear the One About the Irishman?* at Warwick Arts Centre. About five days before we were due to open, our rehearsals were rudely interrupted by an explosion of what Nicholas Ridout has described as laughter that 'bring[s] hands to mouths and force[s] orifices closed against the threat of outburst' (Ridout 2006: 130). It is laughter that is 'not improper on the grand political scale, but improper in the more local sense of being unwanted, untimely and in the wrong place' (Ridout 2006: 129). This is a laughter which is constantly put under conditions of suspension and containment, but which invariably bursts through its confinement. Indeed, the harder suppression is attempted, the greater the chance of failing to do so. In the rehearsal room the actors lost 'it': their characters, their focus, their concentration and that elusive thing, 'presence'.

This moment of laughter collapsed productivity; nothing happened save the laughing. In Ridout's terms this laughter 'destroyed' the rehearsal by 'making a particular moment in a scene the unavoidable occasion for collective giggling' (2006: 131). The corpsing became a repetitive incident which tore apart the fabric of the rehearsed scene at the same moment each time. Typical of much anecdotal evidence of corpsing, the actress Dora Bryan iterates a similar point about the repetitive nature of corpsing:

> Every night after [the first incident of corpsing] it took all the energy and discipline I could muster not to break into laughter again when we reached that same scene.
>
> (Bryan 2005: 53)

This corpsing refers to an oral emanation and physical convulsion which erupts to fracture the prescribed action and so disrupts both the diegetic world and the contract of representation. Corpsing, then, is distinct from laughter which is theatrically done, such as that in *Blasted* discussed in the previous chapter: it is not the sign of laughter but the thing itself. However, there is another peculiar theatrical schism which, while not uncommonly associated with corpsing, is usually given a separate term: 'drying'.[10] Referring to the moment in which an actor forgets their next line of speech, in drying the actor is 'cut adrift from the play [...] dumped out of the textual fabric [which might include action] of the play' (Ridout 2006: 133).

I am not a particularly natural actor and I have had the misfortune to dry spectacularly on a number of occasions. The last (and perhaps most distressing) time was during a production of The Last Days of Mankind *in 2003 (dir. Zoe Waterman). The production required the entire cast, save one, to play multiple parts and to be on stage for the three and a half hours of the piece. I had four characters to play and a number of long speeches to deliver as part of two of those roles. Throughout the rehearsal period it became apparent that I was going to struggle to pull off any kind of believability, let alone a seminal acting display. Not only that but every time I came to certain sections of the piece I simply dried up, becoming frozen in silence, not able to get my lines out, or at best sometimes managing a stumbling hesitation, a sort of bad, actorly paraphrasing. This repetitious failure was so regular that it became self-perpetuating: the more I concentrated on not drying the more I tended to do so; the more I tried to forget the previous gaffs the more I would feel the shudder of remembering them when the lines came around. This drying followed a pattern very similar to that of the corpsing described above: it happened at particular moments in the play each evening, no matter how hard I tried to prevent it. I was caught by 'the Fear', as Anthony Sher has described his own experiences of drying (cf. Sher 2005: 26–27 and passim; and Sher, 1985: passim).[11] I began to fear, as did the rest of the cast, these impending scenes and they constantly circulated in my mind throughout the time I was in the play. Even now, the memory is both embarrassing and returns readily if I even so much as contemplate an audition notice.*

This experience is, of course, widely recognized in the theatre world; drying is not just a problem for the amateur enthusiast. Ian Holm, who had an extreme experience of drying which led him almost to totally abandon stage acting and which manifested itself in something approaching a nervous breakdown, has suggested that drying:

is something which all actors carry around with them, even if they never experience it directly. It can attack the

good, the bad and the moderate. It is both a specific and
a generalized condition, seeming to arise out of singular,
individual circumstances, yet afflicting those it assaults
with an indiscriminate, all-too-familiar carelessness.

(Holm 2004: 123)

While 'drying' and 'corpsing' are often discussed as separate
phenomena, it is productive in the context of the current discussion to bracket them within one term, to which end I am going
to use *failing* from here on. I suggest this amalgamation as both
terms share similarities in their disruption to the live event: both
cause it to fail in various ways. As I will develop, both laughing
and forgetting lines are moments in which the presentation the
performer is making is dislodged and, to return to Goffman, the
line the performer is taking or pursuing is no longer aligned with
the face in which they find themselves. This disjuncture sets the
performer into a schismatic circulation between three versions
of 'self': the moment of failing produces a traumatic schism in
which there is constant movement between what we might call
character-self, actor/professional-self and 'real'/personal-self.

While it is not the main goal of this chapter to determine
why theatrical failing happens, it occurs to me that there is one
possible avenue of exploration on this matter which relates to
my developing argument on the separation of selves caused in
failing. My contention is that the irruption of failure into the
process of playing a role might be properly thought of as an act
of subversion on the part of the unconscious. Thus, it will be
productive to turn briefly to a (Freudian) psychoanalytic reading
of this type of failing in order to postulate a possible cause for
this phenomenon.

Freud argued that throughout life we strive towards the 'resto-
ration' of the 'prior state' of calm before birth (Freud 2003a: 97
and cf. 83–102). In other words, he contends, 'the goal of all life
is death' (2003a: 78). He usefully clarifies that this can be at least
partially achieved in life in his discussion of 'the state that ensues
upon full sexual gratification' which he believes to be 'similar to
dying' (2003a: 137). To achieve this goal, the 'death drive' (also
referred to as *Thanatos*, though not by Freud) is 'charged with
the task of causing animate organisms to revert to an inanimate

state' (2003a: 130). The sexual or life drive, *Eros*, by contrast has
the goal of 'maximizing the complexity of life' (2003a: 131). The
idea of returning to a state of calm can be seen to correspond, in
the context of theatrical failings, to the actors striving to be 'in
character': the point at which they might be seen to be sublimely
'there' and to have left themselves 'behind'. The actor might be
seen to seek *Thanatos*, to relax and become calm, in order to play
another properly: in moving into character the actor might for
a moment find *Thanatos*, only to be violently pulled back to an
awareness of never being left alone. Thus there is an eruption of
Eros into the moment of beautiful placidity in being in character.

The experience of anxiety which is narrated in so many
theatrical anecdotes on failing is precisely to do with the realization that one cannot relax. It is this paradoxical split between a
desire for *Thanatos* and the recognition of its impossibility in the
process of 'being' someone else on stage which might be seen
to cause the failing. Being in role, then, might be seen to correspond with *Thanatos* because it is a transcendent space in which
one can become at rest by being somewhere/someone else and
so for a moment away from your troubles. Being in role can be
figured as a home away from home; however, the unconscious
might be seen to turn in on or subvert itself by making the actor
aware of the unhomely nature of this home away from home.

It is with the rise of the theatrical anecdote (especially prevalent in the contemporary cultural moment I am addressing) that
the phenomenon of theatrical failing has become foregrounded
and articulated as a somehow traumatic experience. The theatre
of countless actors' biographies is constructed as at once excit-
ing and glamorous and, at the same time, psychically risky. The
theatre currently being depicted, *contra* the historical construction of acting as a heroic enterprise and a civilizing process
by figures such as Henry Irving, is one in which the actor is
always in danger of losing themselves. It is seemingly a profes-
sion in which one can become fundamentally traumatized by
the experience of doing one's job.[12] Many accounts of theatrical failing are written precisely within the trauma-tragic mode:
they attempt to articulate (rather than explain or ameliorate)
the experience of what I will argue is a fundamental, traumatic
breach of self.

What is being expressed within these types of narratives is an account of the actor as an isolated individual: in the moment of failure the actor finds themselves alone onstage without anyone to be. It is because being on stage is now perceived to be, in a sense, a place where people feel more exposed, more individualized, more atomized that these stories are being told. This foregrounding of the traumatic, isolating experience of actorly failure can be seen to rhyme quite precisely with my arguments on the flattened, individualized existence of contemporary society made in Chapter 2. The collapse of character-self in the moment of failure corresponds to the collapse of self through the flattening of society in the current, traumatized structure of feeling. One might thus see a possible cultural compensation for this in the notion of celebrity, and everybody believing in the possibility of becoming a celebrity. In 'serious' acting (as opposed to the perceived frivolity of playing/being a celebrity) there exists the possibility of becoming traumatically between selves. In the contract of celebrity the tripartite selves set out above are homologized, pressed very tightly into one self in which there is indistinguishable difference between each. This pressing together can be seen to function as a protection from the traumatic split possible in failing while pretending to be someone else.

Goffman's short essay 'On Face-Work', in *Interaction Ritual* (1967), in which he outlines his model of 'line' and 'face', presents a productive frame through which to continue the discussion of failing in this context. Line and face are central elements in all social interaction and they constitute formal elements of everyday performances (of self) which Goffman discusses in *The Presentation of Self in Everyday Life* (1956). In 'On Face-Work', Goffman suggests that in each instance of 'social encounter' we present to those with whom we are in contact a certain 'line'. The line, according to Goffman, is a pattern of 'verbal' and (importantly in the context of theatre and performance) 'nonverbal' acts by which a person 'expresses [their] view of the situation and through this [their] evaluation of the participants, especially [themselves]' and it is important to note that we will all, always, take a line with or without intention (Goffman 1967: 5). Within these encounters each person claims for themselves a 'positive social value', a 'face', by taking the particular line they do:

> Face is an image of self delineated in terms of approved
> social attributes – albeit an image that others may share, as
> when a person makes a good showing for his [sic] profes-
> sion or religion by making a good showing for himself.
>
> (Goffman 1967: 5)

Goffman goes on to discuss how social interactions are governed
by rules which are specific to the given circumstances of the
group and situation. Furthermore, within each of these contacts
a person will cathect the face they are 'in'; a person's feelings
'become attached to it'. Moreover, rules of 'self-respect' and
'considerateness' ensure that persons usually conduct themselves
so that their face and the face of others is maintained. In what we
might think of as an ecology of face, a productive social encounter is governed by the participants' ability to maintain their face
without detriment to the face of others and so a 'working' mutual
acceptance becomes a 'basic structural feature of interaction,
especially the interaction of face-to-face talk' (Goffman 1967:
6–11).

However, in the moment of failing, this ecology is corrupted
as one or more actors are no longer able to abide by the rules of
the encounter. The actor who fails in this way might be said to
have become 'out of face':

> A person is said to be *out of face* when he [sic] participates
> in a contact with others without having ready a line of the
> kind participants in such situations are expected to take.
> [...]
> When a person is [...] out of face, expressive events
> are being contributed to the encounter which cannot be
> readily woven into the expressive fabric of the occasion.
>
> (Goffman 1967: 8; emphasis is original)

In failing, the actor is unable to sustain the line they are taking
as they cannot stay in face and so, linking Bourdieu back in here,
the performer is no longer able to access their *habitus*. In an
interesting echo of the language of both trauma theorists and of
Holm's and Sher's discussions of drying and 'the Fear' respec-
tively, Goffman states that a person who is out of face 'is likely

to feel ashamed and inferior', and that because a person becomes emotionally attached to the face they present they may, in falling out of that face, 'falter, collapse, and crumble' in both manner and bearing (Goffman 1967: 8). The similarity between accounts of failing and trauma symptoms is, however, more than just in the language of description. Each follows a very similar structure of repetition. Anthony Sher has described the way in which there is always an 'aftershock' post-fail, or even post-near-fail, which results in irrational panic and in him hearing 'babbling voices' which:

> started testing out lines that were coming up [...] another saying I can't take this. In between scenes, I had to go into backstage corners, grimacing, flicking my head, trying to disperse the racket in my head.
>
> (Sher 2005: 26)

Sher discusses these experiences like a traumatic occurrence, a returning, uncontrollable psychic wound which 'takes up residence' and disrupts his ability to function properly as 'the Fear descends, terrorises, and goes. The show finishes, life goes back to normal. And then I start work the next night knowing I've probably got an appointment with The Fear again' (2005: 26). This structure of repetition, which other actors discuss and which Ridout also notes, very closely mirrors the repetitive structure of trauma-symptoms noted in Chapter 1.

Corpsing, according to Ridout:

> annihilates the represented being, leaving the performer alone on stage, helpless, with nothing to fall back on, nothing to do, no one to be. The actor does not 'die' himself, but rather commits an act upon the illusionary character: 'corpsing' it.
>
> (Ridout 2006: 134–135)

Here, Ridout seems to be suggesting that the actor that corpses exposes 'himself', by which Ridout means the actor's personal face, in the destruction of the character. He proposes that corpsing 'might have something to do with the unwanted irruption of the real amid the unreality of the stage fiction' and the actor who corpses 'appear[s] as just himself [sic], not the character he is trying to present' (133). In the context I am discussing here, this seems to me too narrow a reading of the exposure of the relationship between character and actor which happens in the moment of failing.

Failing makes it impossible to keep in play the circulation of selves that an actor who plays a character or persona juggles. By this I mean that they are unable to balance the 'use' of elements of real or private-self, professional or actor-self, and character-self. In the moment of failing, each of these selves collapses and denies the actor access to them; thus the actor becomes caught in a dead space between these selves and is triply out of face. As the actor becomes dislocated from all the selves they usually perform they have, in a more severe way than Ridout suggests, 'no one to be' because they have no access to the face(s) they need to present.

This public, tripartite collapse of face is particular to the mechanisms of theatre presentation and of playing a character. Because of the conscious way in which an actor must embody and represent another person, adding the third 'self', their private and professional selves must, to varying degrees, effectively be put under erasure by this third self for the duration of the performance. However, the relationship is further compli- cated by Schechner's notion that a character is 'not-not-self' which intimates that while character is not-self it is also always bound inescapably to self (cf. Schechner 1985: 112) An actor would not be able to perform the roles they do without recourse to the experiences their other selves have had.[13] (And of course their real selves are always apparent.) Ian Holm, discussing his own experiences, though the sentiment is mirrored in other biog- raphies, claims that:

> [a]ctors don't *like* to work. They *need* to work. And that's because the instrument they use for acting is themselves, so that 'work' and 'self' are, in the end, indivisible. Without acting, actors do not exist.
>
> (Holm 2004: 136)

Herein lies the crux of my argument: when an actor fails there is a flattening or fracturing of the theatrically made self, which mirrors the catastrophic collapse of self experienced in trauma events.

Holm's breakdown and the fear that Sher experiences which led him to seek medical attention are extreme examples of the rupture experienced in failing. Nevertheless, they are part of a continuum of theatrically made traumas which are made possible by entering into the creative act of adding one's selves to another in playing a character. This type of failing, then, seems to be a theatre, as opposed to, say, Performance Art, trauma. The act of acting enforces integration, and at the same time suppression, of professional and personal selves into the creation of character-self which can in turn be collapsed, and so collapses the 'conglomerate self', by the specific conditions and pressures of being on stage.[14]

Theatricalized trauma

Failing is for the most part a minute trauma in comparison to those inflicted on the prisoners of Abu Ghraib. However, just as failing is a trauma which is theatrically made (and theatre specific), the traumas of torture depicted in the many images to come out of the Iraqi prison are equally 'theatrically done'. These two very different types of theatricalized trauma sit at very different ends of a continuum, but on the same continuum nonetheless, that of theatrically made traumatic experience. Similarly, while these two types of theatre trauma are obviously not aesthetic trauma-tragedies in which the point of the performance is to address trauma for a paying audience, they do, however, sit within the realm of social trauma-tragedy which constitutes part of the trauma-tragic loop I proposed in Chapter 2.[15] These theatrically made trauma-tragedies are, likewise, part of our contemporary structure of feeling which is bound up in the traumatic. The trauma depicted in the Abu Ghraib images is explicit, although identifying the theatricality of it requires a slightly deeper reading. The parallel between theatrical failing and contemporary trauma theory is a reading I propose in light of the identifiable current cultural moment in which this book is very much rooted. Both parts of this chapter have addressed an economy of trauma which is identifiable in the structures and mechanisms of theatre and performance. Those mechanisms, and their traumatic possibilities, are identifiable throughout theatre history. However, the economy in which they are discussed here is particularly 'of the moment': a moment in which the emergent structure of feeling is a traumatic or traumatized one and in which an identifiable trope in performance practice is trauma-tragic.

Conclusion: trauma-tragedy and the contemporary moment

Discussing her experience of Societas Raffaello Sanzio's *Genesi: from the museum of sleep* (1999), Helena Grehan writes:

> I got to a point of feeling radically unsettled, a point at which I was driven to reassess my understandings of both the power of theatre and the function of spectatorship in the context of a fraught, media-saturated world.
>
> (Grehan 2009: 3)

Grehan goes on to contend that it is the 'sense of an experience, of excitement, of identification or disruption' which keeps audiences returning to the theatre (3). Here, she is pointing towards a particular type of theatrical experience that is driven by phenomena which impact upon the audience throughout a piece and which return to them again and again, like the intrusive hallucinations of trauma-symptoms, once they have left the performance. It is that element of (the) performance which opens up a schism in our flattened experience of the fraught, media-saturated world to evoke a sense of presence. This, I have been suggesting, offers or stimulates a cathected response to the world around us which is not possible in other forms of art. The trauma-tragic experience – and it need only be one moment in a performance – lifts us from, or pushes us towards, reconsidering our positions within what Fredric Jameson describes as the contemporary metastasis of the psyche (ctd in Anderson 1998: 57). While the trauma-tragic mode operates through multiple mechanisms, its unifying drive is an exploration and possible representation of, and bearing witness to, the traumatic.

In *Modern Tragedy* Raymond Williams' proposition is that 'tragic action, in its deepest sense, is not the confirmation of disorder, but its experience, its comprehension and its resolution. In our own time, this action is general, and its common name is revolution' (Williams 1966: 83). 'Experience' and its ability to provide access to 'comprehension' have been key ideas throughout my arguments and just as they coloured Williams' engagement with structure of feeling and the analysis of 'modern' tragedy, so too have these ideas been central in my engagement with trauma and contemporary performance. However, at the current historical juncture in which the dominant assumption (since c. the 1990s) is that 'political theatre' is now dead, 'revolution' is a tragic action that is no longer truly reflected in either the aesthetic or social realms of the contemporary tragedy I am proposing. Likewise, 'resolution' is no longer the goal of tragic action in our current structure of feeling, particularly in the trauma-tragic mode. Trauma-tragedy may act as a key to later resolution but it is concerned primarily with addressing trauma: it does not propose a world view which could be identified as a resolution, or way to achieve resolution, of traumatic schism. Rather, it presents trauma in ways that reflect the structures of trauma itself. Trauma-tragedy does not imply a performance of violence or shocking imagery, although this may be part of it, but rather it is a mode of performance which attends to trauma through one or many of its key terms, for example: cyclical/repetitious, paradoxical, dichotomous, polysemic, uncomfortable, visceral, emotional, kinaesthetic, uncanny, 'real'.

The idea of trauma-tragedy is, then, tied to the contemporary moment to which it is responding and in which I have developed it. Just as Raymond Williams explored the possibility of modern tragedy in a dramatized society so I am supplementing his arguments to consider the possibility of an artistic figuring of, or response to, trauma in a traumatized society/culture. Trauma-tragedy is a model of contemporary performance that has arisen in response to the de-cathected, individualized and flattened society in which we live at the beginning of the twenty-first century.[1]

Bernard Stiegler formulates a notion of contemporary, late-capitalist consumer society as depersonalized and disembodied

to the point that we exist within a flattened world order in which there is a de-cathected gap between event, its dissemination and consumption, and experience (Stiegler 2003: 41); in other words, experience is now, to varying degrees, wholly mediated. It is this gap which trauma-tragedy seeks to fill by offering the possibility of what I termed first-order experience. Trauma-tragic performances reflect the sociological concerns and traumatized structure of feeling of the contemporary epoch. Working against Debord's claim that what 'was directly lived has reduced into a representation' (Debord 2004: 7), trauma-tragedies present the possibility of cathected experience in a de-cathected society (and so might be seen to offer a certain type of resolution at this level).

Trauma-tragedy articulates the conjoined relationship between a traumatized contemporary society, which we might think of (in Raymond Williams' terms) as the dominant cultural mode, and its performances.[2] It also suggests a performance mode with the potential to resolve the de-cathected experience of existence in contemporary society. So, while the trauma-tragic mode is undoubtedly symptomatic of the dominant structure of feeling, it offers an emergent tool with which to approach the task of addressing trauma in or via performance in the early twenty-first century. It is both an academic discourse through which to consider the efficacy of trauma in representation and a practical framework by which one might produce that efficacy.[3] Trauma-tragedy can help to articulate ways of approaching the question of trauma in performance that facilitate a more authentic encounter with that dichotomous, polysemic phenomenon. While it is emerging out of the dominant structure of feeling, in doing so the conceptualization of trauma-tragedy offers a tool with which we can read, contemplate and reflect on that structure of feeling and potentially thus progress from it at personal and socio-cultural levels.[4]

This, however, leaves us with an old problem. If theatre and performance create a space in which we might begin to consider the world, our position within it and, thus, our position in relationship to others, then we might be seen to be entering into an ethical relationship not only with the people in the theatre (audience and performers) and the images presented, but also, in the context of trauma-tragedy, with the wider concerns which are raised in addressing traumata through performance. Questions about the ethics of representing trauma, especially 'canonized traumas' such as the Holocaust (cf. LaCapra 1996: 19–41), and writing about those representations, pepper the field of Trauma Studies. While the ethics of performance is not a new consideration in general terms – that is to say there have been arguments about what theatre should or should not represent down through the centuries – it is an increasingly explicit area of scholarly investigation in theatre and performance studies. Two useful, recent publications which attest to this rise are Nicholas Ridout's *Theatre & Ethics* (2009) and Helena Grehan's *Performance, Ethics and Spectatorship in a Global Age* (2009). Given the rise in this area of scholarly activity (cognate with my own investigations and relating to questions of ethics which permeate Trauma Studies), I turn now to three entwined areas of the ethical related to this study: the ethics of making, of watching and of writing (about watching).

Critics Jill Dolan (2001) and John Bell (2003) have suggested that theatre and performance might, after all (that is, after the 'death' of 'political theatre'), be able to stimulate social change or, at the very least, should provoke people into considering their position in the world (cf. Dolan 2001: 455–456; Bell 2003: 7). This latter point chimes with my own desire for an efficacy of theatre and with what I believe trauma-tragedy is realizing. In *Theatre & Ethics*, Ridout considers Levinas' philosophical ethics alongside live performance to propose that the latter might be seen to stimulate a way of looking at the world which encourages the spectator to take an ethical position to/for it (2009: 56). This profitably parallels Bell's proposition that performance offers a method towards 'figuring out' where we are in the world (Bell 2003: 7). The idea that performance might help us to identify where we are as a society is precisely the challenge that Raymond Williams asks us to take up in identifying a contemporary structure of feeling in the contemporary moment rather than retrospectively.

In 'Ethics as First Philosophy', Emanuel Levinas proposed an ethics that is oriented around encounters with and responsibility to/for the other (cf. Levinas 1989: 75–87). He argued that 'one has to respond to one's right to be, not by referring to some abstract and anonymous law, or judicial entity, but because of one's fear for the Other' (Levinas 1989: 82). Thus, performance made in relation to or read through Levinasian ethics encourages the spectator, Ridout argues, to 'experience an encounter with someone else' and 'assume ethical responsibility for the fragile life of the other' rather than just regarding it as 'an exploration of [one's] own subjectivity' (Ridout 2009: 8). I have, throughout the book, been writing from a similar perspective: my writing on performance has not only been concerned with elucidating an argument about the relationship between theatre and trauma, but has also been commenting on the world in which we live and the possibility of performance helping to position oneself in it and in relation to the other.

Within trauma discourses there is a recurring concern that in representing trauma, and in writing about those representations, the original events could be trivialized or rendered banal. As an art form which works with and presents bodies, performance is inextricably bound to ethical discourses.[5] Even outside drama-therapeutic concerns, performance makers and thinkers are duty bound, to varying degrees, to contemplate the ethics of the representations they pursue. For example, with *Purgatorio* (2009), Socìetas Raffaello Sanzio presented a performance in which the central fulcrum of action was the paedophilic moles-tation of a young boy at the hands of his father. This, for me at least, poses questions about whether the wider traumas of child abuse and paedophilia are made trivial by such represen-tations. The answers are bound to discussions of the ethics of performance in general, but any ethical position is, importantly, inextricably tied to context, as it is with all representations of trauma. The representations made in *Purgatorio* are in the mind of the spectator: the act happens off stage while a sound track plays out the sounds of the action for the audience (which raises its own ethical dilemmas – was the sound played live and should a young actor be asked to perform lines such as 'stop Daddy, that hurts'?). In this performance, the representa-tion is (overtly) implied rather than explicitly shown. But the representations made in *Purgatorio* do not banalize the traumas referenced: they are, perhaps, over the top or maybe too obvious, yet the performance serves as a potent reminder that these traumas exist and that they must be addressed. Indeed, thinking about Levinasian ethics, I very clearly felt a responsibility to the *traumatized* other here (fictitious on the stage and in the 'real' world), but also a responsibility for the actions of the *traumatizing* other. In this regard, the representation of trauma served to highlight the gravitas of such trauma-events rather than to diminish their importance in any way.

Conversely, the Bolvangar scene in the National Theatre's production of *His Dark Materials* (discussed in Chapter 5) makes a number of representations of trauma within the diegesis which can be seen to detract from the importance of the original event in certain ways. The representations of trauma in this scene are layered, and complicated, by numerous, deliberate significations of social and historically recognizable traumas, in particular Nazi concentration camps, Dr Mengele's experimentation with twins and the Holocaust in general. Jill Bennett has observed that '[t] he fact that we live in a post-Holocaust world is understood to compel us to deal with Holocaust memory, and to account for the ways in which the Holocaust has touched us directly or indirectly' (2005: 6). It is a socio-cultural trauma memory which we continually attempt to bear witness to in various ways: the signification of the Nazi concentration camps, and of other totalitarian regimes, in the National Theatre's production is by no means accidental – in both the books and the plays there are 'hints of Communist Russia and Nazi Germany' (Butler 2003: 71). These 'hints' are designed into the stage adaptation and repeated with such frequency that, for an adult audience at least, it is difficult to categorize them as merely hints; rather, they take centre stage. Pullman's novels make this move too, but the connection is made explicit by the collision of dialogue and scenographic design in the National's production. The austerity of the staging, the institutional quality and intimidating grandeur of the stage buildings, coupled with the Olivier's own stark concrete interior and the archetypal uniforms of the characters, speak explicitly to the numerous images of the Nazi concentration and death camps that pervade film, literature and documentary film and photography.

The images in *His Dark Materials*, however, are employed as allegorical signs for a generic sense of 'evil', rather than specifically attempting to represent the traumas of the Holocaust. The ethical questions about this scene are, then, precisely about the use of specific signs of recognizable traumata as surrogates for all such trauma. By this I mean that the ethics of representation are concerned with the problematic possibility that in using such images, the Holocaust is de-historicized: the specifics of the events are denied and so it comes to stand for a ubiquitous evil or traumatic event of some sort. In such representations the specificity of the original trauma is being banalized through a turn to that referent as a universal sign of suffering: the banalization is concerned with the decision, on the part of the production team, to present images which speak to and of, what we might call, the (traumatic) meta-narrative of the Holocaust.

Returning to Levinas, if we are brought into being as a result of our responsibility to the other, then we must take up this ethical responsibility when appropriating that other, or the memories of that other, in the production of cultural objects. This is not to suggest that the trauma meta-memories which are part of our history and so form part of our structure of feeling cannot be addressed in theatre and performance, but that we have a responsibility to handle that material with care – not because of some sense of political correctness or fear of offending, but because to misappropriate such material is to run the risk of belittling it by denying the particulars of its original context.

Similarly concerned by the possibility of trivializing trauma, Kira O'Reilly commented on the ethics of her own work in this vein when I interviewed her in 2008. O'Reilly suggested that 'all wounds speak. All wounds are a sign that something has happened... some sort of break for better or for worse... [and] so they are performative in that sense'. However, she went on to clarify that, for her, any discussion of wounds and of the performativity of trauma needs to 'exist on a spectrum or continuum' because 'context is really key':

> [T]here is a difference between something that's happening because someone has no choice or something that's happening in a highly designed and very specific time and place and event, as in an art action. For me that is

incredibly important, otherwise it kind of ridicules when horrific stuff happens.

(O'Reilly 2008; personal interview)

The notion of ridiculing the 'horrific' parallels the concerns trauma theorists and survivor-sufferers have regarding the necessity to maintain the 'force and truth of the reality' of the trauma event (Caruth 1995: vii). Yet this concern, for O'Reilly at least, manifests itself in a desire to distance her work from discourses of 'real' trauma and wounding. Discussing a spectator connecting her performance *Succour* (2001, in which she covers her body in multiple small incisions) to Georges Bataille's writing (1989) about the Chinese torture of 'death by a thousand cuts', O'Reilly mentioned her desire to distance her work from the images Bataille published in his writing because:

> there's a sense that this is someone's body, this happened, this is real. [I don't want] to present those images in relation to my work because it might trivialise something which is so horrific by allowing it to be considered for a moment the same, and it's not remotely the same. [...] Collapsing too many things together around bodies being opened and cut can be really detrimental and really without ethics, without space to consider perspective, then it just becomes a misunderstanding of trauma.

(O'Reilly 2008; personal interview)

O'Reilly's position raises a number of points for consideration. Firstly, her desire for a consideration of perspective in approaching trauma parallels the importance of perspectival distance in trying to gain an understanding of trauma, as highlighted in Chapter 1. One cannot recognize trauma for what it is when inside it; it is only afterwards, with a different or distanced perspective, that the event and its impact clarify. This echoes both the paradoxical rotations of trauma theory, such as the gap between trauma-event and symptoms (highlighted in Chapter 1) and in identifying structures of feeling (as discussed in Chapter 2). O'Reilly, however, suggests that without this space there is a possibility that the context of the situation is lost to the point at which, for her, there is an ethical collapse in which the art action and the trauma-event become considered in the same way. The problematic being articulated by O'Reilly is about the possibility of aestheticization creating banalization; while aestheticization should not be mapped with banalization, for they are not necessarily remotely synonymous – the apprehension here is genuine. O'Reilly's practice is concerned to create the aesthetic, cultural object in such a way that it addresses trauma (and other subjects) without collapsing that object into or blurring it with the original event. Secondly, in stating that she wants to distance herself from the torture images Bataille discusses because of a sense of the 'realness' of the photographed bodies and of the situation represented, O'Reilly seems implicitly to deny, or at least treat differently, the ontological position of her own body. Undoubtedly the bodies depicted in the photographs are/were real and we know from Bataille's *Tears of Eros* that death by a thousand cuts did happen. However, O'Reilly posits a complex, paradoxical reading of the ethics of the body here: on the one hand she suggests that her practice (and, by extension, other art practices related to the body) exists on a continuum of wounding, which includes torture, and on the other hand the position she indicates she occupies on that continuum is, for O'Reilly, less 'real' than what is happening in the images of Bataille's book. For O'Reilly there is an ethical impropriety in positioning the two acts together which might be seen to stimulate 'a misunderstanding of trauma'. The two acts are, of course, vastly different in extremity, context and desired outcome; however, just as the body depicted in the photographs we discussed was real, so too is O'Reilly's and, likewise, the incisions she makes into it. The paradox I am suggesting she inhabits is structurally similar to the model of 'homosocial desire' which Eve Sedgwick proposes in *Between Men: English Literature and Male Homosocial Desire* (1985). Briefly, Sedgwick proposes that male relationships exist on a continuum of desire but at the same time within this there is an opposition between the social and the sexual. She argues that the tipping point between the two poles on the continuum is culturally and contextually variable (Sedgwick 1985: 1–5). O'Reilly is occupying a very similar figure here. Crucially, at the heart of her paradox are questions of power and consent. In

O'Reilly's performances both power over the body and consent to the actions which impact upon it are controlled by her; in death by a thousand cuts, and other tortures, power is held by others over the body of the person being cut and as a result consent is not possible. O'Reilly at once acknowledges the position of her performances on a continuum which encompasses torture but at the same time refuses accusations of appropriation of such images. Her move is to position her work within a discourse of the body and 'what it means to have a body' (O'Reilly 2008; personal interview). Crucially, that discourse is facilitated through *her* body; she maintains power over it, unless she consents to a change in that power dynamic as she did in *Untitled Bomb Shelter* (2005),[6] and always consents to incisions made into it. These images/actions might, in turn, be put into focus by, or used as a frame through which to view, traumas such as death by a thousand cuts or other instances of torture: the performance acts as a mechanism to position the spectator as second-tier witness to those traumas while maintaining a first-order experience. While O'Reilly is undoubtedly aware of these sorts of ethical issues and, in her view, slightly problematic readings of her work, she nonetheless understands the importance and, I believe, inevitability of such readings:

> I get a bit worried about [misrepresenting traumas], which is why it's great when people talk about my work as problematic. When someone comes up and says 'well, you know we still have torture in my country' after they've seen *Succour*, it's like a reality check because you go: ok, that's not quite what I'm doing but I really understand that you are plotting a reference point somewhere that's a very necessary one [for the spectator]. The work is problematic, I don't know if it would be so useful if it was easy.
> (O'Reilly 2008; personal interview)

Thus, while acknowledging the possibility and 'usefulness' of 'traumatic' readings of the work, her distancing of any explicit citation of traumas positions such readings as second-order. At the beginning of *Theatre & Ethics*, Ridout suggests that asking of oneself 'how shall I act?' is a basic, yet succinct, way of interrogating the question of ethics in any situation (Ridout 2009: 5): asking how to act as a maker or spectator of performance might thus be considered a key question when addressing trauma in performance. It is clear from the interview that O'Reilly knows how she wishes to act, what she wishes to do with her body, the questions she hopes to interrogate and the representations (or not) that she is playing with. However, while the structures of her performances might hope to manoeuvre the audience into a particular reception of the work, the very fact of slicing into her own flesh and the semiotic and embodied reactions which that invariably motivates means that by acting in this way she is stimulating her audience to read the performance actions as the very representations she sees as unethical. Importantly, however, unlike *His Dark Materials*, O'Reilly is not attempting explicit representational reference to any known, historical trauma: the reading of trauma is made by the spectators, not the artist, and so the ethical responsibility for it is to a large degree placed in their hands.

The ethics under scrutiny here are, then, not the ethics of O'Reilly explicitly attempting to represent any specific trauma but the ethics of spectatorship. This is to do with the way in which the live event, the theatre or performance event – more so than any other cultural practice – positions the spectator as ethical respondent to the presented work and the questions or problems it is grappling with. Not only are spectators at performance events, generally, explicitly aware of their position as spectators (there, in a sense, to pass judgement even if it is only at the level of enjoyment), they are also embroiled in a process of both looking and being looked at. It is, as I argued in Chapter 4, this reciprocal gaze, of other spectators and the performers, which helps to position the audience as witness to the action and so, to varying degrees, complicit within that action and thus ethically responsible to it. In Chapter 2 I proposed that there is, as part of our current structure of feeling, a need to break out of the flattened experience of living in the twenty-first century. Echoing this concern, Ridout proposes, through Hans-Thies Lehmann, that performance might 'reconnect perception and experience, thus perhaps healing wounds which are both personal (psychological) and social (political)' (Ridout 2009: 58). I do not entirely agree with his assumptions on the curative capacity of theatre spectatorship. While all art is therapeutic to some extent (it adjusts us to our world and its possibilities), and thus exists on another culturally constituted continuum, *á la* Sedgwick, the formulation Ridout makes seems to me to suggest a greater healing/therapeutic capacity for theatre spectatorship than I think is necessarily always part of that experience.[7] Nevertheless, the notion that live performance might be able to reconnect perception and experience towards a more cathected experience than that offered by non-live, mediatized performances is a useful one. By re-situating 'precisely the same images as those circulating in the global media [...] in theatrical situations', the theatre might be able to 'awaken in its audience a feeling of ethical responsibility to the people suffering in the images' (Ridout 2009: 58).[8] Ridout goes on to call upon Lehmann's notion of 'response-ability', the implicit idea that in the act of responding to something we take responsibility for it, to argue that 'spectators are called upon to recognise that there is a relationship between what is shown in the theatre and their own experience of the world' (Ridout 2009: 59). In this formulation of what we might call an ethical spectatorship the audience may (*vide* Chapter 4 and a Levinasian reading of the theatrical encounter) come to bear witness not only to their own traumas but also to the historical traumas of others. Jan Fabre's *Orgy of Tolerance* (2009) is just such a performance. The piece very deliberately presented identifiable images from the media, such as those which came out of Abu Ghraib and photographs of the Ku Klux Klan, and contemporary news stories in an attempt to reposition them within the theatrical frame for an audience and so offer an opportunity to engage with them in a different context towards an ethical reconsideration of them. The aestheticization of these images at first appears to banalize the original event; however, as the performance proceeds, the layering of these images suggests a cause and effect reading in which the structures of late capitalism and the way we live our lives within that is seen precisely to cause the types of event being depicted. Thus the banalization is obviated by the layering of aesthetic images of trauma and the (albeit, slightly obvious) reading that comes from this; namely, that the audience might in fact all be responsible for the original events in some way.

In deliberately selecting the performances or moments of performance that I have used to help explicate my arguments, I have been involved in a series of ethical dilemmas in the sense that Kim Solga suggests that audience members attending a performance must develop 'an ethics of encounter' (2007: 249). Solga, discussing the implications of watching Ian's rape in *Blasted* (though the argument is transferable), contends that we have to 'make a choice about the extent to which we are willing to watch [and] to engage' with a performance, its representations and their effects (249). In approaching each of the performances detailed in this volume, I have had to establish an ethical position in relation to it. My choice to continue to reflect and write about those experiences means that I have developed an ethics of encounter in which I have been openly willing to watch and engage with the images presented and their effects. In this position and in attempting to unpick a performance towards an understanding of the relationship between trauma and performance, I become ethically entangled with each performance and my writing becomes an ethical response to my presence at that event. My writing can be seen, in light of Levinas and then Lehmann, to be taking up the challenge of my response-ability to each event. In offering the arguments I do, I am attempting to understand the theatrical event in relation to the current structure of feeling, and vice versa. Adrian Heathfield has asserted that 'how to live?' functions as a 'timeless' ethical question (2001: n.p.). My writing can be viewed within that frame because it is interrogating how theatre and performance, in the trauma-tragic mode especially, can help us to answer this question. Furthermore, I am proposing that theatre in this mode might be part of the answer because it too offers up an ethical relationship with the (traumatized) other. Trauma-tragic performances are making an ethical response to the social dramas with which they form such a close relationship.

So, theatre and performance are embroiled in questions of the ethical on multiple levels, and performances which address trauma doubly so because of the ethical concerns surrounding the representation of trauma-events. I am not hoping or suggesting that attending performance stimulates an audience into action for political change, nor am I proposing that a trip to the theatre should indicate a moral map for the audience to follow as an ancient tragedy might have been seen to do. Rather, with trauma-tragedy, I am proposing a lens through which we can view, define and understand certain instances of contemporary performance which are addressing trauma. Trauma-tragedy offers a mode of performance which not only represents trauma in ways which echo the structures of trauma-symptoms, but also addresses it without moral commentary: trauma-tragedy offers 'the traumatic' to audiences in ways which explicitly respond to and try to break out of the current, de-cathected structure of feeling. In so doing, this mode of performance offers what might be thought of as successive levels of resolution as it tenders both an ethical response to trauma in the twenty-first century in its own right, but also proffers a space in which the audience can move towards considering the ethics of trauma in that encounter. These performances are bound to questions about theatre and performance's relationships and responsibilities to us and our society, and, within and/or because of this, our relationships and responsibilities to the other.

Notes

Introduction

1   *Why Does Tragedy Give Pleasure?* was published in 1996, just one year after the premier of *Blasted*, in the middle of the new wave of 'in-yer-face' writers, to use Aleks Sierz's problematic phrase.

2   A diverse exploration of trauma as a model with which to 'read' or frame performance can be found in *Performance Research: On Trauma*, 16:1 (Wallis and Duggan, eds, 2011).

3   This 'fearing banality', as Luckhurst puts it, is a concern across the field of Trauma Studies in general (Luckhurst 2008: 174). I will return to this issue in concluding the book, when discussing the ethical.

4   While this type of research is not a central concern of my arguments, it is important to highlight that it is a further area of practice in trauma therapy which can be seen to link the performative and trauma. I will attend to this point in a little more detail in Chapter 4, in relation to arguments on catharsis.

5   In the main, where productive, the descriptive sections of writing appear in a different typeface to the rest of the book. In a limited number of cases and where necessary for the developing argument, the writing does attend to the diegesis.

6   This mode of research and writing might be seen to parallel Laurel Richardson's (2005) idea of 'CAP [creative analytical processes] ethnography' (cf. 959–978), in which 'triangulation models… [where there is an] assumption that there is a "fixed point" or an object that can be triangulated' in 'traditionally staged research' are replaced by a crystallization model (963). Here, in order to develop critical understandings of 'the kind of political/social world we inhabit' (962), the same principles of symmetry and substance necessary in academic arguments hold true but also include the 'infinite variety of shapes, substances, transmutations, multi-dimensionalities, and angles of approach' that are more applicable to

creative, analytical processes (963). 'Crystals', Richardson proposes, 'are prisms that reflect externalities and refract within themselves, creating different colours, patterns, and arrays casting off in different directions. What we see depends on our angle of response' (963). While the central imaginary of a crystal is a productive term through which to frame much of the work of this book, nevertheless, within this approach there are specific, local instances of theoretical triangulation, most notably in Chapter 1.

7 Some elements of this section of Chapter 5, along with the full interview, were published in *Studies in Theatre and Performance* (29:3) as part of an article entitled 'The Touch and the Cut: An annotated dialogue with Kira O'Reilly' (Duggan 2009: 307–325).

Chapter 1: Trauma's performative genealogy

1 Interestingly *Blacks Medical Dictionary* also defines traumatology (linguistically meaning, the study of trauma) as the 'branch of surgery specialising in the treatment of wounds and disabilities arising from injuries' (634).

2 See Stamatakou, 1972: 996, 1014, and Dimitrakou, 1969: 1339. My thanks to Dr Antonis Kartsaki and Dr Eirini Kartsaki for pointing me to these sources and for their help with translation.

3 Although not of central importance to my current concerns, it should be noted that hysteria and Charcot, in particular, have come under some scrutiny and criticism from the field of feminism. Hysteria took its name from the imagined site of the hysteric disorder – *hysteron*, Greek for uterus; the very name thus problematically links women to the disorder. One of the principal criticisms of Charcot's theorizations on hysteria (a lineage to which trauma owes much), from feminism, argues that his systematic study of hysterical women (examined later in this chapter) promoted a view of women as 'other', mapping them against and as inferior to a male norm. However, it should also be noted that Charcot did open a small wing for male hysterics in 1882. For a longer engagement with this area, and on the development of hysteria, see Beizer, 1994 (esp. 3–9).

4 'It may happen that a man who has experienced some frightful accident – a railway collision, for instance – leaves the scene of the event apparently uninjured. In the course of the next few weeks, however, he develops a number of severe psychical and motor symptoms which can only be traced to his shock, the concussion or whatever else it was. He now has "traumatic neurosis". It is a quite unintelligible – that is to say, a new – fact. The time that has passed between the accident and the first appearance of the symptoms

is described as the "incubation period", in a clear allusion to the pathology of infectious diseases. On reflection, it must strike us that, in spite of the fundamental differences between the two cases – the problem of traumatic neurosis and that of the Jewish monotheism – there is nevertheless one point of agreement: namely, in the characteristic that might be described as "latency"' (Freud 1964: 67–68).

To explain this a little further: Freud has famously argued that Moses was in fact an Egyptian priest who tried to impose monotheism upon the Jews. Provocatively, he goes on to claim that the Jews, in their impatience with the harsh strictures of his monotheistic religion, murdered Moses. In the phrase 'the problem […] of the Jewish monotheism', Freud is in fact referring to two periods of 'latency'. The first is the time between the point at which Moses had first tried to impose a monotheistic religion on the Hebrews and the moment they accepted and implemented it. The implementation, according to Freud, is due to the guilt the Jews felt at the re-emergence of Moses' murder from collective repression – the gap between repression and re-emergence constitutes the second period of latency.

5   Anecdotally, Richard Schiff, speaking on the BBC's *Breakfast* programme on 2 February 2007, mentioned how a fellow actor and ex-fighter pilot had likened the stress of a dogfight to his experiences of acting. I will explore the idea of theatre-specific traumas in Chapter 6.

6   Phelan goes on to position the self as constructed through and in relation to trauma – 'Maybe bodies come to be "ours" when we recognise them as traumatic' (1997: 18).

7   Lucy Blackman went missing on 1 July 2000 while living in Tokyo. On 11 October 2000, wealthy property developer Joji Obara was arrested, questioned and later charged over her disappearance and murder. On 9 February 2001 Lucy's body parts were discovered in a cave near Tokyo. Steare's interview can be found at http://news.bbc.co.uk/1/hi/world/asia-pacific/6241831.stm.

Chapter 2: Trauma-tragedy: a structure of feeling

1   'Cathected experience' draws on Strachey's translation of Freud's term *Besetzung* as *cathexis* to propose what we might think of as charged, self-invested lived or first-order experience as opposed to a vicarious, second-order or mediated one.

2   The impact of the recession was still being acutely felt in mid-2011 as the Conservative-led coalition government (elected May 2010) increased VAT, radically cut public spending and reduced funding

levels in all areas. The effects of the recession were also being seen in extremely high unemployment figures: 'unemployment rate for the three months to February 2011 was 7.8 per cent of the economically active population [...] 2.48 million [people]' (Office for National Statistics 2011: online).

3   This argument implicitly echoes those made by Marshall McLuhan and Fredric Jameson, among others, regarding a sense of existing in a flattened and de-cathected world, which I will address later in the chapter.

4   In a slightly different, though apposite, context, Marshall McLuhan articulates a similar argument in his discussions of the reception and structures of media, suggesting that it is only when we are 'standing aside from any structure or medium, that its principles and lines of force can be discerned' (McLuhan 2001: 16).

5   I will return to the notion of a collapse in the mimetic order of performance in the next chapter.

6   I make this argument in light of the discussion in the previous chapter and also fully aware of LaCapra's injunction against 'rash amalgamations or conflations' that suggest that 'contemporary culture, or even all history, is traumatic' and of his emphasis on the distinction between historic and structural trauma (1996: x and passim).

7   Duggan and Wallis' 'double traumatic symptom in postmodern conditions' (2011: 14, fig. 2) offers a diagrammatic mapping of a tightly cognate reading of the experience of contemporary society.

8   Diderot suggests that this control of feeling is centrally controlled by the diaphragm and to gain distance from emotions so as to be believable, the actor must gain control of it. Diderot, Roach contends, sees the brain and the diaphragm as '"the two great springs of the human machine", one propelling the mechanism of thought, the other of feeling' (Roach 1993: 131). Roach cites Diderot's contention that: 'If the diaphragm contracts violently a man [sic] suffers and is saddened; if a man suffers and is saddened, his diaphragm contracts violently' (131). Thus in order to control emotion, the actor must control the diaphragm, must centre and control his movements through modulation of that muscle (cf. Roach 1993: 130–132).

9   Especially in the article titled 'A Forum on Theatre and Tragedy In the Wake of September 11, 2001'.

Chapter 3: Mimetic shimmering and the performative *punctum*

1   A definition of mimesis is at best indeterminate but it has commonly been taken to mean representation, imitation, similarity, copy,

expression, adaptation and fake (cf. Kelly, 1998: 232). The indeterminacy surrounding mimesis has frustrated and inspired debate on the subject ever since Plato admonished poetry as imitation thrice removed from the truth in *The Republic* but, as Halliwell forcefully argues, 'the concept of mimesis lies at the core of the entire history of Western attempts to make sense of representational art and its values' (Halliwell 2002: vii). Meanwhile, Michael Taussig suggests that 'mimesis sutures the real to the really made up – and no society exists otherwise' (Taussig 1993: 86).

2   This understanding of mimesis shares similarities with the definition of authenticity set out in the previous chapter.

3   The theatrical or performance event is *always already* both representational, at the level of its fiction, and real, at the level of it happening in the world, just as we sit in the world in the auditorium. Possibly the most fundamental statement of this problematic for our own time, especially in relation to theatre criticism, began with Artaud's *Theatre and Its Double* (1938) and is further articulated and developed in its later critique by Derrida in *Writing and Difference* (1967; particularly 'The Theatre of Cruelty and the Closure of Representation').

4   If we accept, after Derrida, after Heidegger, that words are both inadequate/inaccurate but also necessary within the constraints of available language, then real and representation might be deemed both necessary and inadequate signifiers of specific meanings within this project, and so might be thought of as constantly under erasure.

5   I saw the production in July 2005 and it is to this performance that I shall refer.

6   I am specifically thinking of a passage of movement involving the artist repeatedly collapsing a wooden chair, which was hung round her waist, on to her stomach.

7   The sound is alien to the scene, neither corresponding to a 'naturalistic' sound of wood on flesh nor to any human sound. As such the double beating theatrically elongates the action, paradoxically evoking a greater sense of this as an actual beating in which flesh ruptures, bones shatter and blood spills.

8   I will return to the notion of physical impact and embodied reaction in more detail in Chapter 5.

9   This might be because, in this scene, we are seeing not just 'police' but the whole cultural/political business of *policing*. We might, via Foucault, thus see regimes of truth enfolded with regimes of violence and power (including at the level of representation) (cf. Foucault 1980: 55–62; and Brass 2000: 305–330).

10 While there are many texts which could be recommended here, Rebecca Schneider's *The Explicit Body in Performance* (1997)

eloquently discusses patriarchy/patriarchal gaze in various (performance) contexts.

11   I will return to Barthes and discuss, especially, the notion of *punctum* later in the chapter.

12   For further discussion on this point see Shepherd, 2006: 98–100; and McAuley, 2000: *passim*.

13   This type of audience manipulation is not uncommon in contemporary theatre and performance; SHUNT's *Tropicana* (2005), for example, creates a similar unsettlement. It begins by assembling at a small, unmarked but official-looking blue door in London Bridge station. The audience is eventually ushered into a London Underground worker's 'office' and then through the worker's locker into the 'theatre foyer' and finally into a lift which seems to descend into the bowels of the city. Throughout this production the audience is manipulated around the space, thrown into total blackout, disorientated and finally ejected through the back of the Vaults straight on to the pavement of a busy road in a dimly lit tunnel.

14   Lib Taylor explicates a similar argument around the tensions inherent within looking at 'horrific or frightening image[s]' in relation to encountering what she believed to be a real 'hanging man' on an interstate in America (Taylor 2010: 9 and *passim*).

15   I shall address implication and witnessing in the next chapter.

16   The imputation of the reality of other babies in the world can be seen to operate similarly; i.e. that imputed reality erupts into the first reading of the baby as simply a baby on stage.

17   Later in the performance some of the audience at the head of the bed closed around the headboard to get a better view in a scene eerily reminiscent of Rembrandt's *Anatomy Lesson of Dr. Nicolaes Tulp*.

18   Potlatch has differing definitions but it is taken here, in line with both *The Oxford English Dictionary*, second edition (1989), and *Webster's Third New International Dictionary* (2002), to mean both a gift of magnificence which is intended as 'a display of wealth to validate or advance individual tribal position or social status and marked by the host's lavish destruction of personal property and an ostentatious distribution of gifts that entails elaborate reciprocation', and, more simply, a gift given 'with the expectancy of reciprocation' (both citations from *Webster's*). Marcel Mauss discusses potlatch in depth in *The Gift* (1923–24 [1954, first English translation]) and claims that 'the obligation to reciprocate constitutes the essence of the potlatch [...] the potlatch must be reciprocated with interest' (Mauss 1990: 41–42 and cf. 39–46).

19   This is not to deny that some people find such an experience uncomfortable, even disturbing.

20 The same assumptions can be made of the majority of the venues where this and other of Franko B's works are shown, a complete list of which can be found at www.franko-b.com/Franko_CV.doc
21 In the sense that Edmund Burke, among others, suggested that the sublime might 'excite the ideas of pain, and danger… operat[ing] in a manner analogous to terror' (Burke 1958: 39), but that this was part of a satisfying aesthetic experience, and one which might, as Frances Ferguson suggests in Kelly, produce a 'sense of exertion brought on by a confrontation with the surprising or unfamiliar, with objects of experience beyond an individual's reach' (Ferguson in Kelly 1998: 327 and cf. 326–331).
22 I am not, here, suggesting that *Still Life* be considered *as* a traumatic-event for the audience (although this could be argued), but that it follows a *structure* which mirrors the structure of traumatic event and recurrence of traumatic symptom.
23 Barthes has suggested that the visible presence of bodily fluids (sweat and tears in his analysis) are part of 'an economic order' of performance which might be seen to satisfy a need for a 'verifiable yield' in return for one's ticket price (Barthes 2000: 75–76). The blood in *Still Life* is part of the same economy. We can see that we have had our money's worth, so to speak. But into this equation of fluids the question of waste almost inevitably appears, for while sweat and tears are quantifiable as the results of excellence in the actor's 'physical labor' (*ibid.*), blood is not the product of any imitation or commitment to a role. It is the precious fluid of life and so to give of it for performance seems particularly wasteful if considered within medico-capitalist frameworks – the 'wasted' blood which could be 'banked' etcetera.

Chapter 4: Performance 'texts' as sites of witness

1 I attend to ethics in more detail in the Conclusion of the book.
2 See, for example, Shepherd and Wallis 2004: 207–211; Shepherd 2006: 46; and Fenemore 2003: 107–114.
3 See www.library.yale.edu/testimonies for more information.
4 Undrill is here reviewing three books which have made significant contributions to Trauma Studies: Caruth's *Unclaimed Experience: Trauma, Narrative and History* (1996) and her edited collection *Trauma: Explorations in Memory* (1995), and Bal, Crewe and Spitzer's (eds) *Acts of Memory: Cultural Recall in the Present* (2000).
5 I am defining witnessing, here, in line with the *Oxford English Dictionary* (2003, 2nd edition), which defines a witness as 'a person who sees an event, typically a crime or accident, take place'. The verb 'to bear' is defined as '(i) support; carry the weight of;

(ii) take responsibility for', while 'to bear witness' is defined as 'testifying to'.

6 This second-order witnessing can be experienced, as I argued in Chapter 2, as an authentic, cathected encounter.

7 This might be seen to constitute another sort of shimmering, bound up within mimetic shimmering, in which the audience is caught between responsibility and complicity with the physical actions on stage and their positioning as second-order witness to the dramatic action.

8 The idea of a seemingly accidental discovery to create the spectator as witness maps well with the seemingly accidental discovery of the bloodied bed in *Still Life*, the performative *punctum* that stimulates (reverse) mimetic shimmering.

9 It is worth noting that with all these types of representation there is a problem that they might in some way be banalizing the events themselves. This is less the case with Pinter's work which is testifying to these traumata through abstract, fictitious constructions of the events, but it is certainly problematic in representations of trauma with a discernible history such as the Holocaust. I shall return to this difficulty again in the Conclusion.

10 While I will continue to make some reference to the work of drama therapists, this field of research, because of its predominant focus on curative processes, and on individual survivor sufferers, is not central to my current concerns. It is, however, important to note its connections to my research and its many concurrent/overlapping concerns regarding trauma, witnessing, catharsis and theatre practices.

11 In light of this, we might think of performance as constituting one element in the 'restorative phase' of social dramas.

12 It is also worth noting that Aristotle suggests religious music might also *produce* the 'agitation' he is discussing.

13 *The Room* (first performed in 1957), for example, has recently been restaged in both the United Kingdom (most recently Leeds, April 2007) and America (in a double bill with *Celebration*, written 1999, as part of The Lincoln Centre Festival, New York, July 2001).

14 Bert's only (vocal) contribution to the piece is in the last two pages of script when he speaks about a car journey which might be seen to connote euphemistically a very different scene: Bert says that he 'drove her down, hard' (Pinter 1991: 109) and insists that 'she don't mix it with me' (110). His final contribution to the piece is to attack Riley violently, kicking the blind man's head against a radiator.

15 The production was staged as part of *Artist and Citizen: 50 Years of Performing Pinter*, a conference on and celebration of Pinter's life

and work; the event was curated by Mark Taylor-Batty at Workshop Theatre, University of Leeds (12–15 April 2007).

16 Calle, S., *Exquisite Pain*, performed by Forced Entertainment. Performances referred to here: Soho Theatre, London, April 2007; and West Yorkshire Playhouse, February 2008.

17 *Earthquake* made repetitions both in its structure and imagery/movements but not necessarily in its language. Heathfield has suggested that it is 'a kind of physical testimony' and that 'it is possible [...] to think of all of the actions that take place in *Earthquake* as given and felt in the wake of some unspeakable and multiple trauma. A sense of catastrophe hangs over the piece' (Heathfield 2001: 3–4). Interestingly, although this piece has been quite widely read as 'testifying' to the events of September 11 2001, it was in fact devised and premiered before that date. Heathfield's writing was also completed prior to those events and while he latterly added a footnote both to clarify this chronology and to state that 'the work is uncannily resonant' with those events (2001: 5), it is evident that the piece held resonance with trauma and catastrophe before any retrospective analyses. *Earthquake* thus seems a good articulation of the aesthetic–ritual loop I (re)configured in Chapter 2 (also cf. Bottoms and Goulish 2007: 98–103).

18 There are, of course, certain frames which surround a performance that might be seen to point towards the type of experience one could expect – publicity, venue, company identity, etcetera. However, while these frames might indicate certain expectations about the performance, they might also act as part of the unsettling of an audience. By this I mean that the frames might stimulate another level of shimmering between the perceived knowledge of a performance, and so a sense of safety, and the simultaneous difficulty of fully reading those frames and the possible juxtaposition of that reading against the actuality of the performance.

Chapter 5: Being there: the 'presence' of trauma

1 'In-yer-face' was a term coined by Alex Sierz in his book *In-Yer-Face Theatre: British Drama Today* (2001). The term became prevalent in much thinking concerned with the writers he draws together in the book. However, the all-encompassing nature of the term and the fact that it somewhat denies, or rather ignores, various differences between the writers has meant that it has become increasingly less popular in recent years.

2 This description is of Thomas Ostermeier's production of *Blasted* (*Anéantis*), Avignon, 2005. The hotel room in the first half of the

play was designed so that the bathroom was behind a single, wood-clad wall with an open entrance on either side. The stage was on a revolve so at times the audience was able to see the interior of the bathroom.

3   Warwick Arts Centre, 2000, dir. Russell Whitehead; Avignon Festival, 2005, dir. Thomas Ostermeier; Queen's Hotel, Leeds, 2008, dir. Felix Mortimer; Lyric Hammersmith, 2010, dir. Sean Holmes.

4   Schechner draws a parallel map in *Performance Theory*, suggesting that a disruption of theatrical form (seen increasingly from the late 1960s) creates a 'blurring of the boundaries between categories of performance [aesthetic, ritual, social]' (2003: 194). He argues that this blurring destabilizes people's (makers and witnesses) understanding of where to place the performance in culture: the performance's reading is complicated by the blurring of its performance category caused by a disruption of theatrical form (cf. Schechner 2003: 189–195).

5   The references I make to the production refer to the first, 2004, staging of *His Dark Materials*.

6   Unless otherwise stated, all following citations of the play will be taken from this 'Revised Edition' of the script and page numbers given in parentheses.

7   Pullman's view on this reading of the relationship can be found in Butler 2003: 24.

8   For a reading of this scene in relation to attachment theory and the performative symptoms that erupt from breaking attachment bonds, see Duggan, 2011: 219–238.

9   It is hard to describe Barnett's cry adequately, but his slightly West Country accent seems to elongate 'Lyra' into what might be written as 'Lyyyyyraaaaaa'.

10 In order to arrive at his formulation of a fictive body, Watanabe cites the example of a Noh actor, who, once his performance is over, leaves the stage moving extremely slowly, 'as if his exit was an integral part of the performance. He is no longer in character, because his character's action has finished, but neither is he in his daily reality. He is in an intermediate state. In a certain way, he is performing his own absence. But this absence is performance and is therefore a present absence […] I have called this phenomenon the *fictive body*: not a dramatic fiction but a body which commits itself to a certain "fictive" zone which does not perform a fiction but which stimulates a kind of transformation of the daily body at the pre-expressive level' (ctd in Barba and Savarese 1991: 187; emphasis is original).

11 'Cognitive' here is taken from Lakoff and Johnson's discussion of it as 'conceptual and propositional structures' and meaning-making

processes which occur in 'reference to things in the external world' (cf. Lakoff and Johnson 1999: 11–12).

12   My thanks to Dr Kara McKechnie for her insightful comments and critical engagement with an early draft of this research presented at University of Leeds, April 2008.

13   I am, here, invoking Keir Elam's (2001) model of the stage as a 'syncretic system' (or system of systems) in which each element of the stage – image, light, sound, gesture, speech, etcetera – can be identified as at once a 'mode of signification' (29) and simultaneously 'a weave of radically differentiated modes of expression' (39) towards an ultimate 'act of communication' (29; cf. Elam 2001: 24–50).

14   O'Reilly's views are taken from the transcript of a personal interview I conducted with the artist at the British Library in early 2008. The full interview, along with a short critical essay, can be found in Duggan 2009 (part of which is replicated below) and I shall address other elements of this interview in the conclusion of the book.

Chapter 6: Another view

1   The appropriateness of one's attendance is an interesting point in relation to much of the performance work explored throughout this book; indeed it is perhaps the fundamental aspect that each shares in its disturbance of the audience.

2   'Hoodies' is a term describing a hooded sweatshirt but has more recently been made famous by David Cameron apocryphally suggesting the public needed to 'hug a hoodie', using the term to refer to a person who wears the garment as a means of hiding their face while committing crime.

3   The article implies that Mutar had this sensation while being tortured, rather than making the assessment in light of gaining new knowledge.

4   For a good introduction to and discussion of Bourdieu's theories of *habitus* and *field*, see Swartz 1997: 95–116.

5   American radio presenter Rush Limbaugh famously claimed that the events depicted in the images were 'sort of like hazing, a fraternity prank. Sort of like that kind of fun'. Limbaugh makes his claim as a way of both excusing and explaining the actions of the soldiers. While I do not agree with this aspect of Limbaugh's statement, his assessment of the events as akin to hazing and fraternity rituals does hold weight. It highlights the culture of participation and a theatrical, 'playful' yet humiliating seam of cultural practice which can be seen to underpin certain elements of (formative) American institutions (Limbaugh ctd in Warner 2004: 74).

6   This is not to assume compliance on the part of the prisoners, for while they may be performing subservience with 'diligence', this is not necessarily a sincere face: the adaptive *habitus* which I am discussing might include a strategic disposition to subterfuge – the presentation of an insincere mask, for instance.

7   The term refers to an occasion when someone assaults an unsuspecting victim while an accomplice records the assault on a mobile phone or other recording device: the performance of 'real' violence for entertainment.

8   We might argue that this degradation is a function of the torture and/or that the staged events are intended to wear the prisoners down towards greater compliance (this seems unlikely given the theatricalized content of the images). However, I am explicitly thinking of function in terms of 'knowledge' production; that is, the prisoners are not being interrogated and the torture is not in order to gain 'intelligence' as is historically one of the main functions of torture. See Schulz 2007: 1–12 and 19–27.

9   We might think of the white light of a camera flash as a surface which haptically presses on the body, even through closed eyes or Hessian sacks.

10   For an excellent discussion of the etymology of corpsing and drying, especially in relation to defining the terms, see Ridout 2006: 130–133.

11   Sher's 'Fear' is a mixture of stage fright and moments of drying or almost drying that return to haunt him throughout his acting career. I will return to Sher's experiences later in this chapter.

12   Although a slightly different example to those on failing, the argument of being traumatized by doing the job of acting is further borne out in Daniel Day-Lewis' '*Hamlet* experience' in which the actor became traumatically caught up in the fiction of the play. The '*Hamlet* experience' refers to an incident in which Day-Lewis supposedly was so 'haunted' by the experience of playing Hamlet for an extended run at the National Theatre that he walked off stage mid-performance and has never acted on stage again. The walkout has been reported as being the result of Day-Lewis feeling like he was talking to the ghost of his own father.

13   I do not merely mean in an 'emotional memory' sort of way.

14   Note also that the traumatic experience of failing is further compounded by the knowledge that if the afflicted actor does not recover (sufficiently quickly) the apparatus of representation on which the theatre event relies will collapse and the performance could in theory be brought to a premature end.

15   Indeed, so pervasive have the Abu Ghraib images been and so widely taken up into Western socio-cultural discourse that as

recently as April 2009 they were still being explicitly referenced in performance work: Jan Fabre's *Orgy of Tolerance* recreated a number of the images, notably a pyramid of naked bodies, a man attached to a dog leash and the man attached to electrodes.

Conclusion: trauma-tragedy and the contemporary moment

1   This flattened experience of the world has been identified by such writers as Jameson, McLuhan and Žižek (cf. Chapter 2). More recently (2003), French philosopher Bernard Stiegler has extended the thinking in this area; one can thereby identify it as a continuing and important reading of contemporary society.

2   Here, I am evoking Williams' discussion of dominant, residual and emergent cultural processes. Williams proposes that these concepts offer a framework for understanding the fluid and complex ways in which a culture operates as it perpetually tries to maintain stability while facing continuously changing views within a cultural system. He argues that a culture should not be defined solely by its dominant features but should be aware of the other perspectives which are also contending for meaning, some older or 'residual', some newer or 'emergent' (cf. Williams 1977: 121–127; Brannigan 1998: 40–42).

3   This idea quite closely tracks the project Williams embarked upon with *Koba* (1966), in which he attempted to produce his own artistic tragic efficacy.

4   'Progress' might here be measured both in terms of society 'moving on' or recovering from the dominant, traumatized structure of feeling to the next, emergent structure of feeling (yet to be identified and only possible because of the residues of the current structure of feeling) but also, on a smaller scale, processing and progressing past traumatic experience at a more personal or local level.

5   Alan Read makes a similar argument about the inescapable ethical dimension of theatrical exchange in an early example of scholarly engagement with theatre and ethics (Read 1993: 61).

6   In this one-to-one performance, O'Reilly invited audience members to sit with her and, if they so desired, to slice into her skin with a scalpel. For a more detailed discussion of this piece, see Zerihan, 2006.

7   The language Ridout employs seems to me more definitive of a drama-therapeutic situation in which the purpose of the theatrical encounter, be it watching or making in some way, is *about* the healing of wounds.

8   Note that Ridout's point is not that events can be appropriated into the theatrical frame to signify other, similar events (as with the Bolvangar scene) but that presenting 'precisely the same images' in a theatrical setting might open up a space in which the events depicted can be considered afresh.

Bibliography

Aaron, S., 1986. *Stage Fright: Its Role in Acting*. Chicago & London: University of Chicago Press.

Aeschylus, 1999. *The Oresteia: A Translation of Aeschylus' Trilogy of Plays*. Trans. T. Hughes. London: Faber and Faber.

Anderson, P., 1998. *The Origins of Postmodernity*. London: Verso.

Anderson, T., 2006. *Performing Early Modern Trauma from Shakespeare to Milton*. Aldershot: Ashgate Publishing Limited.

Aristotle, 1981. *Politics*. Trans. T. A. Sinclair. London: Penguin.

———, 1996. *Poetics*. Trans. M. Heath. London: Penguin.

Aston, E. and Savona, G., 1991. *Theatre as Sign-system: A Semiotics of Text and Performance*. London: Routledge.

Auslander, P., 1997. *From Acting to Performance: Essays in Modernism and Postmodernism*. London: Routledge.

———, 1999. *Liveness: Performance in a Mediatized Culture*. London: Routledge.

Bakhtin, M. M., 1981. *The Dialogic Imagination: Four Essays*. Ed. M. Holquist. Trans. C. Emerson and M. Holquist. Austin: University of Texas Press.

Banes, S. and Lepecki, A. eds., 2007. *The Senses in Performance*. London: Routledge.

Barba, E. and Savarese, N., 1991. *The Secret Art of the Performer: A Dictionary of Theatre Anthropology*. London: Routledge.

Barish, J., 1981. *The Anti-Theatrical Prejudice*. Berkley: University of California Press.

Barnett, C., 2003. 'Painting As Performance: Charlotte Salomon's *Life? or Theatre?*'. *The Drama Review*, 47(1), pp. 97–126.

Barthes, R., 1982. *Camera Lucida: Reflections on Photography*. Trans. R. Howard. London: Jonathan Cape Limited.

———, 1997. *The Eiffel Tower and Other Mythologies*. Trans. R. Howard. Berkley and Los Angeles: University of California Press.

———, 2000. *Mythologies*. London: Vintage.

Bataille, G., 1989. *Tears of Eros*. San Francisco: City Lights Books.

Baudrillard, J., 2001. *Selected Writings*. Ed M. Poster. Stanford: Stanford University Press.

————, 2002. *The Spirit of Terrorism.* Trans. C. Turner. London: Verso.

————, 2005. *The Conspiracy of Art.* Trans. A. Hodges. New York: Semiotext(e).

————, 2008. *The Perfect Crime.* Trans. C. Turner. London: Verso

BBC, 2005. 'Abu Ghraib Inmates Recall Torture'. *BBC News* [online]. Available at: http://news.bbc.co.uk/2/hi/americas/4165627.stm (accessed 03 May 2008).

Beckett, S., 1979. *Endgame.* London: Faber and Faber.

Beizer, J., 1994. *Ventriloquized Bodies: Narratives of Hysteria in Nineteenth-century France.* Ithaca: Cornell University Press.

Bell, C., 1997. *Ritual: Perspectives and Dimensions.* Oxford: Oxford University Press.

Bell, J., 2003. 'Performance Studies in an Age of Terror'. *TDR*, 47(2), pp. 6–8.

Benjamin, W., 1999. *Illuminations.* Trans. H. Zorn. London: Pimlico.

————, 2007. *Reflections.* Ed. P. Demetz. New York: Schocken Books.

Bennett, J., 2005. *Empathic Vision: Affect, Trauma, and Contemporary Art.* Stanford: Stanford University Press.

Benvenisti, M. *et al.*, 2004. *Abu Ghraib: The Politics of Torture.* Berkley: North Atlantic Books.

Berninger, M., 2008. 'A Fantasy Epic as a Theatrical Event – *His Dark Materials* at the National Theatre'. In: E. Redling and P. P. Schnierer, eds., *Contemporary Drama in English: Non-Standard Forms of Contemporary Drama and Theatre.* Trier: WVT Wissenschaftlicher Verlag Trier, pp. 153–169.

Billington, M., 2000. 'How do you Judge a 75-Minute Suicide Note?'. *The Guardian*, 30 June.

Bloom, S. L., 1999. *Trauma and Theory (Abbreviated)* [online]. Available at www.sanctuaryweb.com (downloaded 16 November 2004).

Bloomer, K. C. and Moore, C. W., 1977. *Body, Memory and Architecture.* Yale: Yale University Press.

Bottoms, S. and Goulish, M., 2007. *Small Acts of Repair: Performance, Ecology and Goat Island.* London: Routledge.

Bradley, R., 2005. *Ritual and Domestic Life in Prehistoric Europe.* London: Routledge.

Brannigan, J., 1998. *New Historicism and Cultural Materialism.* London: Macmillan Press.

Brass, P. R., 2000. 'Foucault Steals Political Science'. *Annual Review of Political Science*, 3(1), pp. 305–330.

Brennan, C., 2005. *Personal interview at Queen Mary College, University of London.* Conducted 31 March 2005.

Brooks, G., 2008. 'From an Amateur's Angle: The Impact of the Visual Image in Defining Abu Ghraib', *gnovis* [online]. Available at http://gnovisjournal.org/journal/amateurs-angle-impact-visual-image-defining-abu-ghraib (accessed 07 April 2009).

Bryan, D., 2005. *Dora Bryan's Tapestry Tales.* Canterbury Press: Norwich.

Burke, E., 1958. *A Philosophical Enquiry into the Origin of our Ideas of the Sublime and Beautiful.* London: Routledge and Kegan Paul.

Buse, P., 2001. *Drama + Theory: Critical Approaches to Modern British Drama.* Manchester: Manchester University Press.

Butler, J., 1993. *Bodies That Matter: On the Discursive Limits of 'Sex'.* New York: Routledge.

Butler, R., 2003. *The Art of Darkness: Staging the Philip Pullman Trilogy.* London: Oberon Books.

Campbell, P. and Kear, A., 2001. *Psychoanalysis and Performance.* London: Routledge.

Caruth, C. ed., 1995. *Trauma: Explorations in Memory.* Baltimore and London: The Johns Hopkins University Press.

———, 1996. *Unclaimed Experience: Trauma, Narrative and History.* Baltimore: The Johns Hopkins University Press.

Castellucci, C. *et al.*, 2007. *The Theatre of Societas Raffaello Sanzio.* London: Routledge.

Charcot, J.-M., 1991. *Clinical Lectures on Diseases of the Nervous System.* London: Routledge.

Christie, J., Gough, R. and Watt, D. eds., 2006. *A Performance Cosmology: Testimony from the Future, Evidence from the Past.* London and New York: Routledge.

Christy, R., 1887. *Proverbs, Maxims and Phrases of All Ages: Classified Subjectively and Arranged Alphabetically.* London: G. P. Putnam's sons.

Coleridge, S. T., 1817. *Biographia Literaria* [online]. Available at www.english.upenn.edu/~mgamer/Etexts/biographia.html (accessed 6 June 2008).

Crary, J., 1999. *Suspensions of Perception: Attention, Spectacle and Modern Culture.* London: The MIT Press.

Crowther, P., 1993. *Art and Embodiment: From Aesthetics to Self-Consciousness.* Oxford: Oxford University Press.

Csordas, T. J., 1999. 'Embodiment and Cultural Phenomenology'. In: G. Weiss and H. F. Haber, eds., *Perspectives on Embodiment.* New York: Routledge, pp. 143–162.

Debord, G., 2004. *Society of the Spectacle.* Trans. K. Knabb. London: Rebel Press.

De Zulueta, F., 1993. *From Pain to Violence: The Traumatic Roots of Destructiveness.* London: Whurr Publishers.

Derrida, J., 1978. *Writing and Difference.* London: Routledge and Kegan Paul Ltd.

———, 1982. *Margins of Philosophy.* Trans. A. Bass. Brighton: The Harvester Press.

————, 1986. *Mémories: For Paul de Man*. Trans. C. Lindsay, J. Culler and E. Cadava. New York: Columbia University Press.

————, 2004. *Dissemination*. Trans. B. Johnson. London: Continuum.

Di Benedetto, S., 2003. 'Sensing Bodies: A Phenomenological Approach to the Performance Senssorium'. *Performance Research*, 8(2), pp. 101–108.

Diamond, E., 1989. 'Mimesis, Mimicry, and the "True – Real"'. *Modern Drama*, 32(1), pp. 58–72.

Didi-Huberman, G., 2003. *Invention of Hysteria: Charcot and the Photographic Iconography of the Salpêtrière*. Trans. A. Hartz. London: The MIT Press.

Dimitrakou, D. B., 1969. *Dictionary of the Greek Language*. Athens.

Dolan, J., 2001. 'Performance, Utopia and the "Utopian Performance"'. *Theatre Journal*, 53(3), pp. 455–479.

Duggan, M. and Grainger, R., 1997. *Imagination, Identification and Catharsis in Theatre and Therapy*. London: Jessica Kingsley Publishers.

Duggan, P. 2009. 'The Touch and the Cut: An Annotated Dialogue with Kira O'Reilly'. *Studies in Theatre and Performance*, 29 (3), pp. 307–325.

————, 2011. 'Staging the Impossible: Severance and separation in the National Theatre's adaptation of *His Dark Materials*'. In: S. Barfield and K. Cox, eds., *Critical Perspectives on Philip Pullman's* His Dark Material*: Essays on the Novels, the Film and the Stage Productions*. Jefferson: McFarland, pp. 219–238.

Duggan, P. and Wallis, M., 2011. 'Trauma and Performance: Maps, Narratives and Folds'. *Performance Studies*, 16(1), pp. 4–17.

Elam, K., 2002. *The Semiotics of Theatre and Drama*. London: Routledge.

Eldridge, J. and Eldridge, L., 1994. *Raymond Williams: Making Connections*. London: Routledge.

Elkins, J., 1999. *Pictures of the Body: Pain and Metamorphosis*. Stanford: Stanford University Press.

Eng, D., 2002. 'The Value of Silence'. *Theatre Journal*, 54(1), pp. 85–94.

Etchells, T., 1999. *Certain Fragments: Contemporary Performance and Forced Entertainment*. London: Routledge.

————, 2008. 'A Note on *Exquisite Pain*'. *Programme notes for* Exquisite Pain. West Yorkshire Playhouse, February–March 2008.

Fenemore, A., 2003. 'On Being Moved by Performance'. *Performance Research*, 8(4), pp. 107–114.

Fieldman, A., 2004. 'Abu Ghraib: Ceremonies of Nostalgia', *Open Democracy* [online]. Available at www.opendemocracy.net/media-abu_ghraib/article_2163.jsp (accessed 11 June 2008).

————, 2005. 'On the Actuarial Gaze'. *Cultural Studies*, 19(2), pp. 203–226.

Fischer-Lichte, E., 1997. *The Show and the Gaze of Theatre: A European Perspective*. Iowa: University of Iowa Press.

Forced Entertainment, 2008. *Promotional material for* Exquisite Pain *and* Bloody Mess. West Yorkshire Playhouse, February–March 2008.

Forsberg, G. E., 1993. *Critical Thinking in an Image World*. Lanham: University Press of America.

Foster, S. L., 1986. *Reading Dancing: Bodies and Subjects in Contemporary American Dance*. Berkley: University of California Press.

Foucault, M., 1972. *Power/Knowledge: Selected Interviews and Other Writings, 1972–1977*. Ed. C. Gordon. New York: Pantheon Books.

Franko B, 2007. *Interview at Queen Mary College, University of London*. Interviewed by Kamal Ackarie [live]. January 2007.

Freeman, J., 2007. *New Performance/New Writing*. Basingstoke: Palgrave MacMillan.

Freud, S., 1964. *The Standard Edition of the Complete Psychological Works of Sigmund Freud*. Trans. J. Strachey. London: Hogarth Press.

———, 1991. *The Essentials of Psycho-Analysis*. Ed. A. Freud. London: Penguin Books.

———, 1999. *The Interpretation of Dreams*. Trans. J. Crick. Oxford: Oxford University Press.

———, 2002. *The Wolfman and Other Cases*. Trans. L. Huish. London: Penguin Books Ltd.

———, 2003a. *Beyond the Pleasure Principle and Other Writings*. Trans. J. Reddick. London: Penguin Books.

———, 2003b. *The Uncanny*. Trans. D. McLintock. London: Penguin Books.

Freud, S. and Breuer, J., 2004. *Studies in Hysteria*. Trans. N. Luckhurst. London: Penguin Books.

Garner, S. B., 1994. *Bodied Spaces: Phenomenology and Performance in Contemporary Drama*. New York: Cornell University Press.

Geertz, C., 2000. *The Interpretation of Cultures*. New York: Basic Books.

Goffman, E., 1967. *Interaction Ritual: Essays on Face-to-Face Behaviour*. New York: Pantheon Books.

———, 1986. *Frame Analysis: An Essay on the Organization of Experience*. Northeastern University Press.

———, E., 1990. *The Presentation of Self in Everyday Life*. London: Penguin Books.

Grehan, H., 2009. *Performance, Ethics and Spectatorship in a Global Age*. Basingstoke: Palgrave Macmillan.

Griffiths, T. R. and Wheeler, W. J., 1992. 'Staging "The Other Scene": A Psychoanalytic Approach to Contemporary British Political Drama'. In: A. Page, ed. *The Death of the Playwright? Modern British Drama and Literary Theory*. London: MacMillan, pp. 186–203.

Gumbel, A., 2007. 'Soldier Breaks Down During Graphic Account of Girl's Rape'. *The Independent*, 22 February.

Halliwell, S., 2002. *The Aesthetics of Mimesis: Ancient Texts and Modern Problems*. Princeton: Princeton University Press.

Hand, R. J. and Wilson, M, 2002. *Grand-Guignol: The French Theatre of Horror*. Exeter: University of Exeter Press.

Handler, R., 1986. 'Authenticity'. *Anthropology Today*, 2(1), pp. 2–4.

Heath, M., 1996. 'Introduction'. In: Aristotle. *Poetics*. Trans. M. Heath. London: Penguin.

Heathfield, A., ed., 1997. *Shattered Anatomies: Traces of Body in Performance*. Bristol: Arnolfini Live.

———, ed., 2000. *Small Acts: Performance, the Millennium, and the Marking of Time*. London: Black Dog Publishing.

———, 2001. 'Coming Undone' [online]. Available at www.adrian-heathfield.com/cu.pdf (accessed 20 October 2008).

———, ed., 2004. *Live:Art and Performance*. London: Tate Publishing.

———, 2006. 'Writing of the Event'. In: J. Christie, R. Gough and D. Watt, eds., *A Performance Cosmology:Testimony from the Future, Evidence from the Past*. London and New York: Routledge, pp. 179–182.

Henri, E. J., 1966. *Methods of Torture and Execution*. London: Walton Press.

Herman, J. L., 2001. *Trauma and Recovery: From Domestic Abuse to Political Terror*. Rivers Oram Press.

Hesford, W. S., 2006. 'Staging Terror'. *TDR: The Drama Review*, 50(3), pp. 29–41.

Hirsh, M., 2004. 'Editor's Column: Collateral Damage'. *PMLA*, 119(5), pp. 1209–1215.

Hoad, T. F., ed., 1986. *The Concise Oxford Dictionary of English Etymology*. Oxford: Clarendon.

Holm, I., 2004. *Acting My Life: The Autobiography*. London: Bantam Press.

Holmes, J., 1993. *John Bowlby and Attachment Theory*. London: Routledge.

Johnson, M. L., 1999. 'Embodied Reason'. In: G. Weiss and H. F. Haber, eds., *Perspectives on Embodiment*. New York: Routledge, pp. 81–102.

Jones, A., 2006. 'Rupture'. In: J. Christie, R. Gough and D. Watt, eds., *A Performance Cosmology: Testimony from the Future, Evidence from the past*. London and New York: Routledge, pp. 71–78.

Jones, D. H., 1998. 'Response to "Marsyas – running out of skin"'. *Information Society Network* [online]. Available at http://shl.stanford.edu:3455/3/98 (accessed 13 April 2008).

Kafka, F., 1949. *In the Penal Settlement*. Trans. E. Muir and W. Muir. London: Secker and Warburg.

Kane, S., 2001. *Sarah Kane: Complete Plays*. London: Methuen.

Kear, A., 2005. 'The Anxiety of the Image'. *Parallax*, 11(3), pp. 107–116.

Kelleher, J. and Ridout, N., eds., 2006. *Contemporary Theatres in Europe: A Critical Companion.* Oxon: Routledge.

Kelly, Michael, ed., 1998. *The Encyclopaedia of Aesthetics, vol. 3.* Oxford: Oxford University Press.

Kleist, H., 1810. *On the Marionette Theatre* [online]. Trans. T. Parry. Available at www.southerncrossreview.org/9/kleist.htm (accessed 20 May 2008).

LaCapra, D., 1996. *Representing the Holocaust: History, Theory, Trauma.* New York: Cornell University Press.

———, 2001. *Writing History, Writing Trauma.* Baltimore and London: The Johns Hopkins University Press.

Ladly, M., 2007. 'Being There: Heidegger and the Phenomenon of Presence in Telematic Performance'. *International Journal of Performance Arts and Digital Media,* 3(2 and 3), pp. 139–150.

Lakoff, G. and Johnson, M., 1999. *Philosophy in the Flesh: The Embodied Mind and Its Challenge to Western Thought.* New York: Basic Books.

Laub, D., 1992. 'Bearing Witness, or the Vicissitudes of Listening'. In S. Felman and Laub, D., eds., *Testimony: Crises of Witnessing in Literature, Psychoanalysis, and History.* London: Routledge, pp. 57–74.

———, 1995. 'Truth and Testimony: The Process and the Struggle'. In C. Caruth, ed. *Trauma: Explorations in Memory.* Baltimore: The John Hopkins University Press, pp. 61–75.

Layder, D., 1981. *Structure, Interaction and Social Theory.* London: Routledge and Kegan Paul Ltd.

Lehmann, H.-T., 2006. *Postdramatic Theatre.* Trans. K. Jürs-Munby. Oxon: Routledge.

Levinas, E., 1989. *The Levinas Reader.* Ed. S. Hand. Oxford: Blackwell.

Leys, R., 2000. *Trauma: A Genealogy.* Chicago: The University of Chicago Press.

Lifton, R. J., 1973. *The Broken Connection: On Death and the Continuity of Life.* New York: Simon and Schuster.

Luckhurst, M. ed., 2006. *Modern British and Irish Drama 1880–2005.* Oxford: Blackwell Publishing.

Luckhurst, R., 2003. 'Traumaculture'. *New Formulations,* 50, pp. 28–47.

———, 2008. *The Trauma Question.* London: Routledge.

McAuley, G., 2000. *Space in Performance: Making Meaning in the Theatre.* Michigan: University of Michigan Press.

McLuhan, M., 2001. *Understanding Media.* London: Routledge Classics.

MacDonald, L., 2007. 'Imagining *His Dark Materials* as a *Gesamtkunstwerk*'. *Studies in Musical Theatre,* 1(2), pp. 199–211.

Mahon, A., 2005. *Eroticism and Art.* Oxford: Oxford UP.

Malpede, K., 1996. 'Teaching Witnessing: A Class Wakes to Genocide'. *Theatre Topics,* 6(2), pp. 167–179.

Mauss, M., 1990. *The Gift: The Form and Reason for Exchange in Archaic Societies.* Trans. W. D. Halls. London: Routledge.

Mey, K., 2007. *Art and Obscenity.* London: I. B. Tauris.

Mitchell, M. ed., 2007. *Remember Me: Constructing Immortality. Beliefs on Immortality, Life, and Death.* London: Routledge.

Mitchell, W. J. T., 2005. 'The Unspeakable and The Unimaginable: Word and Image in a Time of Terror'. *ELH,* 72(2), pp. 291–308.

Moreno, M., 2008. *Revenger's Tragedy Workpack.* London: The Royal National Theatre Board.

Munt, S., 2011. 'After the Fall: Queer Heterotopias in Philip Pullman's *His Dark Materials* Trilogy'. In: S. Barfield and K. Cox, eds., *Critical Perspectives on Philip Pullman's* His Dark Material: *Essays on the Novels, the Film and the Stage Productions.* Jefferson: McFarland, pp. 202–217.

Nathan, J., 2004. 'Review of *His Dark Materials*'. *Jewish Chronicle, Theatre Record* 1–28 January, p. 18.

Nelson, T. G. A., 1990. *Comedy: The Theatre of Comedy in Literature, Drama, and Cinema.* Oxford: Oxford University Press.

Nuttall, A. D., 1983. *A New Mimesis: Shakespeare and the Representation of Reality.* London: Methuen.

———, 1996. *Why Does Tragedy Give Pleasure?* Oxford: Oxford University Press.

O'Reilly, K., 2008. *Personal interview at British Library.* Conducted 19 March 2008.

Office for National Statistics, 2011. *Labour Market: Employment* [online]. Available at www.statistics.gov.uk/cci/nugget.asp?id=12 (accessed 4 May 2011).

Onions, C. T., ed., 1966. *The Oxford Dictionary of English Etymology.* Oxford: Clarendon.

Page, A., 1992. *The Death of the Playwright? Modern British Drama and Literary Theory.* London: MacMillan.

Page, H. W., 1883. *Injuries of the Spine and Spinal Cord and Nervous Shock.* London: J. and A Churchill.

Phelan, P., 1993. *Unmarked: The Politics of Performance.* London: Routledge.

———, 1997. *Mourning Sex: Performing Public Memories.* London: Routledge.

———, 2002. 'Francesca Woodman's Photography: Death and the Image One More Time'. *Signs: Journal of Women in Culture and Society,* 27(4), pp. 979–1004.

Pollock, G., 2006. 'PRESENT: Art/Trauma/Representation'. In: Bath ICAS Symposium. Bath, England. Unpublished keynote, 13 May 2006.

Pullman, P., 2007a. *Northern Lights.* London: Scholastic.

———, 2007b. *The Subtle Knife*. London: Scholastic.

———, 2007c. *The Amber Spyglass*. London: Scholastic.

Ragland, E., 2001. 'The Psychical Nature of Trauma: Freud's Dora, The Young Homosexual Woman, and the *Fort! Da!* Paradigm'. *Post Modern Culture*, 11(2).

Read, A., 1993. *Theatre and Everyday Life: An Ethics of Performance*. London: Routledge.

Read, R., 2007. 'Representing Trauma: The Case for Troubling Images'. In: M. Mitchell, ed. *Remember Me: Constructing Immortality. Beliefs on Immortality, Life, and Death*. London: Routledge, pp. 227–242.

Reinelt, J. G. and Roach, J. R., eds., 1992. *Critical Theory and Performance*. Michigan: University of Michigan Press.

Richardson, L. and St. Pierre, E. A., 2005. 'Writing: A Method of Inquiry'. In N. K. Denzin and Y. S. Lincoln, eds., *The Sage Handbook of Qualitative Research (3rd Edition)*. London: Sage Publications, pp. 959–978.

Ridout, N., 2006. *Stage Fright, Animals, and Other Theatrical Problems*. Cambridge: Cambridge University Press.

———, 2009. *Theatre & Ethics*. London: Palgrave Macmillan.

Roach, J., 1993. *The Players Passion: Studies in the Science of Acting*. Michigan: University of Michigan Press.

Rokem, F., 2002. 'Witnessing Woyzeck: Theatricality and the Empowerment of the Spectator'. *SubStance*, 31(2 and 3), pp. 167–183.

———, 2006. 'Witnessing the Witness'. J. Christie, R. Gough and D. Watt, eds., *A Performance Cosmology: Testimony from the Future, Evidence from the past*. London and New York: Routledge, pp. 168–172.

Román, D., 2002. 'Introduction: Tragedy'. *Theatre Journal*, 54(1), pp. 1–18.

Román, D. *et al.*, 2002. 'A Forum on Theatre and Tragedy in the Wake of September 11, 2001'. *Theatre Journal*, 54(1), pp. 95–138.

Rothberg, M., 2000. *Traumatic Realism: The Demands of Holocaust Representation*. Minneapolis: University of Minnesota Press.

Royle, N., 2003. *The Uncanny*. Manchester: Manchester University Press.

Saunders, G., 2002. *Love Me or Kill Me: Sarah Kane and the Theatre of Extremes*. Manchester: Manchester University Press.

Schechner, R., 1985. *Between Theatre and Anthropology*. Philadelphia: University of Pennsylvania Press.

———, 2003. *Performance Theory*. London: Routledge Classics.

Schneider, R., 1997. *The Explicit Body in Performance*. London: Routledge.

Schulz, W. F., ed., 2007. *The Phenomenon of Torture: Readings and Commentary*. Pennsylvania: University of Pennsylvania Press.

Sedgwick, E., 1985. *Between Men: English Literature and Male Homosocial Desire*. New York: Columbia University Press.

Seltzer, M., 1997. 'Wound Culture: Trauma in the Pathological Public Sphere'. *October*, 80, pp. 3–26.

Shepherd, S., 2006. *Theatre, Body and Pleasure*. London: Routledge.

Shepherd, S. and Wallis, M., 2004. *Drama/Theatre/Performance*. London: Routledge.

Silk, M. S., ed., 1996. *Tragedy and the Tragic: Greek Theatre and Beyond*. Oxford: Oxford University Press.

Solga, K., 2006. 'Rape's Metatheatrical Return: Rehearsing Sexual Violence among the Early Moderns'. *Theatre Journal*, 58(1), pp. 53–72.

———, 2007. '*Blasted*'s Hysteria: Rape, Realism, and the Threshold of the Visible'. *Modern Drama*, 50(3), pp. 346–374.

Sontag, S., 2001. *Against Interpretation*. London: Vintage Books.

———, 2003. *Regarding the Pain of Others*. London: Penguin.

———, 2004. 'Regarding the Torture of Others'. *The New York Times* [online]. Available at www.nytimes.com/2004/05/23/magazine/23PRISONS.html?ex=1400644800&en=a2cb6ea6bd297c8f&ei=5007&partner=USERLAND (accessed 28 November 2007).

Stamatakou, I., 1972. *Dictionary of Ancient Greek Language*. Athens.

States, B. O., 1985. *Great Reckoning in Little Rooms: On the Phenomenology of Theatre*. Berkeley: University of California Press.

———, 1992. 'The Phenomenological Attitude'. In: J. G. Reinelt and J. R. Roach, eds., *Critical Theory and Performance*. Michigan: University of Michigan Press, pp. 369–379.

———, 1996. 'Performance as Metaphore'. *Theatre Journal*, 48(1), pp. 1–26.

Stephens, J. and McCallum, J., 1998. *Retelling Stories, Framing Culture: Traditional Story and Metanarratives in Children's Literature*. London: Routledge.

Stephenson, H. and Langridge N., 1997. *Rage and Reason: Women Playwrights on Playwriting*. London: Methuen Drama.

Stewart, E., 1990. 'The Integrated Text and Postmodern Performance'. *MTD: A Journal of the Performing Arts*, Summer 1990, pp. 2–9.

Stiegler, B., 2009. *Acting Out*. Stanford: Stanford University Press.

Swartz, D., 1997. *Culture and Power: The Sociology of Pierre Bourdieu*. London: The University of Chicago Press.

Taussig, M., 1993. *Mimesis and Alterity: A Particular History of the Senses*. London: Routledge.

———, 2008. 'Zoology, Music, and Surrealism in the War on Terror'. *Critical Enquiry*, 34 (Winter Supplement), pp. 99–116.

Taylor, L., 2010. 'The Hanging Man: Death, Indeterminacy and the Event'. *Performance Research*, 15(1), pp. 4–13.

Taylor-Batty, M., 2008. *Personal interview at Workshop Theatre, University of Leeds.* Conducted 3 November 2008.

Tinker, J., 1995. 'The Disgusting Feast of Filth'. *Daily Mail*, 19 January 1995, p. 5.

Trilling, L., 1972. *Sincerity and Authenticity.* London: Harvard University Press.

Turner, V., 1974. *Dramas, Fields, and Metaphors: Symbolic Action in Human Society.* New York: Cornell University Press.

Undrill, G., 2000. 'Book Review'. *Performance Research*, 5(3), p. 133.

Van Leeuwen, T., 2001. 'What is Authenticity?'. *Discourse Studies*, 3(4), pp. 392–397.

Wald, C., 2007. *Hysteria, Trauma and Melancholia: Performative Maladies in Contemporary Anglophone Drama.* New York: Palgrave MacMillan.

Wallis, M., 2005. 'Translating Bodies: Siddons, Cowley and the Stage Sublime'. *Performance Research*, 10(1), pp. 68–80.

Wallis, M. and Duggan, P., 2011. 'Editorial: On Trauma'. *Performance Research*, 16(1), pp. 1–3.

Warner, B., 2004. 'Abu Ghraib and a New Generation of Soldiers'. In: M. Danner, ed. *Abu Ghraib: The Politics of Torture.* Berkeley: North Atlantic Books, pp. 71–86.

Weiss, G., and Haber, H. F., 1999. *Perspectives on Embodiment.* New York: Routledge.

Weiss, P., 1983. *The Persecution and Assassination of Jean-Paul Marat as Performed by the Inmates of the Asylum of Charenton Under the Direction of The Marquis de Sade.* New York: Atheneum.

Whitmore, J., 1994. *Directing Postmodern Theatre: Shaping Signification in Performance.* Michigan: University of Michigan Press.

Williams, R., 1996. *Modern Tragedy.* London: Chatto and Windus.

———, 1977. *Marxism and Literature.* Oxford: Oxford University Press.

———, 1987. *Drama From Ibsen to Brecht.* London: The Hogarth Press.

———, 1989. *The Politics of Modernism: Against the New Conformists.* Ed. T. Pinkney. London: Verso.

———, 1995. *Writing in Society.* London: Verso.

Wilshire, B., 1982. *Role Playing and Identity: The Limits of Theatre as Metaphor.* Indiana University Press.

Wright, N., 2003. *His Dark Materials.* London: Nick Hern Books.

———, 2004. *His Dark Materials.* Revised ed. London: Nick Hern Books.

Zarilli, P. B., ed., 2002. *Acting (Re)Considered: A Theoretical and Practical Guide.* 2nd ed. London: Routledge.

Zerihan, R., 2006. 'Intimate Inter-actions: Returning to the Body in One to One Performance'. *Body, Space and Technology Journal*, 6(1) [online]. Available at http://people.brunel.ac.uk/bst/vol0601/rachelzerihan/zerihan.pdf (accessed 1 July 2009).

Žižek, S., 2002. *Welcome to the Desert of the Real.* London: Verso.
———, 2004. 'Between Two Deaths: The Culture of Torture'. *ARTicles* [online]. Available at www.16beavergroup.org/mtarchive/archives/001084print.html (accessed 23 November 2007).
———, 2006. *The Parallax View.* London: MIT Press.
———, 2008. *Violence.* London: Profile Books.

Index

Note: 'n.' after a page reference indicates the number of a note on that page.
Plays and performances can be found under authors'/practitioners' names.

Index

Kristeva, Julia 131

LaCapra, Dominic 4–5, 23–24, 176,
190n. 6
Laub, Dori 89, 97, 99, 110–112
laughter 118–123, 128, 163–164
see also corpsing
Lehmann, Hans-Ties 30, 47, 63–64,
183–184
Lepage, Robert 33
Dragon's Trilogy 33–34
Levinas, Emanuel 176–179, 185
Luckhurst, Roger 4–5, 17–18, 25, 117

McLuhan, Marshall 48–49, 190n. 4
mimesis 24, 59–61, 63–65, 73, 75,
82–84, 95–96, 190n. 1
mimetic shimmering 73–75, 83–84,
92, 111

Neilson, Anthony 7, 22, 91–92, 98
Normal 21–22, 91–92
Penetrator 98–99

O'Reilly, Kira 11, 141–147, 179–183
other, the 51, 89, 176–177, 179, 186

Page, Herbert W. 17–19
pain 51–3, 77–78, 110, 123, 125,
135–136, 139, 154–155, 159
Phelan, Peggy 27, 29, 54, 118, 189n. 6
phenomenological experience 128,
131–132, 138–141, 144
phenomenology 11, 130–131, 150
Pinter, Harold 31, 99, 102
The Room 99–103
Post Traumatic Stress Disorder 7,
22–23
presence-in-trauma effect 111–112,
139–140, 150
Pullman, Phillip
His Dark Materials 129–141

reality 8, 41, 43, 48, 50–53, 56, 61–73,
79–84

Ridout, Nicholas 65, 67, 72, 163–164,
169–170, 176–177, 183–184
ritualization 131–132

Schechner, Richard 42, 46–47, 50–51,
56, 119, 170
self, the 17, 22, 27–30, 54–55, 73, 107,
111, 120–121, 132–133, 148,
162, 165–171
September 11 2001 37, 50, 56, 195n.
17
Shepherd, Simon 70–71, 89–90, 108,
148–149
Simmons, Pip
An Die Musik 2–3
Societas Raffaello Sanzio 66, 71, 78,
173, 177
BR.#04 66–75, 152
Purgatorio 177–178
Sontag, Susan 52, 56
spectator 3, 9, 30, 59, 66–68,
73–75, 81–82, 86–93, 102–104,
112–113, 124, 128, 135–137,
139, 145, 147–148, 152–153,
176–177, 182–184

Taussig, Michael 60–2

uncanny 72–73, 83, 147
echo 131–132, 136–138, 140,
150–151
undecidable 74, 155, 160
see also indecidability

violence 40, 51, 67, 70–73, 92,
98–99, 101–103, 118, 125–128,
174

Wallis, Mick 131–132
Williams, Raymond 7–8, 34–36,
38–43, 57, 174
Witnessing 21, 26, 85–90, 94, 96–97,
108–110, 135, 148–149

Žižek, Slavoj 50, 52–53, 154

Lightning Source UK Ltd.
Milton Keynes UK
UKOW06f0432300915

259546UK00001B/35/P